W0018210

# TAN CHUNG

# CHINA
## A 5,000-YEAR ODYSSEY

Los Angeles | London | New Delhi
Singapore | Washington DC | Melbourne

*First published in 2017 by New World Press, Beijing*

*This edition published in 2018 by*

**SAGE Publications India Pvt Ltd**
B1/I-1 Mohan Cooperative Industrial Area
Mathura Road, New Delhi 110 044, India
*www.sagepub.in*

**SAGE Publications Inc**
2455 Teller Road
Thousand Oaks, California 91320, USA

**SAGE Publications Ltd**
1 Oliver's Yard, 55 City Road
London EC1Y 1SP, United Kingdom

**SAGE Publications Asia-Pacific Pte Ltd**
3 Church Street
#10-04 Samsung Hub
Singapore 049483

Published by Vivek Mehra for SAGE Publications India Pvt Ltd, typeset in 11/14 pts Bembo Std by Fidus Design Pvt. Ltd., Chandigarh and printed at Chaman Enterprises, New Delhi.

**Library of Congress Cataloging-in-Publication Data**
Name: Tan, Chung.
Title: China : a 5,000-year odyssey / Tan Chung.
Description: New Delhi: SAGE Publications; Thousand Oaks, California: SAGE Publications India, 2018.
Identifiers: LCCN 2018011528| ISBN 9789352807246 (print pb) | ISBN 9789352807253 (e pub 2.0) | ISBN 9789352807260 (e book)
Subjects: LCSH: China—Civilization.
Classification: LCC DS721 .T263 2018 | DDC 951—dc23
LC record available at https://lccn.loc.gov/2018011528

**ISBN:** 978-93-528-0724-6 (PB)

**SAGE Team:** Manisha Mathews, Alekha Chandra Jena, Madhurima Thapa, and Ritu Chopra

The figures in this book are provided by CNSPHOTO, Li Chenxi, Tan Chung, and Zhao Yue.

# CONTENTS

# FOREWORD

The rise of India and China over the past two decades has led to numerous books and articles about the future security architecture of Asia. When it has become clear that the world's economic growth centers have shifted from the North Atlantic to the Indo-Pacific, it is time to retell the story of the region's interstate and cultural relations over the past millennia. Tan Chung's new book sets out to do that for what he calls China's odyssey, for 5,000 years of it. What is exceptional about the book is that a Chinese scholar who deeply loves and understands India is offering a new perspective on China's history.

I first met Tan Chung half a century ago. When I realized that he was the son of Tan Yun-shan, someone my father greatly admired, the story of what the young Tan Chung was doing in India came doubly alive. My father told me that he was teaching in 1927 at the Chinese High School in Singapore when he heard that Tan Yun-shan had met Rabindranath Tagore, and that he was greatly awed to learn that Tagore was so impressed that he invited Tan Yun-shan to teach the Chinese classics at Visva Bharati in Shantiniketan. My father's account of Tagore's pioneering effort to build an Indian center of excellence that was not dependent on the British view of history and culture has stayed in my imagination ever since.

The Tan father-and-son story is an extraordinary one. Born in Malaya in 1929 and educated in China, Tan Chung joined his father in 1955 and, like his father, was soon immersed in the world of Indian civilization. Teaching Chinese to generations of Indian students and drawn to the genius of India, he developed a portrait of Chinese history that could only have come from looking north across the Himalayas and down the river systems of the Huang He and the Yangzte. The result was, as he suggests, it enabled him to conceive of two parallel civilization-states that defied the challenge of the nation-state systems coming out of the Mediterranean political cultures.

Tan Chung first threw down the gauntlet in 1973 against the contemporary dominance of the nation-state framework soon after he completed his PhD from the University of Delhi in 1973 and submitted his paper "On Sinocentrism: A Critique," followed by "The Britain–China–India Trade Triangle" the next year. The full context was then set out when his book *China and the Brave New World* was published in 1978. Since then he has refined and developed the critical points that he had made, but he remains consistent in challenging the Eurocentric narratives of postcolonial historiography even as these are being revised.

I also commend the added dimensions that have come from Tan Chung's growing interest over the past two decades in what Tagore and his father had earlier emphasized—the fruitful ancient civilizational ties between India and China. There had been a deep and rich reservoir of connectedness that drew from many springs, and he has been exploring China's store of documentary and archeological materials to depict the many layers of that story. Thus, what he calls an odyssey envisages China and India rising again in a different world from that which Tagore and Tan Yun-shan had known. Tan Chung offers a new take on China's history from a perspective enriched by his own half-century studying, teaching, and writing practices in India.

He does not claim to know how much the history that future Indian historians may come to write will share in common with that of China or whether those historians will proceed along an altogether different path possibly closer to that of the modern West. Also, he is right in expecting that there would always be people from both countries who would share Tagore's lofty hopes. Tan Chung has encapsulated it in Tagore's own words and has quoted him with the utmost respect:

We must learn to defend our humanity against the insolence of the strong, only taking care that we do not imitate their ways and, by turning ourselves brutal, destroy those very values which alone make our humanity worth defending.

**Wang Gungwu**
National University of Singapore

# PREFACE

Dear readers, I am telling you a story of my China. I say "my China" because I am the scion of Chinese parents and I grew up in China, spending a quarter of a century of my childhood and youth there, and I have "Chineseness" (now fashionably described as "Chinese characteristics") in my DNA. According to me, anything that takes place in China is logical, resonating to some historical or current circumstance, as well as some internal or external factors. I don't see any "China puzzle" in any scenario of China vis-à-vis international development. I also find observations that pitch the "admirable China" against the "abominable Chinese," or the "amicable Chinese" against the assertive China to be irrational. In my story of my China, there is no cause for fear or worry, or dismay.

I have been living outside China for more than six decades, which was a whole lifetime for the ancients.[1] I have spent these decades almost single-mindedly thinking about China, reading about China, watching China's developments, and pondering upon its problems. I have also appointed myself as a spokesman of "my China" to whosoever wanted to know China or share my views on China. It is a special situation for me to see my China from a distance and see at close quarters how the world sees my China. This situation so often brings anguish and anxiety to me as I see so many images of my China, which are so different from the true picture in my mind. Therefore, it motivates me to share my picture of my China with the world.

There are nearly 1.4 billion people claiming "my China," squeezing "my" China into a tiny spot of existence. There is only one China, not 1.4 billion of it; hence there should be only one true picture of China. To my surprise, there are myriad pictures of China among the 1.4 billion of my countrymen. Obviously, some of these pictures are questionable, distorted, and even untruthful. Mistaken conceptions of

---

[1]There is a millennial Chinese description of the age of 70 as *guxi* 古稀 meaning "a rarity from the time immemorial."

China among its people are not new, because of long-term traditional biases. Many foreigners have seen it and I see it clearly as well. In October 2017, my book on Chinese civilization written in Chinese language was published (Chinese title 简明中国文明史 meaning "concise history of Chinese civilization") along with a relatively simplified English version separately titled *China: A 5,000-year Odyssey*. More and more people in China have started sharing the picture of my China. Now, SAGE is bringing out this volume so that people all over the world can share the picture of my China.

If we compare the world to a forest, China is the tree that is the oldest among the lush green, flower blossoming and fruit bearing ones having survived five millennia of hurricanes and tornadoes. It is both a unique and common phenomenon. After all, China has not come from another planet, but has evolved on our earth. Chinese people, both ancient and modern, are humans, just like the humans of other countries. But they have united into a common entity for millennia in a special Chinese manner, with tremendous energy of appetency creation. I trace the origin of this energy to the dynamics of the third longest river, Yangtze, and the fifth longest river, Huanghe (the Yellow River) which carved out the contours of China on earth, long before the appearance of the man-apes. The inhabitants in and around the valleys of Yangtze and Huanghe quickly shed their tribal mentality and eliminated the identities of races and nations. In the picture of my China, we cannot find a Chinese "nation-state." My macro picture shows that China was, is, and will be a "civilization-state," which does not stage the tragic trilogy of rise–apex–decline like what the Roman Empire and British Empire did. It is for the same reason that China did not and will not follow the beaten track of the Soviet Union. By the same logic, China will not become a world hegemon or a colonial power. This is the picture of my China in a nutshell.

As I own only one out of 1.4 billion shares of "my China," I don't monopolize China. I go a step further to proclaim that China belongs to all Chinese and also to the entire world. In my perspective, China is "created by Heaven and constructed by Earth 天造地设" as the Chinese saying goes. China owes a lot to the world and has redeemed its gratitude to the world through some Chinese inventions. The Chinese inventions of tea culture and porcelain culture have immensely enriched the people's living standards universally. The British scientist and philosopher Francis Bacon famously observed in his *Instauratio Magna* (great instauration) that the Chinese invention of "gunpowder" had "altered the face and state of the world" in "warfare"; but the Chinese never invented gunpowder! What they had invented is called *huoyao* 火药 meaning a "concoction for fire." Known as "fireworks powder," it was used to enrich China's hedonistic merrymaking by creating the effect of an explosion and smoke in entertainment shows. This "fireworks powder" industry has accumulated more than a millennium of expertise so much so that today almost all the fireworks displayed all over the world are made in China. It was Genghis Khan, the Mongol conqueror of Eurasia, who had set up a special unit of captured Chinese soldiers in his army to use this fireworks powder for the purpose of blasting defensive barriers (in fact, scaring the enemy to death) in Eurasia, and thus, the concept of "gunpowder" was born. If, in fact, the concept of "gunpowder" had been the brainchild of the Chinese, would not the people of Song Dynasty taken advantage of its "made-in-China" fire powder to repulse the attacks of the horsemen of the Khitan, Nurchen, and Mongol nation-states and emerged victorious? It was not Chinese stupidity but China's odyssey along the civilization highway (coupled with the hedonistic merrymaking of the Song ruling elite) that resulted in the two great tragedies of the 12th and 13th centuries, which I have illustrated in Chapter 6 of this book.

I leave it to my readers to conclude whether the world has really seen the true picture of China—my China, your China, and the world's China. I thank SAGE for the wonderful service of helping the world see it.

# INTRODUCTION

Let me begin by introducing myself. I was born of Chinese parents in Malaya (now Malaysia) in 1929, but lived in China until I was 25 years old. I am a product of Chinese civilization. Later, I lived, studied, and taught in India for 45 years (1955–1999). India welcomed me as a sort of spokesman of Chinese civilization, and I shared whatever little I knew of that with my Indian friends and students. Circumstances seem to have molded me into an intermediary between Chinese civilization and Indian civilization, and promotion of China–India cultural friendship and understanding has become part and parcel of my career. While living in retirement in the United States, I have continued to delve into the development of Chinese civilization from time immemorial until today. Decades of direct and indirect dialogue with international China experts created in me a strong urge to write a book that tells the story of China. That is why I am now connecting with you through these pages.

Since publication of *The Middle Kingdom: A Survey of the Geography, Government, Education, Social Life, Arts, and History of the Chinese Empire and Its Inhabitants* in 1883 by the renowned American missionary, diplomat, scholar, and pioneer of China studies in the United States, Samuel Wells Williams (1812–1884), there have been a good number of quality and influential books in English with a holistic perspective on China. They are all authored by non-Chinese scholars except *China: Its People, Its Society, Its Culture* written by my late friend Professor C. T. Hu 胡昌度 (1920–2014) of the Columbia University (I may be culpable for the intentional omission of Lin Yu-tang's 林语堂 *My Country and My People* and my unawareness of the writings of young Chinese scholars in the past two or more decades). C. T. Hu's book is not so well known, making practically no impact. Thus, I see only non-Chinese scholars telling the story of China in international circles. No wonder China's international image has so often been distorted!

On November 22, 2015, the Chinese press reported a speech of mine at the inaugural session of the 6th World Forum on China Studies xiv

in Shanghai. I herewith quote the translated portion of a news report on my speech as follows:

> … Since all scholars present here have made excellent contributions to China studies, I am on the stage to receive this award on your behalf. I have had long accumulated feelings while pursuing China studies abroad. For instance, in the United States, those who research Russia read the books of Russian authors, those who research France read the books of French authors, and those who research India read the books of Indian authors. Strangely, those who research China read the books of American, not Chinese, authors. An eminent example is the world famous writings of John King Fairbank, late professor at Harvard University. If he were alive today, this World Forum would have surely offered him an award for excellent contributions to China studies.
>
> In the absence of great Chinese masters in China studies, the vast majority of foreign students know nothing of the views of Chinese scholars, leading to international misunderstanding about China. For instance, those who now discuss whether China will rise peacefully are inclined to quote John King Fairbank. Fairbank wrote a famous book on "China's world order," emphasizing "Sinocentrism" (and misleading people). Of course, we don't blame Fairbank for international misunderstanding about China, and for the distortion of China's international image. We must blame ourselves for doing a poor job telling the story of China. We have no Chinese scholars producing books on China in English and other foreign languages that are as popular as those of Fairbank. China did an excellent job organizing the 2008 Beijing Olympics, the 2010 Shanghai Expo, and the 2014 Beijing APEC Summit. In September 2016, China successfully hosted the G20 Summit in Hangzhou. I am sure, in the near future, there will be books on China in English and other foreign languages written by Chinese scholars and well received worldwide. That will be the real contribution to China studies.[1]

CHINA: A 5,000-YEAR ODYSSEY

---

[1] For the Chinese original, see *Social Science Weekly* (社会科学报), November 23, 2015, p. 1.

I was given only three minutes to speak at the inaugural ceremony of the 6th World Forum on China Studies, unable to read my prepared eight-minute speech. I just said something extempore. I am sure that the afore-mentioned words reported by the press were from my mouth, but they are somewhat different from what I wished to say. I have always regarded John King Fairbank's (1907–1991) "Sinocentrism" theory as the theoretic basis of the international fear of China's rise. Perhaps, Chinese academia has not clearly seen this. In addition, Chinese public opinion, including many authoritative views, has provided supporting evidence for Fairbank's "Sinocentrism." There is an impression that China will become another hegemon, like the United States, even replacing the United States as number one superpower. This is a serious problem that could stand in the way of establishing a "new type of great power relationship" between China and the United States, make China's neighbors insecure, and result in China's not being loved by many. Thus, as many books as possible should be written to refute "Sinocentrism" and clearly, objectively, and correctly communicate China's civilization development to dispel international fear of China.

I have yet to see a good Chinese publication that clearly, objectively, and correctly communicates China's 5,000-year civilization development. Some Chinese books portray the "frog-in-the-well" mentality, while others focus on major issues of international concern and carry on a dialogue with foreign opinions, as if defending China's position in an international forum, which is not sufficiently persuasive.

Moreover, there is always a feeling in China that foreign friends cannot decipher the China conundrum. But, have Chinese scholars really understood China? It is a big question! This book I write on China's 5,000-year civilization is not only for foreign readers but is also for Chinese readers (including Chinese intellectual elites). Only after understanding China themselves can Chinese intellectual elite tell a good story of China. By telling a "good" story, I don't mean sharing only the good news and hiding the shortcomings, let alone trying to masquerade the bad as good. People should see China as it is.

The main thrust of Fairbank's "Sinocentrism" is summarized by another American scholar as follows:

> Probably the most ethnocentric people in the world, the Chinese considered their realm the center of the universe, the Middle Kingdom, and regarded all cultural differences as signs of inferiority. All who were not Chinese were, obviously, barbarians. Europeans and Americans were distinguished from Inner Asian tribesmen only by the fact that they approached from the east and by sea, as opposed to those who came from the northern steppes. The fact that barbarians should come to China in quest of the benefits of civilization did not surprise the Chinese, who were prepared to be generous—provided the outsiders behaved with appropriate submissiveness.[2]

These words are from the famous historian and expert on Sino-American relations of the University of Maryland, Warren I. Cohen's celebrated book *America's Response to China: An Interpretative History of Sino-American Relations* (first published in 1971 and now in its fifth edition). I have always marveled at Professor Cohen's easy and impassioned description of "the barbarians from the northern steppes" and their coming "to China in quest of the benefits of civilization" without sympathy or empathy for the millions of Chinese lives lost and billions of properties looted by them in the over 2,000 years from the Xiongnu (Huns) days to the days of Mongol Yuan and Manchu Qing. The Chinese people have, indeed, been "generous" in their toleration of such barbarity and their total forgiveness for the misery wrought by the "Europeans and Americans who approached from the east and by sea" in modern times! Nevertheless, Cohen's lack of empathy for Chinese suffering is one thing and the truth of his remark is another. If we think about this calmly, though this quote is not free of exaggeration, it is not out of order and is somewhat reflective of the arrogant attitude of Manchu rulers in China when dealing with emissaries from the

---

[2] I quoted, 30 years ago, these words from Warren I. Cohen's first edition (New York, 1971) of *America's Response to China: An Interpretative History of Sino-American Relations*, 2–3. See Tan Chung, *Triton and Dragon: Studies on Nineteenth Century China and Imperialism* (Delhi: Gian Publishing House, 1986), 337–338.

West. Seeing this acknowledgment of China's own drawbacks, why must we refute "Sinocentrism"?

The crux of the issue lies in the mind-set. We see the afore-mentioned quote describing the Chinese people as "the most ethnocentric people in the world." This "ethnocentric" tendency has been endemic in the world of "nation-states," including several centuries in Europe and all the United States' history. In the ethnocentric world of "nation-states," it was common to treat foreigners as "barbarians." This very word, said with a sense of contempt, was the Roman Empire's designation for all foreigners. Indeed, for over 2,000 years, the Chinese called foreigners *Hu* 胡 or *Yi* 夷 without the abusive connotation of the Roman word "barbarian." During the Tang 唐 and Song 宋 dynasties, the Chinese government demonstrated its warm hospitality by building guesthouses for foreigners, naming these guesthouses *Yiguan* 夷馆/*Yi*-houses obviously meaning no insult. Qishan 琦善 (1786–1854), the governor-general of Guangdong and Guangxi, visited Hong Kong in 1843. He attended a banquet hosted by the British governor of Hong Kong and reported this to the Chinese Emperor, describing it as *Yiyan* 夷宴/*Yi*-banquet. Did he use the word *Yi* 夷 to insult himself? Of course not! All this seems like a puzzle of Chinese history that is difficult to decipher internationally. China has never been a "nation" of any ethnicity and thus could never have been "ethnocentric." Perhaps, we could call the Chinese people "civilization-centric," which, again, will not be comprehensible to other peoples. Ethnocentric "nation-states" were always restive, using force to conquer, rule, or influence "barbarians." China has never done this. Actually, many international China experts are well aware of this fact, though few of them, if any, would rush to remove the "Sinocentric" stigma from China.

In today's interconnected world, China will be the odd man out if the "Sinocentrism" theory prevails. People would be squirming about the advent of people of Chinese origin, even Chinese commodities, and fear that their interests and security may be threatened. I know such feelings exist in India and the United States. "Sinocentrism" makes China radioactive and untouchable, and hurts its relations with the rest of the world. It was on the pretext of "Sinocentrism" that some countries would suddenly tear up signed agreements with China. The mischief of

"Sinocentrism" has created unnecessary political apprehension in other countries when considering Chinese investment and tenders, preventing foreign governments from the normal consideration of pure merits and economic gain. Many big companies in the world have intimate connections with their native governments. They merrily go about their business and are well received worldwide. The only exception is Huawei Company of China (华为). Not that Huawei actually has the alleged "military connection," but "Sinocentrism" has made it look suspicious. Though China has ingenuously inserted itself into the globalization of "nation-states" without reservation, many in the "nation-states" world have balked at accepting China. "Sinocentrism" has caused China to be feared like a specter.

I want to write this book and unfold China's 5,000-year odyssey along the civilization highway beyond the rhythm of the "nation-state." This is of supreme importance. The world has always been in tune with the rhythm of the "nation-state." In remote times, vibrant nations can be likened to troupes performing on stage, attracting followers, enlarging their spheres of influence, and becoming "nation-states." They fought endless wars among themselves, with victors creating empires after crushing and vanquishing others, but ending in their own ruin.

The "nation-state" concept was born at the Westphalia Conference in Europe in 1648. The "Peace of Westphalia" aimed to use "diplomacy" (i.e., ostensibly organizing congenial parties, clinking glasses, and hugging dancing partners while clandestinely stealing intelligence, recruiting spies, and engaging in sabotage) to transform the notorious warring continent that was Europe into a "peaceful" world by using a dagger hidden in a smile. The enlightened and progressive international experts call such a world order the "Westphalian Regime." Today, all countries of the world are developing along such a "nation-state" path.

This "nation-state" path advocates individualism, subjugating culture to the law of the market with "free" competition to introduce "survival of the fittest" into humanity. As the pie of a national economy grows larger, fewer and fewer get the lion's share. The "nation-state" flexes its muscle before other countries and develops horizontally, grabbing territories and treating other countries, especially neighbors, as competitive rivals and potential enemies.

Big "nation-states" are typical performers of the trilogy of "rise–apex–decline." The British Empire that used to enjoy the "sun-never-sets" glory (meaning as Britain had a foothold in all parts of the world, there was no moment when the Union Jack was not under sunshine) is now a virtual loner on the three isles. The United States of "liberty," initially allergic to the institution of the president, subsequently succeeded Great Britain as the hegemon, climbing to the top of the world, but now in the second phase of its arch trajectory. The Soviet Union was born of the international proletarian revolutionary movement, but has strayed onto the road of "nation-state" and is now an ephemeral nightmare, even without ruins for a trace. Japan, the rising sun a century ago that endeared many a Chinese patriot (like Sun Yat-sen 孙中山 and Lu Xun 鲁迅), turned out to be a ferocious monster indulging in atrocities in China and other countries. The sun ultimately fell into the sea and the monster committed seppuku. All "nation-state" roads have ended up in a blind alley.

While the entire world has conformed to the rhythm of the "nation-state," China and India have not. Human civilization started at the riverside. The Nile River is the longest river on earth. The Nile flows north into the Mediterranean from its source in Central South Africa. With plentiful supply of water from the upper stream, the Nile frequently flooded in its lower stream and enriched the fertility of the soil in the river valley. The Egyptian civilization was thus born. This was the earliest venue for wheat cultivation, with buffalo introduced from Asia. Its script, architecture, and sculpture developed much earlier than China's. It was the earliest star of human civilization on earth. The Greeks envied the prosperity of Egypt. Herodotus (484?–425 BCE), the Greek historian, described Egypt as "the gift of the Nile." Unfortunately, Egypt was repeatedly conquered by the "nation-states" of Europe, and its initial glitter has faded forever.

Among the five longest rivers on earth, the Nile ranks first, the Amazon and the Mississippi of the American continent rank second and fourth, respectively, and the Yangtze and the Yellow River

(Huanghe) rank third and fifth, respectively. As a gift of the Yangtze and Huanghe, China was the earliest rice producer in the world. For 5,000 years, China has grown from strength to strength. Today, its international status is much higher than Egypt's because Egypt has been a weak member of the "nation-state" world, while China embarked on an odyssey along the civilization highway beyond the development of "nation-states." This different outcome has something to do with the special feature of the two great rivers, the Huanghe and Yangtze, which I will spell out in this book.

In my opinion, the kind of arrogance previously exhibited by China was "civilization-centric" rather than "ethnocentric." As a no "nation-state," China had consistently eliminated ethnic identities and differences. By contrast, every Western country is a "nation-state" and every Westerner has a "nation-state" mind-set; hence the word "nation" is actually coterminous with state or country.

Since modern China is interconnected with the world, Chinese people today often mix the concept of state or country with the concept of nation. What is important is not faultfinding, but making a clear distinction between China and "nation-state." Without that, the slogan of rejuvenation of the Chinese nation (*zhenxing Zhonghuaminzu* 振兴中华民族) will be nothing less than providing supporting evidence for the "Sinocentrism" accusation. People would say: "Look how passionate they are about rejuvenating the Chinese nation! Isn't that a sign of ethnocentrism?" All this indicates that we must thoroughly understand China in order to tell a good story about it. To do this, we must discard the prism of "nation-state" and see China through the prism of civilization.

China is gradually building the "Shanghai Cooperation Organization Community of Common Destiny," "China–India Community of Common Destiny," "China–South Asia Community of Common Destiny," "China–ASEAN Community of Common Destiny," "East Asia Community of Common Destiny," "BRICS Community of Common Destiny," and the "Eurasian Community of Common Destiny." With perseverance and hard work, the "Community of Common Destiny" may eventually cover the entire world. In this way, the age-old Chinese ideal of "When the great Dao prevails, all under heaven becomes one community" (大道之行也，天下为公) can materialize. We can wipe away all tears from the eyes of people in the world and make our suffering globe a new world of prosperity and happiness. Let peach flowers smile with the spring breeze in every nook and corner of the earth! This is my purpose in writing this book. I hope readers will bless me by reading it and giving me critiques.

# CHAPTER 1
# COMMON GEOGRAPHICAL ENTITY OF CHINA

CHINA: A 5,000-YEAR ODYSSEY

# I. China—The "Enchanting Bride"

This is our northern country,

A billion square-feet in deep freeze,

And snowflakes over thousands of leagues.

Look, outside and inside the Great Wall

Everything lies under Almighty's thrall.

Our enormous Yellow River

A surging fury reduced to soft murmur.

Mountains meander like silver serpents

And tablelands stand like wax elephants,

Vying to match Heaven's height.

Wait till Sunny days come next

When red flowers dressed in white

Perform a wondrous sight.

What an enchanting bride,

For heroes who woo her with craving eyes!

(北国风光，千里冰封，万里雪飘。望长城内外，惟馀莽莽；大河上下，顿失滔滔。山舞银蛇，原驰蜡象，欲与天公试比高。须晴日，看红妆素裹，分外妖娆。江山如此多娇，引无数英雄竟折腰。)

This is my translation of a portion of the renowned poem entitled "Snow 雪," composed by Mao Zedong 毛泽东 (1893–1976), when he saw a huge snow storm in North China for the first time in his life in 1936. Mao was one of the innumerable heroes who wooed the Enchanting Lady (as China is referred to in the poem) and won her hand. Thus, the poem is a part of Chinese history, displaying China's enchanting attraction to her "would-be" rulers.[1]

---

[1]The other part of Mao's poem mentions four famous imperial rulers of China: Qin Emperor Shihuang, Han Emperor Wu, Tang Emperor Taizong, and Song Emperor Taizu, as well as the Mongol Yuan Emperor Genghis Khan.

China is perceived as an exotic combination of "hill 山" and "river 河" ("river 河" alternates with "water 水"). China is a land of more hills than plains. It is interwoven with hills and rivers, fields, and lakes and ponds, presenting a gorgeous landscape of tremendous variety. China has two celebrated rivers: Huanghe 黄河/Yellow River and Yangzijiang 扬子江/Yangtze River. The term "he 河" often refers to Huanghe (Yellow River), and the term "jiang 江" stands for Yangtze River. The phrase "shanhe 山河" also alternates with the phrase "jiangshan 江山" and is used in Mao's poem to represent China.

When dealing with China as US Secretary of State, Hillary Clinton used to quote a famous couplet by the renowned Song Dynasty poet Lu You 陆游 (1125–1210), which says: "After endless mountains and rivers that leave doubt whether there is a path out, suddenly one encounters the shade of a willow, bright flowers, and a lovely village." Kudos to Hillary (or her secretary or advisor) that she indeed grasped the essential charm of China as a country.[2] This is a very realistic feeling of a traveler in China. I often had this sentiment when I traveled long distances on foot during my boyhood in China. Hillary quoted these lines figuratively (as the Chinese always do) to indicate that the solution to a problem is always there when the situation appears to be hopeless. But, I share this traveler's feeling with my readers to reiterate Mao's metaphor of China as "an enchanting bride." China's enchantment is a combination of natural charm and human activities. The natural charm is created by the landscape of hills and rivers. Part of the joy of traveling in China is arriving at a village to meet new friends and enjoying the hospitality of the local people. Judging from my personal experience, traveling in China can feel like an endless, but enjoyable, journey.

---

[2]The title of the poem is "My Visit to the Village West of the Hill 游山西村." The translation differs slightly from the original couplet in Chinese, which is pronounced as *shan qiong shui fu yi wu lu, liu an hua ming you yi cun* and spelt as 山穷水复疑无路，柳暗花明又一村. A literal rendering in English would be "I thought I had traveled past all hills and rivers and there was no road ahead to go further, suddenly, the new vista of shady willows and bright flowers of a village appeared before me."

Chapter 1: Common Geographical Entity of China

Before modern modes of transport were made available, no one had been able to travel to every nook and corner of China. For millennia, the shade of willow trees, bright flowers, and lovely villages have been common sights in China. A "village" is a general description of a group of houses accommodating both local residents and occasional passersby. As early as the first century of our Common Era, Indian and Central Asian Buddhist monks arrived in China and chose to live and preach, erect temples, and build societies on hilltops and in remote locations. They built villages and townships to disseminate Buddhist dharma. Next, Buddhist pilgrims came to visit these places, and poets arrived to carve their masterpieces on rocks or leave them in Buddhist temples to add to the charm of the villages and townships.

The arrival of the Indian monk "Huili 慧理" was a most remarkable phenomenon of charm creation in China. Though we cannot find any reference to him in Indian history, his story is often told in Chinese literature. Chinese records maintain that he sailed from "West heavenly India 西天竺" and arrived in China in the 320s. He settled in Hangzhou 杭州 of Zhejiang 浙江 province, which was then a remote place with villages sparsely scattered throughout. He used to meditate atop a rock of a hill beside West Lake 西湖, which has become one of the hottest tourist attractions in the world today. Gradually, he gained a small following and told the local people that the hill had been a familiar spot in India called "Lingjiushan 灵鹫山" (this *lingjiu* 灵鹫 is the Chinese translation of the Sanskrit word *Gṛdhrakūṭa* meaning "hill of the sacred kite" or, as it is generally translated, "vulture peak," which I don't like). Indian readers will be familiar with this geographic name, which was alleged to be Buddha's favorite retreat located at Rajgir in Bihar. The story goes that the Indian monk Reverend Huili, whose original name might be Matiyukta, told the local people, who were mostly his followers, that the hill on which he was meditating was part of the Magadha Kingdom (known in China as "central heavenly India 中天竺") and that it had flown to Hangzhou through the divine power of Buddha. The locals were mystified and not a little skeptical. Seeing their reaction, Reverend Huili or Matiyukta declared he

could prove what he claimed because he knew the hill very well and even that his old friends lived there. In fact, he told them that he would call his old friends out to prove it.

Then, he made some strange calls and down came a troop of monkeys from the jungle right into their midst. The locals were convinced and news that a "hill was flown here from India 飞来峰" spread far and wide. Now I don't believe this story any more than you do, but you must join me in recognizing the Chinese geographic name "Feilaifeng 飞来峰/the hill flown here from India." Feilaifeng has also been called the "hill of heavenly India 天竺山."

The poet Bai Juyi 白居易 (772–846) used to be the governor of Hangzhou. He wrote a poem titled "Three Years as Governor 三年为刺史" describing how he had led a hard life "drinking ice and eating the stump 饮冰复食檗." He was not a corrupt man, but confessed to having done one thing to satisfy his personal desire. He had picked up two pebbles from the "hill of heavenly India 天竺山" that he thought had "the value of 1,000 pieces of gold" (此抵有千金), yet his "honesty and integrity remained unimpaired" (无乃伤清白). For many centuries, there has been a Chinese saying: "As there is Devapura in Heaven, there are Suzhou and Hangzhou on earth" (上有天堂，下有苏杭). Bai Juyi governed both Suzhou (苏州) in Jiangsu (江苏) province and Hangzhou in Zhejiang province. These stories show that both nature and people, including locals as well as foreign travelers and settlers, such as Indians, have contributed significantly to the allure of China.

The world's climates can be divided into three groups: the frigid zone, the temperate zone, and the tropical zone. China sits on all three zones and has all features associated therewith. The horizontal mobility and migration of plantations facilitate creation of a three-zone synthesis that adds to the glamor of the country. There is always a benign coexistence of the northern wheat culture with the southern rice culture, northern horsemanship

**Feilaifeng: "The Hill Flown Here from India"**

with southern boatmanship, and the northern brawn with the southern brains. Historically, it has been northern China's assertiveness dominating the political stage and southern China's opulence sustaining economic prosperity.

One thing to remember about China is that it's a huge country (about the size of Europe) featuring centripetal dynamics. A Chinese saying goes that "when the east is dark, the west is shining 东方不亮西方亮," which can be seen as a variation of the "sun-never-sets" brag of the 19th-century Britain. Another Chinese saying goes: "When one segment is in trouble, support comes from all other segments" (一方有难，八方支援). In general, China has managed to stay in unity with backing from all parts of the country. In turn, unified China has often taken care of problems in particular periods of time. China is a unified whole made up of different parts having their own characteristics.

The parts love the whole, while the whole endears the parts. The parts support the whole, while the whole oversees all parts. This is also where China's glamor lies. In this book, I will focus on China's centripetal dynamics.

## II. The Himalaya Sphere

When you sleep in a train, you are in static mode even though you know you are moving quickly. When you sleep at home, you think you're static, but the cosmonaut sees you moving with the Earth. The Earth revolves around its axis and the sun. Few, if any, view China through the cosmonaut's goggles as I am about to do by rewinding to millions of years ago.

It's the Earth's revolution that has touchingly revealed the story of China. The Earth's double revolutions created movement and drastic change in its crust. It is the only planet in the Solar System that holds a lot of water for sustaining life. Billions of years ago, there were only two huge land masses on the Earth: Laurasia and Gondwana. Laurasia was our present Eurasia in addition to North America, while Gondwana split into Australia, Africa, and South America. Then, Africa joined the western end of Eurasia, and South America joined North America. The continental plate of India was originally a part of Africa. It migrated across the Paleo-Tethys Ocean to embrace the continental plate of China. The front of the former ran into the bottom of the latter and pushed it up, creating the Himalayas, the Qinghai–Tibetan Plateau 青藏高原, and two great rivers—Huanghe and Yangtze. This change took place 240 million years ago and is called "Himalayan orogeny" by scientists. At that time, south of the Yangtze was sea. Then, 180 million years ago, another great change called "Indosinian orogeny" took place and the land of present South China was created along with present Southeast Asia. The Yangtze was still separated by the sea from the newly created land. Then there was a third great change in the Earth's crust 135 million years ago, when the northeastern corner of Eurasia received a shock causing disappearance of the inland sea south of the Yangtze.

If we use a compass to draw a circle on Earth, with one leg pointing at the center of Himalaya and the other at Kanyakumari (Cape Comorin), the southern tip of the Indian peninsula, we get the Himalaya Sphere that encompasses the entire continental

South Asia and Southeast Asia, a large part of the valleys of the Yangtze and Yellow rivers, Central Asia, and West Asia (including the "Fertile Crescent"). This Himalaya Sphere is the native home to half the flora and fauna on earth, and the homeland of humans. India is home to 90,000 vegetation species and 45,000 animal species. Most plants of the Northern Hemisphere can be found in China. India and China are, therefore, the twin major civilizations of the Himalaya Sphere.

People of the Himalaya Sphere drink the water of rivers mainly created in the Himalayan glaciers. Four great rivers stood out and shaped Indian and Chinese civilizations: Indus, Ganga, Yangtze, and Huanghe. Ganga flows from Himalaya and the Qinghai–Tibetan Plateau into the Bay of Bengal, while Indus flows from the same area into the Arabian Sea. These two rivers carved the contours of the Indian common geographical entity for various tribes and races of the Indian subcontinent to develop the Indian common civilization entity. The Indian subcontinent never really embarked on a "nation-state" path from the dawn of civilization to the eve of colonial British rule: This is because the Indian common civilization entity didn't allow any nation to grow and indulge in unlimited horizontal expansion to establish a "nation-state" until the British conquest.

Like India, China went through the dual process of creating the common geographical entity and then the common civilization entity. The Huanghe and Yangtze rivers originate from the same Himalaya and Qinghai–Tibetan Plateau. Huanghe flows from the Bayan Har mountain range, and the Yangtze flows from the nearby Tangula mountain range. They part ways with one flowing north and the other south. Huanghe flows through Qinghai, Sichuan, Gansu, Ningxia, Inner Mongolia, Shaanxi, Shanxi, Henan, and Shandong before flowing into the sea. The Yangtze flows through Qinghai, Sichuan, Tibet, Yunnan, Sichuan again, Hubei, Hunan, Jiangxi, Anhui, and Jiangsu before flowing into the sea. The two rivers are connected by the Huai River, forming a garland and making Huanghe inseparable from the

Yangtze and vice versa. Thus, they carved the Chinese common geographical entity just as Indus and Ganga carved the Indian common geographical entity.

The Chinese describe the phenomenon as "conceived by heaven and constructed by earth," thereby meaning that China was not originally created by Chinese, but by two great rivers. Among the 10 greatest rivers on earth, eight are internationally shared. Only the Yangtze and Huanghe are not. No other country has ever contested China for sovereignty of any portion of the Yangtze or Huanghe. The Chinese people never had to fight wars over water disputes relating to the Yangtze and Huanghe. From early times until today, the population in the valleys of the Yangtze and Huanghe has always embraced the common identity that is China.

The contours drawn by the two great rivers create an enormous space. The total drainage area of the Yangtze is 1.8 million square kilometers and that of Huanghe is 0.795 million square kilometers, totaling 2.595 million square kilometers (almost 80 percent of the present size of India). During the days of primitive transportation, it took a Chinese traveler 10 hours to cover 50 kilometers (as was my personal experience when I was young). If he or she traveled non-stop, he or she could travel 18,250 kilometers in a year or 912,500 kilometers in 50 years. Chinese ancients seldom lived that long, and no one would travel all his or her life. To ancient Chinese, China was, indeed, huge and unbounded.

Human civilization always emerges from rivers. The two great rivers carved the contours of China and nursed human development in China. Conventional wisdom used to see Asia as key to the origin of humans. From the 20th century onward, scientists have started to prove humanity being "born in Africa." I am neither a ticktock traditionalist nor a revolutionary discoverer. I have no expertise to judge the "born in Africa" theory. Two decades ago, I visited Chuxiong 楚雄 County, now Chuxiong

The first mainstream looks like an epic about the offspring of the Lantian Ape Man, who lived in a lush green environment with giant pandas, elephants, tigers, and deer. People could fashion rough stone instruments, hunt, and gather fruit, seeds, and vegetables. The "Lantian Ape Man" began a new age of Paleolithic culture in the Huanghe valley (in its middle stream). During the Neolithic Era, the Central Plain had a large area of sustained cultural development in the middle and lower streams of the Huanghe, including a succession of Yangshao 仰韶, Longshan 龙山, and Anyang 安阳 civilizations.

The "Yangshao Civilization 仰韶文化" was a Neolithic civilization[3] spreading from Gansu to Henan provinces from 5000 BCE to 3000 BCE. Most unearthed sites are in Henan and Shaanxi provinces. Here was a civilization with fairly advanced agriculture in proso millet (粟) and broomcorn millet (黍), as well as animal husbandry of mostly pigs.

The "Longshan Civilization 龙山文化" was a Neolithic civilization in its late phase spreading in Shaanxi, Henan, Shanxi, and Shandong in the middle and lower streams of the Huanghe during about 4350–3950 BCE. Shandong province is crucial to discovery of the "Longshan Civilization." There is also the discovery of the "Dawenkou Civilization 大汶口文化" on the banks of Dawen 大汶 River, 30 kilometers south of Taian 泰安 City in Shandong, which existed 4,000–5,000 years ago.

---

[3]Readers may find it interesting how the Chinese people's script preserves information of living conditions during the early Neolithic and even Paleolithic Age. There is the visual for "cave" (穴 in modern writing), and 冂 (the entrance of a cave) in Oracle Script, the oldest script in China. People of the Yangshao Civilization commonly lived in caves. Even today, cave residence is still common in Shaanxi and Gansu provinces. There is another visual for "to smell" (嗅 in modern writing) and 𡧛 (in Oracle Script) which is a two-part combination with the upper part 𠂤 drawing a nose and the lower part 犬 drawing a dog (there is a varied drawing of 犭 dog in Oracle Script). Today, police in most countries use dogs to detect drug trafficking as dogs have the sharpest sense of smell. The Chinese people had this information during the Neolithic Age and kept dogs as important helpers during hunting: No wonder the Chinese are the world's first people to keep dogs as pets. The modern English phrase "running dog" is an adoption of the pejorative description from modern Chinese literature.

Fast wheel pottery technology was the highlight of the Dawenkou Civilization. This same technology was adopted by the Longshan Civilization to produce polished, thin black pottery.

According to archaeological convention, a newly discovered ancient civilization is christened after the name of the site where it is first excavated. Thus, the Yangshao Civilization takes the name of Yangshao Village in Mianchi 渑池 County of Sanmenxia 三门峡 City in Henan province where the first archaeological site is located. The Longshan Civilization takes the name of Longshan Town (now the Longshan Street Office) in Zhangqiu 章丘 County of Jinan 济南 City in Shandong province, where the first archaeological site is located. This does not mean the two sites are the centers of their respective civilizations. As a matter of fact, the areas of these two early civilizations overlap. From a holistic perspective, we should regard them as the overall civilizational development of the Central Plain.

The "Anyang Civilization 安阳文化" was a milestone for ancient Chinese civilization in three ways. First, it was the successor to the Yangshao and Longshan civilizations by evolving from the primitive Stone Age into the more advanced Bronze Age and Iron Age. Second, it discovered the ruins of Yin 殷, the capital of the Shang-Yin/Yin-Shang Dynasty, which means China's archaeological discoveries are converging with the age-old literary tradition of Chinese history thousands of years before invention of archaeology.[4] Third, Anyang Civilization also features the Oracle Script, marking the beginning of literacy in China.

We are increasingly enriched by the information learned about ancient China through archaeological discoveries, which China excels at. Unlike Indians, who cremated their dead seniors, along with their mementos, the Chinese built underground

---

[4]This tradition began with the Yellow Emperor 黄帝 through the abdication period, Xia Dynasty establishing the Great Yu, then the Shang Dynasty. Thus, the literary tradition of Chinese history becomes reliable and respectable. Such a feat of archaeological discovery supporting ancient literary tradition is remarkable in the history of world civilization.

**The visual of 家/home in Oracle Script**
**(A picture of a pig inside a house to depict "home, sweet home")**

In the more advanced Small Seal Script, the visual is simplified into 𩠐, now written as 家 (the upper part 宀 represents the roof and the lower part 豕 represents the pig). This indicates that ancient Chinese conceived the idea of "home" when they began animal husbandry, with the pig occupying primary importance. It is certain that Chinese "pig culture" was first developed in the Yangtze valley, borne out by the following picture.

**A black pot unearthed from Hemudu**
**7,000–9,000 years ago**

Such a pretty design demonstrates the warm affection Neolithic Chinese in the Yangtze valley had for the pig. We know the "pig culture" was prominent in the Yangshao–Longshan–Anyang civilization chain and must have spread from the Yangtze valley. Combination of the rice and pig culture created self-sufficient agriculture and animal husbandry and made people of the Yangtze valley more homebound than people in the Huanghe valley, which took a longer time to free itself from a nomadic lifestyle. Nurtured by rice and pork, Chinese people lived in densely populated townships and were slower to become politically oriented and to assume an expansive role than people in the Huanghe valley.

## IV. China–India Resonance

The new star of the Yangtze mainstream of development in the Neolithic Age is, no doubt, the Sanxingdui 三星堆 Civilization discovered in the Chengdu 成都 area of Sichuan province. This was an ancient civilization living 3,000–6,000 years ago (2800–1000 BCE). Excavation is still being carried out. One site is located in Guanghan 广汉 City, 40 kilometers from Chengdu, and another site is at Jinsha 金沙, within Chengdu City, where 90 percent of excavation is yet to be done. Since the discovery became public, it has attracted growing international attention. The incredible nature of this discovery has led many foreign commentators to describe it as a civilization of "aliens from another planet." This was a two millennia Yangtze valley civilization, matching the Yangshao–Longshan chain. It was more developed economically than its contemporary Central Plain Neolithic civilizations. It had an industrial orientation with a large number of bronze and jade wares, as well as some gold products. In addition, there is evidence of highly developed commerce and trade, including foreign trade.

It is my firm opinion that the Sanxingdui Civilization started the Silk Road and was why China became known as the "country of silk." Sichuan is the home of silk, and the Sanxingdui Civilization contributed greatly to the export of raw silk, silk fabrics, and even silkworms (supposedly a great trade secret). My conclusion is based on the following quote from *Arthashastra* (a treatise on statecraft), authored by Chanakya (who is also known as Kautilya or Visnu Gupta), the founder and prime minister of the Maurya Empire in ancient India.

*Kauseyam cinapattasca cinabhumijah*

(Chinese cocoons and Chinese fabrics are the products of China.)

**Chapter 1: Common Geographical Entity of China**

**A humanoid bird sculpture of Sanxingdui**

My visit to the Guanghan exhibition of Sanxingdui gave me a deep impression about the humanoid birds among the bronze sculptures. They seemed to be the Sanxingdui version of the legendary Indian bird Garuda. There were many birds on the bronze sculptures, with some having human or animal heads. I saw animal feet shaped like the bird's tail. These sculptures combined with the four Garuda-type sun birds at the Jinsha exhibition led to the opening of a new door in mythology study. The Indian legend of Garuda is millennia old, but I have never seen a very old artifact of Garuda in India, certainly not as old as the Sanxingdui exhibits. I'm sure Indian historians and archaeologists would be interested in an in-depth study of this phenomenon.

We can extend this topic of Garuda to the Chinese mind-set in the Yangtze valley millennia ago. There was another ancient Chinese artifact, a T-shaped silk painting (205 centimeters long, 92 centimeters wide in the upper portion, and 47.7 centimeters wide in the lower portion) unearthed at Tomb Number One at the Mawangdui 马王堆 site in Changsha 长沙. This Mawangdui silk painting can improve our familiarity with the ideas of ancient Chinese sun worship.

One will notice the prominent sun bird in the upper right corner and the long-winged bird with an animal head carrying a large structure on its shoulders in the center. This picture surely presents the worldview of Chinese people in the Yangtze valley, although we are unable to explain it in detail. Surely, the Garuda and Dragon (Chinese incarnation of the Indian Naga) dominated the scene. There were no dragons in the Sanxingdui exhibitions, which were a couple of millennia older than the Mawangdui.

**Silk painting of Tomb One unearthed at Mawangdui**

The human facial features of the Sanxingdui bronze sculptures, with big eyes and high noses, resemble present-day Indians much more than present-day Chinese, who have small eyes and flat noses. If anyone wants to identify Sanxingdui as an ancient Indian civilization, it would seem logical. But, Sanxingdui is very much within China, while Indian territory, in historical times, was very far away. Of course, during that period, 5,000 years ago, identities of China and India were hardly established. Discovery of the Sanxingdui Civilization indicates that Chinese and Indian civilizations had been resonating a long time before they became distinguishable from one another.

We shall look at another ancient Chinese artifact on which facial features resemble the Sanxingdui exhibits. This piece was

**A piece of bronze sculpture**

Chapter 1: Common Geographical Entity of China

Image of Buddhas Xiangtang Unit
(a modern Chinese artist's rendering)

Uma—Goddess of Himalaya. There is a fascinating story of King Mu of Zhou 周穆王 (reigned in the 10th century BCE) traveling to Mount Kunlun 昆仑 (Himalaya) to rendezvous with this goddess. Many decades ago, I visited the famous "Celestial Lake 天池" a few hours by road from Urumqi 乌鲁木齐, capital of Xinjiang 新疆: This is said to be the resort of Goddess Xiwangmu. I think her Chinese name Xiwangmu should be read as *xi* (west) + *wangmu*, with the second part being the Chinese term for *uma*. It is possible the Indian legend of Uma (wife of God Shiva and Goddess of Himalaya) reached China via Central Asia. During its travel, Uma was changed to wangmu. Perhaps a scholar knowing some Central Asian language can help explain the process of change. Today, devout Hindus make pilgrimages to Mount Kailash and Manasarovar Lake to pay homage to God Shiva and Goddess Uma. In the Chinese legend of Xiwangmu, she resides by the lake called the "Jade Lake 瑶池" or "Celestial Lake 天池" in Chinese. The former is the Manasarovar Lake of Tibet (in Himalaya) and the latter is at the location near Urumqi where I had the honor to pay homage to Goddess Xiwangmu/Uma.

There is yet another story that illustrates resonance between early Chinese and Indian civilizations. The story of Pangu 盘古

**Image of Goddess Xiwangmu/Uma
(A modern Chinese artist's rendering)**

circulated in China much later than the story of Fuxi–Nüwa and Goddess Xiwangmu/Uma, probably from the 3rd century CE. Pangu is described as creator of Heaven and Earth. He was initially a small man, but grew fast. Initially, there was neither Heaven nor Earth. Heaven rose as high, and Earth thickened as much as he grew. After 18,000 years, both Heaven and Earth took shape. He died after living 80,000 years, his eyes became the sun and moon, and other parts of his body were transformed into mountains, rivers, vegetation, and animals on Earth. In modern times, some scholars believe he looked like a Chinese version of the Indian legend Purusa, from Vedic literature, who was a cosmic man whose sacrifice by the gods created all life in the universe. Like Pangu, Purusa's eye also became the sun. Also, Pangu was like Nüwa, having a human head and snake body.

# CHAPTER 2

# THE CHINESE COMMON POLITICAL ENTITY

From the gray areas of our knowledge about early Chinese civilization, we follow the footsteps of the Chinese march into a new common political entity. You have probably noted the absence of powerful tribes, nations, and nation-states within Chinese civilization. Sanxingdui Civilization was probably the most developed and advanced among the Neolithic communities in the Yangtze and Huanghe valleys, but it did not become a force of war and conquest. It mysteriously disappeared and sank into oblivion after a pacific existence lasting nearly two millennia. We know nothing about the community identity and political entity in the absence of a script. Today, scholars describe it as the ancient "Shu 蜀" state, mainly through conjecture. The earliest reference to "Shu 蜀" reticently appears in the first Chinese chronological history, *Shiji* 史记 (records of a historian), compiled by renowned historian and "China's Herodotus" Sima Qian 司马迁 (145–90 BCE).

## I. Yu Created the Common Political Entity

Sima Qian had no idea the earth was a globe, nor did he know any ape men existed in China hundreds of thousands of years ago, nor anything about the Yangshao, Longshan, Sanxingdui, or other Paleolithic and Neolithic civilizations, nor any of the archaeological discoveries made in modern China. However, he was more conversant than us in terms of China's literary tradition. According to him, the earliest Chinese rulers were the "celestial sovereign 天皇," "terrestrial sovereign 地皇," and "harmonious sovereign 泰皇" (a variation on the last is "human sovereign 人皇"). Sima Qian initiated an ancient Chinese discourse on the so-called "three sovereigns and five emperors 三皇五帝" with no consensus about their identities. Modern Chinese scholars describe the earliest Chinese political history as the "age of the three sovereigns and five emperors," which is in fact an unknown time and space. It is clear that ancient Chinese legends came from various origins: Those of the Huanghe valley substantially differ from those of the Yangtze valley. The most prominent case

is the phenomenon of the dual ancestors of modern Chinese people, "Huangdi 黄帝/Yellow Emperor" and "Yandi 炎帝/Yan Emperor." Today, Chinese people like to designate themselves as "Yan-Huang zisun 炎黄子孙" (progeny of Yandi and Huangdi). Huangdi/Yellow Emperor (the cultural hero of the Huanghe valley) is quite well known internationally. Yandi/Yan Emperor (the cultural hero of the Yangtze valley), though less known abroad, was the peer of the Yellow Emperor as a cultural hero in China. The visual of the latter's name "yan 炎" in Chinese script presents the double symbol of "fire 火." The Yan Emperor is, thus, the Chinese version of a solar deity. Worship of the Yan Emperor has been popular in the Yangtze valley (he must have had his altar in the sun worshipping time of Sanxingdui, but we still need to prove that). But, we know he was "god of agriculture 神农." The Yellow Emperor ushered in the three famous ancient rulers of Yao, Shun, and Yu in the Central Plain of the Huanghe valley.

Yao 尧 was an ancient king of the Central Plain according to Chinese tradition. He voluntarily abdicated his ruling position to Shun 舜, who, in turn, abdicated his position to Yu 禹. Tradition is meant to be believed, not scrutinized. Yao died in 2259 BCE at age 118, after having ruled his kingdom for 70 years. At age 90, he wanted to find a virtuous successor. Popular opinion favored Shun, who was from a poor family. Yao provided decent accommodation for Shun, with attendants to serve him and observe his conduct. After Shun's credibility was affirmed, Yao vacated his seat of king for, and also married his two daughter princesses to, Shun. After some time, a veteran officer named Gun 鲧 failed to harness the rivers and caused a disastrous flood. Shun, the new king, dismissed Gun and appointed Gun's son to the job. The son spent over a decade dredging water channels and digging canals to resolve the serious flooding problem, transforming his father's miserable failure into a remarkable success and winning universal praise. This achievement made the country prosperous and its people happy. King Shun was greatly impressed and abdicated his kingship to this popular hero—the "Great Yu 大禹."

Chinese tradition highlighted Yao, Shun, and Yu as examples of sage rulers, tantamount to celebrating the convention of the king choosing his successor and handing over his reign to that successor while still alive. However, this practice was ceased by Yu, the greatest of the three sage rulers. Yu was the founding father of the hereditary system of government in China. From a realpolitik perspective, this was an improvement that created stability in that a ruler's successor was to be decided within the ruling family rather than by way of the king's personal choice devoid of rules and regulations. Thus, Yu was the founding father of a new political era in China.

The great Indian epic Ramayana is a biographical account of Rama, a legendary cultural hero and king of ancient India. The Chinese story of the Great Yu resembles that of Rama. While pious Indians have not been inquisitive about Rama's historical details, the secular Chinese have had a prolonged controversy about the Great Yu for 2,000 years. The controversy was initiated by the great historian Sima Qian who remarked: "Yu rose from Western Qiang 禹兴于西羌." However, Chinese orthodoxy and conventional wisdom always regarded the Great Yu as a great man hailing from the Central Plain.

Since ancient times, the folklore of the Qiang 羌 nationality of Sichuan province has owned the Great Yu as a local hero. In the 1980s, I went to Chengdu 成都 to study the issue of ethnic minorities and met with Professor Zhou Xiyin 周锡银, director of the Institute of Nationality Studies of Sichuan. He reiterated that the Great Yu was a Qiang 羌 from Sichuan and presented his book[1] to me. Later, when I presented this new perspective in international seminars, overseas Chinese scholars vehemently challenged my view that the Great Yu was a Sichuan Qiang national.

There was no consensus among Chinese academics about Zhou Xiyin's proposition until the devastating Wenchuan 汶川

---

[1]Zhou Xiyin 周锡银 and Liu Zhiron 刘志荣, *Qiangzu*《羌族》(Qiang nationality) (Beijing: Nationality Press 民族出版社, 1993).

earthquake of 2008 awoke people from their diehard Central Plain prejudice. Volunteers from various places in China went to help with reconstruction for earthquake victims and discovered the special sentimental attachment of Wenchuan's Qiang community to the Great Yu. Still, many Chinese found it hard to believe this new story spreading across China. People wondered, "How did the Great Yu of Henan (Central Plain) suddenly transform into a Qiang national of Sichuan?"

Meanwhile, the Beichuan 北川 Qiang Autonomous County, under the jurisdiction of Mianyang 绵阳 City in Sichuan, tried its best in the last 30 years to pursue study of the Great Yu and develop tourism as the home of the Great Yu. They discovered the existence of the 142nd descendant of the Great Yu—Professor Si Yuanyi 姒元翼 of Harbin Medical University. Thus, the theory of Great Yu's Qiang origin is further strengthened. The central government has paid special attention to Qiang culture, as severe damage to Qiang historical assets resulted from the great earthquake of 2008. During this process, the age-old prejudice of the Central Plain has been corrected. Today, there is consensus throughout China, and two "Yu monuments 禹穴" are recognized as the cultural heritage of China. The first is the birthplace of Yu at the foot of Jiulongshan 九龙山 in Beichuan County, Sichuan, and the second is the "Tomb of Yu 禹陵" at the foot of Mount Huijishan 会稽山 in Shaoxing 绍兴 City, Zhejiang. In 2007, Beichuan was conferred as the "home of the Great Yu culture." In 2011, the Yu legend was recognized as the state-level "intangible cultural heritage."

The story of Qiang-ethnicity Yu, who was born in interior Sichuan and died in the east coast province of Zhejiang, as the founding father of the common political entity established in China's Central Plain (thousands of miles from Yu's birthplace) is a significant indication that the Chinese common civilization entity is transforming into a common political entity.

Sichuan, home of the Wushan Ape Man and Sanxingdui Civilization, played an important role in this transformation. The

story of the Great Yu also reflects input of the Yangtze valley civilization into the political construction of the Huanghe valley. The interplay of geography and politics is paradoxical. The valley of Yangtze has always had an advantage over that of Huanghe because the Yangtze is a larger river than Huanghe, providing more fertile soil and economic prosperity and less natural calamity. But, politically, the valley of Huanghe always shows greater initiative and accomplishment. However, we should not forget the interdependence and interconnectivity of the two rivers. The Great Yu was a son of Sichuan, where there was the brilliant Sanxingdui Civilization during his time. He must have injected aspirations of the Yangtze valley into the Huanghe valley. Conversely, if Yu had remained in his home place and never gone to the valley of Huanghe, he would have sunk into oblivion along with the Sanxingdui in history. He helped the Central Plain rise as a great political entity and the Central Plain made him the "Great Yu."

The Great Yu was truly great due to his deed in harnessing the Huanghe and other rivers over 4,000 years ago. It was a crucial

**The Great Yu fighting with the dragon to harness rivers (painted by Lu Honggang)**

event in making the Central Plain a good place to live. It is no surprise that the great deed gave rise to fairytales that the Great Yu commanded a huge contingent of laborers and fought with dragons to carry out his project. Remoteness in time does not provide us with details of historical facts. One story that must be true is that in a time period spanning 10 years, the Great Yu led his huge contingent of workers, crisscrossing the country, tackling the problems of the rivers. He passed his own house three times but did not enter and say hello to his near and dear ones. For thousands of years, this story has inspired Chinese people to devote themselves to their duties in a selfless spirit.

The renowned German historian Karl August Wittfogel (1896–1988) wrote voluminous books and articles on China. He coined a special word, "hydraulic" (instead of "hydro"), to characterize the special nature of Chinese politics and society. While Wittfogel used "hydraulic" to characterize Chinese bureaucracy, we will use it to strengthen our perspective on the Chinese common entity. You will agree that the "hydraulic" enterprise, invented and initiated by the Great Yu, befittingly responded to the two great rivers' creation of the common geographic entity. The two great rivers wanted people who lived in their valleys to live up to their expectations and construct the Chinese common entity. They gave Chinese people a huge challenge and opportunity. Yangtze was a very friendly and beneficial river that provided a harmonious life for its residents. Huanghe challenged its residents by creating trouble. The Great Yu used his Yangtze heritage to achieve economic prosperity and political solidarity. He used his "hydraulic" effort to brighten the Chinese economic image and went a step further to brighten the Chinese political image. He created the common political entity in China.

## II. The Three Dynasties Before Unification

At the time when King Yao vacated his seat to see the virtuous Shun succeed him as ruler, the kingdom must have been rather small. But the Great Yu created a huge area free from flooding and was vindicated as ruler after a great expansion of the regime, which became the Xia Dynasty 夏朝 (about 2070–1600 BCE). Since 1952, Chinese archaeologists have worked hard to excavate the "Erlitou Civilization 二里头文化" at Dengfeng 登封 in Henan province, in the hope of discovering something more about the Xia Dynasty capital. Two hundred sites around Zhengzhou 郑州 and Luoyang 洛阳, in a vast area covering southern Shanxi and western Henan, have been excavated. The area was reminiscent of an erstwhile palace and gave people the impression that it used to be the site of a political center. However, absence of written scripts and lack of evidence make it impossible to draw any conclusions.

The new era ushered in by the Great Yu resulted in the creation of a confederation of sorts on Chinese soil. This confederation was essentially a two-tier polity. In the higher tier, there was the "son of heaven 天子" and the realm directly under his rule. In the lower tier, there were the "lords 诸侯," who also had a kingdom directly under their rule. The Great Yu and his successors in the dynasty were "sons of heaven" ruling the leading kingdom. They were also tutelary leader of the "lords" of the confederation. Externally, the Xia confederation was one solid political entity. Though non-members came to join the confederation, there was no foreign state to threaten its security and existence. Internally, the "son of heaven" only ruled his own kingdom and refrained from interfering with the domain of the "lords." The lords had two obligations to the son of heaven: paying tribute to contribute to the revenues of, and rushing troops to defend, the latter's kingdom.

According to tradition, Yu passed the son of heaven kingship to 14 consecutive successors, and the Xia Dynasty lasted 500 years. When Yu became the son of heaven, he gathered all the lords of the confederation to perform a swearing-in ceremony to mark formal establishment of the confederation. This is known historically as the Tushan Conference 涂山之会. The venue was

in Huaiyuan 怀远 County, Bangbu 蚌埠 City, Anhui province. The conference was famous for the scene of "ten thousand 万" (meaning innumerable) warriors (heads of the states within the confederation) bringing jade and cloth (meaning gifts) for exchange, instead of clashing with their weapons. This historic event is the origin of the famous Chinese saying "transforming weapons into jade and cloth 化干戈为玉帛" (meaning to stop war and negotiate peace). Here, we see that the Great Yu created the Chinese confederation peacefully (lords attended the conference voluntarily and the Great Yu never used force against any of them). It was said that Yu was unwilling to pass kingship to his son Qi 启, but the lords were in favor of Qi. After Qi ascended to the throne as the "son of heaven," he also held a swearing-in ceremony which all lords of the confederation attended.

From tidbits revealed in early Chinese books, we see that after the Great Yu and his son and successor Qi, all the "sons of heaven" of the Xia Dynasty were mediocre or bad. Still there were, altogether, about 15 rulers to sustain for 500 years. Such a development would not be possible during the later Chinese "empire." This shows that the Xia Dynasty was just a loose alliance of autonomous states which collectively ensured continuation of the status quo. In those early years, there was no strong state in China's neighborhood to challenge the stability of the Chinese confederation under the banner of Xia. Finally, there emerged the final son of heaven of the Xia Dynasty, whose name was Jie 桀 (reigned 1652–1600 BCE). He was actually a capable man, a warrior, well cultured, and held the throne for 52 years. But then, Tang 汤, ruler of a subordinate state in the confederation, rose and destroyed the Xia and established a new dynasty. King Jie, captured and banished by Tang, eventually starved to death.

The Shang Dynasty (about 1600–1046 BCE) was founded by King Tang, who was as capable as the Great Yu and had the advantage of living over half a millennium later than Yu. We see this new dynasty marking the progress of Chinese civilization

into the Bronze Age from the Chalcolithic Age. The Shang Dynasty, which lasted for over 500 years under 31 kings, covering the Longshan and Anyang civilizations, also saw the development of the Chinese script. However, China remained a confederation, the only change being that a new ruling family had replaced the erstwhile family of the Xia Dynasty. One theory, based on the assumption that indigenous China did not develop a bronze culture, suggested that this new ruling family from the northern steppe had brought a bronze culture to the Central Plain. But recent discovery of the Sanxingdui and Tanheli civilizations, as seen in Chapter 1, makes it hard to support that assumption.

The city culture that was introduced by the Shang Dynasty has been a distinctive feature of China, until it was overtaken by Western countries in modern times. Luoyang 洛阳, in Henan province, was one of the earliest millennial prosperous urban centers in China. The Shang Dynasty changed its capital eight times, but always kept it near the Luoyang area. Ruins of early Shang palaces unearthed in Luoyang indicate that handicrafts and commerce developed substantially in China during the second half of the third millennium BCE. It was a development that caused China to become an open space with easy horizontal mobility across state boundaries.

History seems to have repeated itself when the Shang Dynasty was overthrown by the Zhou[2] (which means the Chinese confederation had a new ruling family to act as its son of heaven

---

[2]An unusual episode related to the founding of the Zhou Dynasty is worth narrating here. Two brother noblemen, Boyi 伯夷 and Shuqi 叔齐, pleaded for peace as King Wu of Zhou was about to wage war with the last ruler of the Shang, King Zhou 纣 (ruled 1075–1046 BCE). King Wu turned a deaf ear to their pleading, fought a big war, overthrew the Shang Dynasty, and established the Zhou Dynasty. The two proponents for peace went to the jungle and lived on wild vegetation to sever their connection from King Wu's reign, which was founded on violence. Later, people told them even the jungle and wild growth belonged to King Wu of Zhou, the reigning son of heaven. They stopped eating and died of starvation. Confucius complimented the noble spirit of the two, who came to be regarded as sages in Chinese civilization. Though an isolated episode, it reflects the peace-loving social atmosphere of ancient China.

and tutelary leader). The hero of this change was King Wu of Zhou 周武王, who reigned in the 1040s BCE. In Chinese tradition, King Wu of Zhou was just one of the three eminent sage personalities of the same family with the title of Zhou 周. They were: the father, King Wen of Zhou 周文王 (1152–1056 BCE), and the two sons, King Wu and Duke of Zhou 周公 (dates unknown). Confucius observed that "great was King Wen of Zhou: He is my model 郁郁乎文哉郁郁乎文哉，吾从周." King Wen of Zhou was revered as a sage ruler, while Duke of Zhou was regarded as a good administrator who greatly helped King Wu of Zhou's reign.

The Zhou Dynasty 周朝 had 35 rulers and lasted nearly 800 years (1046–256 BCE). The prime years of this new dynasty was during its first phase called "Western Zhou 西周" (1046–771 BCE). The Chinese confederation worked fine until the end of Western Zhou. During the three dynasties, subordinate autonomous states were depended upon for revenue and defense, mainly to protect the son of heaven who had only a small state to rule. In the capital that was the seat of the son of heaven, "beacon towers 烽火台" were built for emergency communication with subordinate states. Whenever an enemy attack was spotted, fires would be set in the beacon towers to alert the soldiers on guard duty, who would then beat the alarm drums so that army commanders would send in troops for defense. This was an ingenious system that had ensured the safety and stability of the Chinese confederation three to four millennia earlier. The system was destroyed by a bad son of heaven of the Zhou Dynasty— King You of Zhou 周幽王 (reigned 795–771 BCE). His queen, Baosi 褒姒 (791–? BCE), was a beautiful lady who never smiled. After failing to make her smile by all means, the king set fires in the beacon towers and took the queen to the rampart to see the fun. When friendly forces from neighboring areas rushed over to defend the son of heaven against the invaders, what they saw instead was the king and queen laughing at them from the rampart.

Chapter 2: The Chinese Common Political Entity

When the trick worked in making the queen smile, King You of Zhou repeated it a couple more times to the fury of the lords of the confederation. When there did come a genuine foreign attack in 771 BCE, King You was killed by the invaders because no one was there to rescue him. As a result, the Zhou Dynasty virtually collapsed. Zhou nobility revived the dynasty by establishing a new capital in the east (present Luoyang in Henan), known in history as the "Eastern Zhou 东周" (770–225 BCE). The Eastern Zhou period was also known as the periods of "Spring and Autumn 春秋" (770–476 BCE) and "Warring States 战国" (475–221 BCE), which was followed by China's unification. China was no longer a solid confederation and the son of heaven (of Zhou) was no longer in a position of command, even symbolically.

During the Warring States period, there were only seven states with a son of heaven as figurehead. The seven states vied to gain hegemony or maintain survival. They engaged in cold and hot wars. Five lords rose to prominence, consecutively: King Huan of Qi 齐桓公 (ruled the state of Qi from 685 BCE to 643 BCE), King Xiang of Song 宋襄公 (ruled the state of Song from 650 BCE to 637 BCE), King Wen of Jin 晋文公 (ruled the state of Jin from 636 BCE to 628 BCE), King Zhuang of Chu 楚庄王 (ruled the state of Chu from 613 BCE to 591 BCE), and King Mu of Qin 秦穆公 (ruled the state of Qin from 659 BCE to 621 BCE). Finally, the Qin state vanquished the other six and unified China.

**The ancient Chinese "beacon tower"**

## III. Confucius and the "Hundred Schools"

Politically, the Eastern Zhou (Spring and Autumn, as well as Warring States) saw the collapse of the three-dynasty Chinese confederation. However, culturally, there was renaissance in China with the phenomenon of "various masters and a hundred schools 诸子百家." The Chinese term *zi* 子, suffixing a surname, is akin to the Indian "ji" (like in "Gandhiji") in showing respect and means "master." "Kongzi 孔子" means "Master Kong," "Mengzi 孟子" means "Master Meng," "Zhuangzi 庄子" means "Master Zhuang," and "Sunzi 孙子" means "Master Sun." Laozi or Laotze 子 (Master Lao) was an outstanding scholar whose surname was probably Li 李, and whose life we know practically nothing about. He left behind a short text full of gems we call *Laozi/Laotze* or *Daodejing/Tao-the-king* 道德经, which is internationally well known. The text is a collection of isolated sentences, each of which is a meaningful adage somewhat puzzling and subject to different interpretations.[3] Here is one example:

In Laozi, there is a short sentence: *zhizhebuyan, yanzhebuzhi* 知者不言，言者不知. Superficially, it may be understood as "Those who know don't speak, and those who speak don't know." Clearly, this would not have been the true meaning of the adage. The true meaning depends on how one interprets it. We know ancients often used the word *zhi* 知 to mean "wise/wisdom," as is the case with this adage. Thus, the adage can be

---

[3]Here are a couple of more examples: "Disaster foretells good fortune while good fortune has the potential to lead to disaster 祸兮福所倚，福兮祸所伏." Laozi also observed: "The sage does not accumulate. One becomes richer after helping others get rich, and one owns more after sharing with others 圣人不积，既以为人己愈有，既以与人己愈多." I think the observation is meant both spiritually and materially. Another example: "The weak will prevail over the strong and the limber will overcome the hard 弱能胜强，柔能胜刚." There is enormous wisdom in such simple observations, potentially helpful in dealing with life's complicated situations. Laozi, the real master, must have been a great thinker who distilled such wisdom through rich life experiences.

**Chapter 2: The Chinese Common Political Entity**

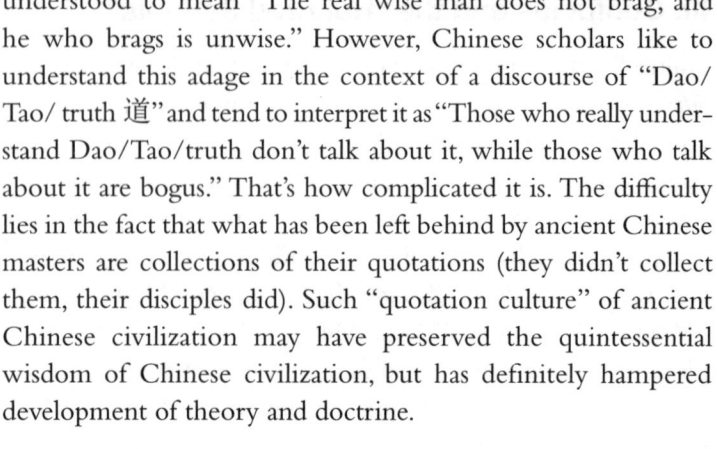

understood to mean "The real wise man does not brag, and he who brags is unwise." However, Chinese scholars like to understand this adage in the context of a discourse of "Dao/ Tao/ truth 道" and tend to interpret it as "Those who really understand Dao/Tao/truth don't talk about it, while those who talk about it are bogus." That's how complicated it is. The difficulty lies in the fact that what has been left behind by ancient Chinese masters are collections of their quotations (they didn't collect them, their disciples did). Such "quotation culture" of ancient Chinese civilization may have preserved the quintessential wisdom of Chinese civilization, but has definitely hampered development of theory and doctrine.

Zhuangzi or Master Zhuang (369?–286? BCE), whose full name was Zhuang Zhou 庄周, spent some time in government service, but lived as a freethinking commoner. He was opposed to top-down imposition of moral norms (as proposed by the Confucian school). His famous observation is:

> People's hearts (minds) are more precipitous than mountains and rivers; more inaccessible than Heaven. Heaven shows its variations of seasons, day, and night, but the human heart hides deep behind benign countenance.
>
> (人心险于山川，难于知天。天犹有春秋冬夏旦暮之期，人者厚貌深情。)

He left behind many fairytales, including the most famous, known as the "Butterfly Dream 蝴蝶梦." In this dream, he offered the well-known dialectic observation that Zhuang Zhou (himself) could become a butterfly and a butterfly could become Zhuang Zhou.

Mozi or Master Mo 墨子 (died in the early 4th century BCE), a late contemporary of Confucius, was a prominent officer in one of the states, just as Confucius was in another. He was famous for propounding a theory of "universal love 兼爱" (love without discrimination) and "pacifism 非攻." In the 1980s, I met a leading China expert from the Soviet Union at an international conference in Hamburg who thought Mozi was the world's earliest socialist thinker.

Xunzi or Master Xun 荀子 (313–238 BCE), an ancient Chinese version of a realist, had an open debate with Mencius, a disciple of Confucius' grandson, about human nature. Han Feizi or Master Han Fei 韩非子 (280–233 BCE) was one of the world's earliest proponents of rule of law.

Gongsunzi or Master Gongsun 公孙子 (320–250 BCE), whose full name was Gongsun Long 公孙龙, was ancient China's logician. Originating from ancient Greek philosophy, logic is an inquiry into inference and a study of the form of arguments. What Gongsun Long propounded exactly was that. He raised the question of whether a "white horse" is a horse and his answer was both yes and no. His famous saying "A white horse is not a horse 白马非马" was controversial among his contemporaries. His analyses are threefold. First, "horse" is a generic term and "white horse" a specific term. Second, the specificity of "horse" is the body of the animal, while the specificity of "white horse" is the color of the animal. So there is a difference. Third, a brown horse or black horse is a "horse," but a "white horse" is not a brown horse or black horse. Therefore, the white horse does not fit into the brown horse or black horse = horse equation. Another famous argument of Gongsun Long is known as "separation of hard and white 离坚白." He argues that one cannot say a "hard, white stone" in the same breath. There can be a "hard stone," which is the conclusion drawn about the stone's material through touch. There can also be a "white stone," which is the conclusion drawn about the color of the stone through sight. The two propositions should be separated, not integrated. Though not as famous as other "masters" of his time, Gongsun Long's influence on the thinking of later intellectuals has endured.

**Chapter 2: The Chinese Common Political Entity**

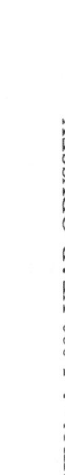

There were also two ancient military strategists in the same family tree known as Sunzi or Master Sun, that is, Sun Wu 孙武 (545–470 BCE) and Sun Bin 孙膑 (Sun Wu's descendant separated by several generations) and they both authored books on war strategy (Chapter 9).

Of course, the most important among these ancient Chinese thinkers was Confucius, the Latin form of the Chinese "Kongfuzi or Guru Kong 孔夫子," also called "Kongzi 孔子" (551–479 BCE). His status in Chinese civilization is similar to that of Jesus Christ in Christianity. He was a wonderful ancient thinker and a tireless teacher. The "Four Books 四书" of China (*Great Learning* 大学, *Golden Mean* 中庸, *Analects* 论语, and *Mencius* 孟子) are all collections of Confucian quotations, except the last, which is a collection of the words of Mencius, disciple of Confucius' grandson. The "Five Classics 五经" (*Book of Odes* 诗经, *Book of History* 书经, *Book of Change* 易经, *Book of Rites* 礼记, and *Spring and Autumn* 春秋) also contain important input from Confucius. No study on Chinese civilization can be fruitful without involving Confucius. The English word "Mencius" is also a Latin form of the Chinese "Mengzi or Master Meng 孟子" (372–289 BCE). His historical status in relation to Confucius is just like that of the modern Indian philosopher Vivekananda

**A portrait of Confucius**

(1853–1902) in relation to Ramakrishna (1836–1886). In other words, Mencius, who had higher popularity among the kings of various states than Confucius, contributed greatly to the dissemination of the teachings of Confucius.

Confucius frequently traveled in his state of Lu 鲁 (present-day Shandong province) with his disciples, inquiring about how people lived. One day, as he and his students passed through Mount Tai 泰山, they saw a woman weeping sadly at a grave-yard. Confucius asked a student to get off their bullock cart and find out what was going on. The woman said that a tiger in the locality had killed her father-in-law, her husband, and most recently, her son. Confucius then asked her why she would not move to a safer place, away from this dangerous tiger. The woman's reply was that she liked the place better because there was no tyranny there. Confucius then came to the conclusion that "Tyranny is more ferocious than the tiger 苛政猛于虎."

Confucius was a great thinker and educator, but many of his teachings went missing or were not recorded. Only fragmented quotes of what he said have come to light, which is strange for a civilization famous for maintaining historical records. Moreover, fragmented Confucian quotes have not been treated as quintessential wisdom, but have been parroted for over 2,000 years without developing a social science theory. As I discussed while quoting *Laozi*, there has been a permanent problem in understanding classical Chinese adages. For example, in the *Analects*, Confucius said, "*zhao wen Dao xi si ke si yi* 朝闻道夕死可矣." Many interpret it literally as "I can die at night if I hear Dao/Tao/truth in the morning." The great master spent his entire life advocating "Dao/Tao/truth," talking about and discussing "Dao/Tao/truth" all the time. He would not have made a trivial remark like "I can die at night if I hear Dao/Tao/truth in the morning." We need to delve into the depths of Confucius' mind to understand the real meaning of this adage.

**Chapter 2: The Chinese Common Political Entity**

Confucius said further in the *Analects*, "From the state of Qi evolved the state of Lu, from which, in turn, the Dao evolved 齐一变至于鲁, 鲁一变至于道."[4]

The "Essay on Grand Harmony 大同篇" in the *Book of Rites* contains an observation that "When the great Dao prevails, the selfless public spirit will prevail throughout the universe 大道之行也天下为公." If we think about what Confucius said in these two observations, we will feel Confucius expressing his longing for an ideal Chinese universe more advanced than the state of Lu (famous for its civility) and selfless public spirit throughout the universe. Thus, what Confucius was actually trying to say was that if he gets the good news of emergence of such a society in the morning, he would die without regret at night. By saying that, Confucius was actually lamenting that such an ideal society was far from reality.

Overall, ancient Chinese philosophy, represented by Confucius, molded "harmony ethics" as opposed to "struggle ethics." I think the main difference between Eastern and Western civilizations is the former's reiteration of "harmony ethics" and the latter's obsession with "struggle ethics," that is, hunger for power. What Laozi propounded (e.g., "the weak will prevail over the strong and the limber will overcome the hard") could have developed into a powerful counter-Western and anti-nation-state ideology, which would have become a benign influence for global development.

---

[4]It is worth mentioning that Qi 齐 and Lu 鲁 were two different states within the Zhou Dynasty at the time of Confucius. Qi was strong and assertive, but less cultured, while Lu was weaker and more cultured. Qi may be likened to Germany in the late 19th and early 20th centuries, while Lu may be compared to Germany after World War II. Germany may have potential to lead Europe to the destination of a common entity of destiny. If that happens, it would be the Dao of Confucius' dream.

# IV. "Tianxia" and "Zhongguo"

In the final quote from the "Essay on Grand Harmony" in the *Book of Rites*, I translated the original term *tianxia* 天下 into "universe." Hereafter, I shall refer to it just as "Tianxia" as it is a basic Chinese concept reflecting the world view of Chinese civilization. Literally, *tianxia* 天下 denotes "under the heaven" or "all under heaven." Chinese history books say during the time of the Great Yu (4,000 years ago), "there were '10,000' states in Tianxia 天下万国" under his tutelary leadership. Thus, it is clear the concept of Tianxia is the same as the Chinese common entity within the contours drawn by the two great rivers. It was the Chinese common geographical entity in the beginning, then the Chinese common civilization entity, and then, the Chinese common political entity that was the Chinese confederation during the Xia, Shang, and Zhou dynasties.

From a new perspective, Confucius was as much the ideologue and proponent of Tianxia as Tianxia was the ideology of the preunification Chinese confederation. The greatest contribution of Confucius to China's cultural development was the process he prescribed for development of the individual and collective, as he stated in the *Great Learning*. The process he propounded began from the "cultivation of personal virtue 修身" and advanced toward "creation of a harmonious family 齐家" and further toward "good governance of the state 治国," and even further toward the goal of "a pacific and blissful Tianxia 平天下." Such a Confucian dynamic stimulated individual endeavors for career advancement, but tied up individual ambition with the happiness of the family, not neglecting or renouncing it. A Chinese family always included at least two generations, parents and children: There must be love and family warmth among them. Confucius made it clear that *jia* 家 (family) and *guo* 国 (country/state) are collectives of the same nature, family being a small collective and state a greater collective. Every individual has to integrate his/her own happiness and future into these two collectives. All individuals contribute to construction, consolidation, and maintenance of these two collectives. In the final part of this Confucian process, *pingtianxia* 平天下 (creation of a pacific, blissful Tianxia/universe), Confucius only meant the universe within the Chinese common entity, not beyond.

Mencius observed that a gentleman had three things to enjoy but "to be *wang* (ruler 王) over Tianxia" was not one. He said it was a gentleman's pleasure to "have the cream of Tianxia as disciples 得天下英才而教育之" (and to have his entire family healthy, his own honesty, and integrity). This observation echoed another popular saying that a good teacher who taught the cream of society is like a garden reaping "peaches and plums all over Tianxia 桃李满天下." From this, we see a picture of elite Chinese intellectuals refraining from power struggle and being passionate about education as they strive to turn the Chinese Tianxia into a fruitful orchard. His reference to the Chinese concept of *wang* (王) leads us into the deep waters of Chinese civilization.

The Chinese character *wang* (王) is a very meaningful construction, with the three horizontal strokes representing heaven, earth, and humanity, respectively, and the vertical stroke indicating a force integrating the three.

This was the ancients' definition of a "ruler 王者" (*wang zhe*, literally, the person who rules as king). While *wang zhe* acted as the harmonizer of Tianxia, the people of Tianxia vindicated him without reservation. In early Chinese classics, one can easily find observations such as "Just as there is no second sun in Heaven, there is no second *wang zhe* on land 天无二日，土无二王" or "All land of Tianxia belongs to the *wang zhe*, all people from land to the sea coast are subjects of the *wang zhe* 普天之下莫非王土，率土之滨莫非王臣." Such observations easily make Western scholars like Fairbank, who was obsessed with the nation-state, imagine a *wang*-centered world order.

Much as I would hesitate to say, it was a fact that Fairbank did not know enough Chinese to pursue his China studies. He had to depend on a large number of Chinese scholars to translate for him. The deficiency of his research assistants and disciples in understanding Chinese civilization contributed to his erroneous theory of "Sinocentrism." Let me give a concrete example. A Fairbank disciple (a Chinese scholar), named Immanuel C. Y. Hsu (Chinese "Chung-Yueh Hsü/Xu Zhongyue 徐中约 [1923–2005]), obtained his doctoral degree from the Harvard University. He translated the aforementioned quote as: "Under the wide heaven, there is no land that is not the emperor's, and within the sea-boundaries of the land, there is none who is not the subject of the emperor."[5] Hsu's translation looks harmless, but there is a grave mistake, if not a deliberate twist of history. The quote (from *Shijing* 诗经, Book of Songs) was 1,000 years earlier than the emergence of the first Chinese emperor (221 BCE), after the appearance of dozens, if not hundreds, of people claiming to be *wang zhe*. I'm sure Hsu didn't understand the historical background of this quote. Had Fairbank's Chinese disciples and research assistants, like Immanuel C. Y. Hsu, told him the true Chinese civilization story, the Sinocentrism theory might not have existed at all. In Chinese classics, phrases that are similar to or synonymous with "Tianxia" include "four seas 四海" or "within the (four) seas 海内."[6]

Because of the common geographical entity, "Tian 天" (heaven) has been a common asset of Chinese civilization from its inception. In Oracle Script (oldest script in China), the visual

---

[5]C. Y. Hsu, *China's Emergence into the Family of Nations* (Cambridge, MA: Harvard University Press, 1970), 6.

[6]Following the thinking that after Han Emperor Wu attacked the Xiongnu (discussed in Chapter 4), Chinese soldiers and diplomats reached Lake Baikal (in present-day Russia) and lakes in Central Asia to the West. Such experiences added to the Chinese knowledge of a sea on the east and south to create an impression that China was surrounded by sea. The ancient Chinese concept of "four seas" or "within the four seas," like "Tianxia," indicates the ancients' awareness of the limits of the Chinese common entity rather than a belief that China was at the center of the world.

**Chapter 2: The Chinese Common Political Entity**

of "tian 天/heaven" draws a horizontal stroke above the visual for "human" (人), indicating that "heaven" is a reality, space, and force above humans and greater than human ability. But, if the horizontal stroke is put below "人" (in Oracle Script, and modern script "立"), it draws a picture of a human standing on the ground, hence, the concept of "stand/establish." In these two ideographic visuals of Chinese script ("Tian 天" and "立"), we find the three basic substances of the world in the specific Chinese mind-set: heaven, earth, and humanity. *The Book of Change* 易经 contains this observation: "Yin and Yang are the ways of building heaven 立天之道, 曰阴曰阳," "suppleness and solidity are the ways of building earth 立地之道, 曰柔曰刚," and "human love and righteousness are the ways of building humanity 立人之道, 曰仁曰义." Mencius 孟子 went a step further to conceive these three substances as "celestial seasons 天时," "terrestrial resources 地利," and "human harmony 人和."

Let us understand these three propositions with Mencius' annotation, which is not complicated. When ancient Chinese conceived "Yin and Yang are the ways of building heaven," they also had in mind sunny days represented by yang, and cloudy and rainy days represented by yin. Thus, the Chinese "ways of building heaven" include people's acclimatizing to changing weather and temperature variations to pursue agricultural production. Similarly, "suppleness and solidity are the ways of building earth" reminded ancient Chinese of the "terrestrial resources," namely, how and where to undertake planting and mining. This helped development of the economy, essentially agriculture and industry. The last proposition of "human love and righteousness are the ways of building humanity" was the corollary of the first two. Living within the common geographical entity, people had to maintain "human harmony" by observing the norms of "human love and righteousness."

In *Laozi* 老子, there is an observation: "Dao/Tao/truth creates one, one creates two, two creates three, and three creates all beings on earth 道生一，一生二，二生三，三生万物." This can also be explained easily. The "one" created by Dao is "Tianxia"—the Chinese universe. The "two" created by "one" is Yin and Yang. The "three" created by "two" is heaven, earth, and humanity. Thus, what is expressed by Laozi is: "Dao/Tao/truth creates Tianxia or Chinese universe; the Tianxia or Chinese universe creates Yin and Yang; Yin and Yang create Heaven, Earth, and Humanity; and Heaven, Earth, and Humanity create all beings on Earth." This observation explains the ways of building heaven, earth, and humanity. For ancient Chinese, Tianxia was a common entity of heaven, earth, and humanity. It was through this conception of the common entity that innumerable local tribes, races, communities, and ethnic, linguistic and cultural idiosyncrasies blended together as a civilization and subjected themselves to one political authority. Thus, the Chinese concept of Tianxia reached far beyond the development of a nation and nation-state.

"China is always the Middle Kingdom!" This remark is frequently expressed in international media to propagate the theory of "Sinocentrism"—suggesting the Chinese name for

**Mister He's vessel; 3,000 years old**

Chapter 2: The Chinese Common Political Entity

China, that is, Zhongguo 中国, automatically puts China in the center of the world. This is, of course, a misconception. The earliest appearance of Zhongguo 中国 was an inscription on a bronze vessel named Hezun 何尊 (Mister He's vessel) from the early Zhou Dynasty unearthed in Shaanxi in 1963, which says: "The Zhou King Wu conquered the big state of Shang and invoked the Heaven with these words: 'I am now residing in this Zhongguo (中国) and rule over the people from here'." We know Zhongguo was coterminous with Zhongtu 中土 (literally, central land) and Zhongyuan 中原 (Central Plain), all of which first appeared in the official Zhou Dynasty documents highlighting the status (central importance and primacy) of its son of heaven. Initially, the state of Zhou was a subordinate state under the tutelary leadership of the Shang Dynasty, and it conceived itself as "western land 西土." It only began to claim its position as "central state" after the establishment of the Zhou Dynasty. Its geographic position remained the same. The change from western to central signified the change of political status. Clearly, the origin of Zhongguo/Central State/Middle Kingdom was the specific description of the state directly ruled by the son of heaven, which later extended to all of China, and does not indicate that China was the center of the world.

In fact, when we peruse Chinese documents, we see the term Zhongguo mostly used by Chinese Buddhists to translate the Indian word "Madhyadesa/central state," Central India, known in Chinese historical writings as *zhong Tian zhu* 中天竺/central heavenly India." The great Buddhist master of the Tang Dynasty, Daoxuan 道宣 (596–667) wrote in his classic *Shijiafangzhi* 释迦方志 (literally, gazetteers of Sakyamuni land) that "south of Himalaya is named Zhongguo/Middle Kingdom/Central State" (雪山以南名为中国), making India, not China, the Middle Kingdom/Central State. We know in the past China was always named after the title of the ruling dynasty, not Zhongguo. Only after China was humiliated by the Opium War did Chinese begin to use Zhongguo. It is evident that if the Sinocentrism theory is built on the term Zhongguo/Middle Kingdom/ Central State, it is flawed.

# CHAPTER 3

# A UNIFIED EMPIRE SANS IMPERIALISM

Thus far, we have gone from the time of Great Yu to the academic environment of Confucius, who propounded the *Qi-Lu-Dao* evolution predicting that China would become increasingly weaker, but more cultured, until it reached the ideal situation of "grand harmony." What we see now is the "city-sack Ares" (god of war), worse than the days of Confucius when the state of Qi flexed its muscles and earned unfavorable comment from the sage teacher. History is an eternal satire on civilization. Two hundred and fifty years after the *Dao*-dreaming Confucius had passed away, troops of Qin started conquering the valleys of the two great rivers and created the first great empire on Earth. This development was anti-Confucian but exactly what Chinese civilization needed to march forward. Evolution of China from the common geographical entity progressed a stage further through the common civilization entity and common political entity to the common entity of destiny. China was unified, became an empire, and claimed sovereignty over the valleys of the two great rivers. China transformed itself to a collective with centripetal force. China made itself unbreakable and undividable.

With the establishment of the Qin Dynasty 秦朝 (221–207 BCE), China became Asia's great empire 200 plus years earlier than the Roman Empire. Had it embarked on the "nation-state" development path, it would have ceaselessly expanded externally, conquered other states, and ultimately staged the trilogy of "rise–apex–decline," like the Roman Empire. In 22 centuries, from the time the Qin Dynasty unified China to the recent past, China has had only four dynasties capable of external aggression and expansion: Qin 秦 (15 years); Han 汉 (422 years minus 20 years at the end during the "Three Kingdoms" disintegration); Sui 隋 (38 years); and Tang 唐 (288 years), totaling 743 years. The Ming 明 Dynasty (268 years) did not have the requisite power to pursue world hegemony. The Song 宋 Dynasty could merely maintain its territorial integrity during its first 168 years (out of a 319-year existence). For one millennium, China was either ruled by a non-Chinese race or maintained its sovereignty only south of the Yangtze, ceding North China to foreign rule.

Do you think China really qualified for staging the trilogy of "rise–apex–decline" on the stage of the "nation-states" world in historical times with these political assets?

## I. Qin Emperor Shihuang Created the Chinese Empire

In the second half of the 4th century BCE, Alexander the Great (356–323 BCE), a disciple of the great Greek philosopher Aristotle, became the first famous world "conqueror." He inaugurated the "nation-states" world's development path of conquest and waging sanguinary wars on other nations. He inspired innumerable ambitious careerists of the world for more than two millennia. His name has been taken by innumerable people of various countries—proving he has been universally loved and admired. For over 2,000 years, people have called him Alexander the Great.

The personal name of Qin Emperor Shihuang 秦始皇 (259–210 BCE) was Yingzheng 嬴政. He became the King of Qin at age 13 and Emperor of China at 39. He gave himself the title of *huangdi* 皇帝 by combining *huang* 皇 and *di* 帝, both words meant deities in ancient Chinese tradition. He was probably the first ruler on Earth to honor himself in the name of a god. He also named himself "shihuangdi 始皇帝" (beginning emperor) as a wish that his descendants inherit the throne forever, not imagining that his son and successor would be overthrown after three years of rule. But, he was truly the "Beginning Emperor" of not only China, but also the world. He initiated a new era of Chinese civilization. From his time until today, China has, with several intermissions, been the most continuous, sustainable political entity, with the largest population and innumerable world firsts, in the world. Here was a marvelous hero who fought as brilliantly in war as Alexander the Great, but was a much greater political player, with outstanding achievements, than Alexander. But, no one called him "Qin Emperor Shihuang the Great," nor was any mermaid inquiring "Is Qin Emperor

Chapter 3: A Unified Empire Sans Imperialism

Shihuang alive?"[1] Though it was a big achievement that the Qin Emperor annihilated six big states and unified China, few people seem to have been impressed, and even fewer sang hymns for him. Few, if any, scholars in China or the world have noted the Chinese trilogy of a common civilization entity evolved from the common geographical entity and further evolving into a common entity of destiny with integrated sociopolitical, economic, and cultural development in China.

The Qin 秦 state was initially an inconsequential member of the loose confederation under the Zhou 周 Dynasty outside the Central Plain, in the western corner (present-day Shaanxi and Gansu). The name "Qin 秦" was not a national insignia, but a civilization badge, as were the names of the other six states vanquished by the Qin. There have been different opinions about the ethnic origins of Qin. Generally, people of Qin are regarded as progeny of "Eastern foreigners 东夷." Meng Wentong 蒙文通 (1894–1968), expert on the ethnicity of Qin, thought people of Qin were likely progeny of Qiang 羌, which begets affinity with the Great Yu. There is the world famous Shaanxi "Terracotta Exhibition 兵马俑" (an archaeological discovery of the terracotta soldiers of Qin Emperor Shihuang) thronged by tourists from all over the world today. From the great variety of facial features of these Qin soldiers, we see the multinational composition of the Qin state and Qin Dynasty.

The rise of Qin state began with King Mu of Qin 秦穆公 who ruled between 659 and 621 BCE. He distinguished himself as a strong man of the Eastern Zhou confederation during the Spring and Autumn period in competition with "King Huan of Qi 齐桓公" (ruler of the state of Qi in 685–643 BCE), "King

---

[1]There is a 1,000-year-old Greek fable narrating that in a storm, when sailing at sea, a mermaid would appear and ask the captain, "Is King Alexander alive?" If the captain answered, "He is alive, well, and rules the world," the mermaid would disappear and the sea would calm. If the answer was different, the mermaid would drag the ship to the seafloor, drowning everyone aboard.

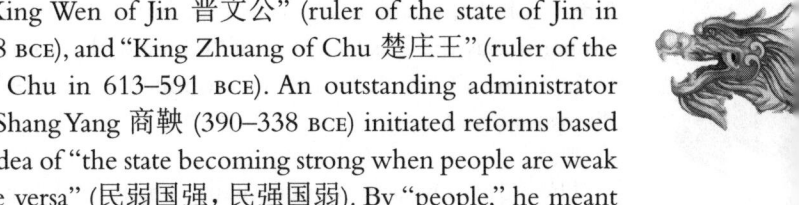

Xiang of Song 宋襄公" (ruler of the state of Song in 650–637 BCE), "King Wen of Jin 晋文公" (ruler of the state of Jin in 636–628 BCE), and "King Zhuang of Chu 楚庄王" (ruler of the state of Chu in 613–591 BCE). An outstanding administrator named Shang Yang 商鞅 (390–338 BCE) initiated reforms based on the idea of "the state becoming strong when people are weak and vice versa" (民弱国强，民强国弱). By "people," he meant influential higher-ups and wanted to stop unruly behavior by the dominant groups of the society and strengthen the state. In the meantime, he encouraged common people to increase production. He had a policy of protecting farmers' interests while restraining merchant profiteering. All this made the Qin state prosperous and powerful. The state of Qin was a dark horse among the seven states of the Warring States period: King Yingzheng led it at the top, making himself the "Beginning Emperor" and creating an earth-shaking change in Chinese politics. No other historical figure in China has surpassed Qin Emperor Shihuang in political feat. Had he been in the "nation-states" world, he would have been a great hero. In China, he was forever infamous. Shadows on the image of the Qin emperor was not his own making: He was crucial to the development of Chinese civilization, which innately disliked him because of his bigotry, abuse of power, and violence.

Chinese political commentary has two descriptions for Qin Emperor Shihuang: "One emperor in a millennium 千古一帝" and "Tyrant 暴君." The two are like cathode and anode that reject each other, yet they are forever inseparable in the evaluation of this historical personality. The Chinese common geographical entity took tens of thousands of years to become a common civilization entity and common political entity, but the Qin Emperor converted them into a common entity of destiny overnight. He created a unified country with specific policies for writing with one script 书同文, carriages with one width 车同轨, and social behavior with one moral code 行同伦. Today, in comparison with India, we see China's great advantage of a unified script. We also see the merits of an expansive China

Chapter 3: A Unified Empire Sans Imperialism

having a universal moral code (his Indian contemporary, the Great Ashoka, could have done this, but did not). The Qin Emperor was the great creator of "Chinese characteristics" or "Chineseness," which figures so prominently in international discussions on China today.

The Qin Dynasty conceptually changed China's land ownership from king's ownership 王有 to state ownership 国有. This change of land ownership indicates an advancement in Chinese politics. Before Qin, the "mandate of heaven 天命" was rather obscure. The Qin Emperor made a seal known as "the jade seal for ruling the state 传国玉玺".

**The Qin emperor's seal**

Graphs on the seal, reading *shou ming yu tian, ji shou yong chang* 受命于天，既寿永昌 (ordered by heaven, long life and eternally thriving), were the handwriting of Qin Prime Minister Li Si 李斯 (284–208 BCE) in "Great Seal 大篆" style. It was the epigraphic presentation of the mandate of heaven (certifying the legitimate authority of the Chinese ruler). This seal became the most precious object for post-Qin rulers of China. As people scrambled to obtain it, it was lost. Though the seal was lost, the aforementioned epigraph was preserved in various Chinese documents; hence the Qin emperor's claim of "ordered by heaven" was passed down as an established Chinese political tradition—the Chinese tradition of the mandate of heaven. This seal of the Qin Emperor illustrates the Chinese ideology of humanity in Tianxia, humanity for Tianxia, and Chinese Tianxia for itself.

The Qin Emperor's conquest went beyond the pre-Qin limits of China. After he vanquished the southernmost Chu 楚 state, he further annexed a large area of the Yangtze valley into his domain. He conquered *lingnan* 岭南 (present-day Guangdong 广东 and Guangxi 广西) in 218 BCE. There was difficulty supplying food and grain to the rapidly advancing troops during the expedition. The Emperor sent an officer, Shi Lu 史禄, to construct a canal linking the Xiang 湘 and Li 漓 rivers at a spot in today's Xing'an 兴安 County, Guangxi Zhuang Autonomous Region. The canal has linked the Yangtze and Zhujiang 珠江 (pearl) rivers, making Guangdong and Guangxi part of the Yangtze valley. During 214–213 BCE, the Emperor sent troops to fight the Xiongnu 匈奴, which harassed the northern border area of China. Then, he built the Great Wall to prevent swift incursions into North China by Xiongnu horsemen. The Qin state had been a political power that arose in the northwest, a little far from the Central Plain. The Qin Emperor made Xianyang 咸阳 (present-day Shaanxi province) the capital of China and moved some of the wealthy people from the Central Plain to the suburbs of the capital. Later, the Han Dynasty emulated the Qin and created a new capital at Chang'an (now Xi'an), keeping China's political center in the western part of the country. The Qin Emperor also extended his rule to Sichuan. Territorial expansion of the Qin and Han dynasties, initiated by the Qin Emperor, created a new and centralized political entity with expanded territory within the contours of the two great rivers.

The world was, and is, dominated by the "nation-state," with the strong bullying the weak and a gigantic China managing to stay away from that threat. Unification has been the prerequisite condition for China to sustain for over two millennia. The Qin

Emperor reigned for only 12 years (221–210 BCE), yet we credit him for China's over 2,000-year existence because no other 12 years in China's history could be weightier than during the Qin Emperor's rule.

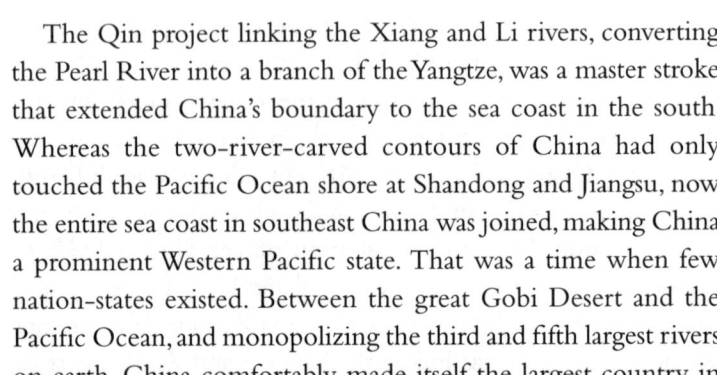

The Qin project linking the Xiang and Li rivers, converting the Pearl River into a branch of the Yangtze, was a master stroke that extended China's boundary to the sea coast in the south. Whereas the two-river-carved contours of China had only touched the Pacific Ocean shore at Shandong and Jiangsu, now the entire sea coast in southeast China was joined, making China a prominent Western Pacific state. That was a time when few nation-states existed. Between the great Gobi Desert and the Pacific Ocean, and monopolizing the third and fifth largest rivers on earth, China comfortably made itself the largest country in Eurasia. This fact has never been disputed by any nation or civilization.

While alive, Qin Emperor Shihuang enjoyed maximum authority over humankind. But, following his death, no one would listen to him. Those surrounding him (Prime Ministers Li Si, Zhao Gao 赵高, and others) destroyed his edict and asked Prince Fusu 扶苏 to rush back to the capital and take charge of his funeral and other matters. They failed to reveal the Emperor's will to name the youngest prince Huhai 胡亥 as successor. Most pathetic of all, as part of the scheme to block news of the Emperor's death, the body of Shihuang traveled hundreds of miles in scorching heat from Pingtai 平台 (present-day Guangzong 广宗 County in Xingtai 邢台 City, Hebei province) back to the imperial capital in Shaanxi. His body was laid to rest weeks after it was completely decomposed, smelling awful. He did not deserve such an undignified end. All great people of the world have their untold mishaps: The Qin Emperor was no exception to the Chinese saying that "there is no perfect human being in the world." Do you think the Qin Emperor's achievements condone his mistakes?

## II. Tyrant or "Once-in-a-millennium" Emperor?

Which description, "once-in-a-millennium emperor" or "tyrant," is more befitting for the Qin emperor as we look at his four great construction projects: The Great Wall, the Great Highway, the Great Palace, and the Great Underground Palace (his tomb)? Each involved hundreds of thousands of workers. Each inch of the Great Wall was said to have been "made with a catty (over half a kilogram) of mud" carried on human shoulders from distant places. Due to constant dearth of available labor, a huge percentage of Qin's able-bodied men were forcibly recruited to construct the Wall and the other three projects. The story of Meng Jiang looking for her lost wall-building husband (孟姜女万里寻夫) has been the theme of numerous operas, movies, and TV shows. Her husband, a laborer recruited to build the Great Wall, was never found. The story is a vivid reminder of the Qin Emperor's construction projects and how hundreds of thousands of laborers shed their sweat and blood while their loved ones shed tears for the projects. Today, Chinese and foreigners pride themselves on visiting the Great Wall, seldom noticing the sweat, blood, and tears that contributed to this—one of the "seven wonders of the world."

The Great Highway was meant for the Qin Emperor and his entourage to travel from the imperial palace to other parts of China, especially in North China. It also had strategic importance for movements of troops and transport of goods. Unlike the Great Wall, it disappeared long ago with no trace remaining. The Great Palace is known as the "E Pang Palace 阿房宫," which was both real and legendary. Today, tourists can visit Xi'an in Northwest China to tour the historic site of this famed ancient palace. A new project costing about $5.5 million is underway to make it a greater tourist attraction by remaking its 2,200-year-old former self. However, the glory of E Pang Palace cannot be recreated because scholars have found that only part of the Qin emperor's original project was actually completed and the conventional belief that the palace was exceptionally magnificent did not match reality.

**Chapter 3: A Unified Empire Sans Imperialism**

Qin Emperor Shihuang's Great Underground Palace (his tomb) is not legendary, but is a unique, highly valuable portion of our globe. It is deliberately preserved 30 meters below the earth's surface by order of authorities in China. The Qin Emperor began constructing his grave at age 13, right after he had become king. The project wasn't completed until 39 years later, or two years after his death (208 BCE). According to modern archaeologists, the underground palace is a large complex 51 meters high and over 1,700 meters in circumference. As indicated in historical documents, the complex included many palaces packed with precious treasures. Hundreds of underground group burials surround this complex (400 confirmed by archaeologists). The recently unearthed Shaanxi "Terracotta Figures" is but one of the hundreds of surrounding burials of the Qin Emperor's tomb. Chinese authorities are in no hurry to excavate them as underground treasures could suffer erosion when exposed to light and air.

Once the entire Qin underground palace is safely excavated, the Qin Emperor will certainly gain in historical importance and prestige. Maybe even Qin Dynasty history will have to be rewritten. However, I'm less sure how to evaluate the Qin Emperor's construction projects. Chinese civilization would have looked much poorer without them, but they have certainly cost the country a fortune in material resources and human lives. The Qin Emperor's tyrannical repression of the common people cannot be overlooked. Chinese history books have recorded a lot of the Emperor's tyrannical acts, including "book burning 焚书" and "live burial of scholars 坑儒."[2] The books that got burnt were those authored by Confucius and other pre-Qin scholars (213 BCE). The government also issued an order prohibiting

---

[2]"Live burial of scholars" allegedly occurred in 212 BCE. It was recorded that over 460 scholars were ordered buried alive. However, there have also been controversies about the truth of the event and about the number of victims involved. One theory claims that the Emperor was punishing sorcerers who had tricked him with their "secrets of immortality." Another asserts that the victims were scholars who had been propagating Confucian teachings. Whatever the reasons, it was extremely cruel to bury people alive.

concealment of such books, which was not lifted until after the early Han Dynasty. When the ban was finally lifted, some senior Han government scholars recited the Confucian classics and had them transcribed into "classics in modern script 今文经." Still later, when some ancient houses were demolished, a number of pre-Qin classics people had hidden inside their walls were discovered. These were the so-called "classics in ancient script 古文经." The Qin Emperor's "book burning" was obviously an anti-civilization act that did great harm to China's cultural development. His motivation, however, is unclear as no serious investigation into this has ever been conducted.

There is no simple "yes" or "no" answer to the question whether Emperor Qin Shihuang was a tyrant. We must view it against the background of the time. The earth-shaking feat of the Qin Emperor destroyed innumerable, powerful, vested interests waging life-and-death struggles against him. Offspring of rulers in all six states vanquished by the Qin Emperor frantically employed assassins to take his life. Violence was inevitable. The Qin Emperor's abuse of force and repression compounded the peril he faced. It is the basic law of physics that the greater the pressure the stronger the rebound. One phenomenon of the Qin Dynasty was the massive number of criminals overcrowding jails. Liu Bang, founding father of the Han Dynasty, was a junior official of Qin escorting convicts from one jail to another. In one trip, some convicts escaped. Liu Bang knew that, at the end of the trip, he would be locked up. So he set the rest of the convicts free and joined the rebel army. There was a scholar, an expert linguist named Cheng Miao 程邈 (dates unknown), who was jailed for a minor offense. He saw jailors having a hard time using the Small Seal script invented by Li Si for record-keeping. He spent years in jail to invent an easier simplified script greatly needed by the Emperor to improve administrative efficacy. The Emperor adopted his invention called *lishu* 隶书 (the "junior official's script") and put Cheng Miao in charge of jail administration. This episode shows the humane side of the Qin Emperor, and not just that of a muddleheaded tyrant.

**Chapter 3: A Unified Empire Sans Imperialism**

The country was in turmoil as soon as the Qin Emperor passed away, indirectly indicating the capability of a ruler whose high-handed reign had ended with his death. The Han Dynasty, which inherited the political structure of the Qin, learned the lesson and eased all repressive measures against the people, consolidating unification of China. All reforms of the Han Dynasty underwrote the tyranny of the erstwhile Qin Dynasty. Han was a successor Dynasty that learned lessons from the predecessor's negative examples. The Qin Dynasty led the way with both successes and failures.

We know that before adopting policies, the Qin Emperor would ask his courtiers to discuss and make suggestions, but the final decision was his. There was no paper, so words had to be written on strung-together wooden or bamboo sheets, known as "bamboo books 竹书." In Oracle Script, it was written as "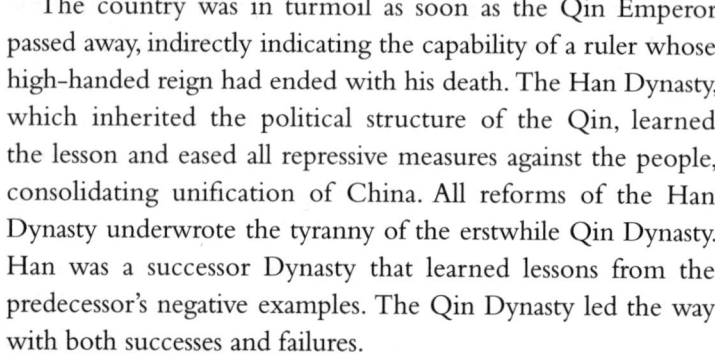" (in modern Chinese script, "册"). Government documents laid on the Qin Emperor's desk were such bamboo books. The Emperor made it a rule that he had to read 120 catties (60 plus kilograms) of bamboo books before he went to sleep. This was commendable.

From a holistic perspective, all imperial rulers of China were selfish, cruel, and condescending tyrants. To single out the Qin Emperor as a tyrant from a couple hundred emperors would mean he was the worst among all tyrants. The Qin Emperor cannot be rated so low, even considering the alleged cruelty of "burying scholars alive."

## III. Liu Bang and the New Dynasty

The Han Dynasty 汉朝 (202 BCE–220 CE), a successful successor, eclipsed the glory and diminished the importance of its predecessor, the Qin Dynasty. This is why many things connected with China have adopted the badge of "Han" today. Chinese are called Han people, Chinese language is called Han language, and Chinese script is called Han script, and so on. The term "Han nation" was established after the imperial order in China was overthrown in the beginning of the 20th century, although this book considers it a misnomer.

Han scholar Jia Yi 贾谊 (200–168 BCE) wrote a famous essay called "A Critique of the Qin Dynasty 过秦论" analyzing causes of the downfall of Qin. It says:

> The (Qin) administration ruled with an iron hand. Awards and punishment were unjust. Taxation was excessive. Tianxia was in turmoil beyond the control of the government. People had a hard time, but the apathetic Master did not observe restraint. Misrule and fraud exploded, but the government, at all levels, shied away from responsibility. Convicts multiplied and everywhere there was corporal punishment and killing. Tianxia suffered greatly. Panic gripped minds from administrators to commoners. Poverty and suffering prevailed and no one felt at ease in his position. All this led to the downfall.

Liu Bang 刘邦 (256–195 BCE) was a subject of the Qin before he founded the Han Dynasty. He may have "shied away from responsibility," initially but eventually rose to overthrow the Qin. In 209 BCE, officials and commoners in Pei County 沛县 (present-day Feng County 丰县 under the jurisdiction of Xuzhou 徐州 City of Jiangsu) killed the magistrate and rose in rebellion. They elected Liu Bang, who had already been absconding, as their leader. We know that after the death of Qin Emperor Shihuang, China was in great chaos. Descendants of rulers of the erstwhile states vanquished by Qin saw there was opportunity for restoration of pre-Qin order. Xiang Yu 项羽 (232–202 BCE), grandson of a famous general of the Chu 楚 state, was the leading figure among them. Xiang Yu was a born warrior over 8 feet tall with enormous strength in his arms. In addition to war strategy that he learned from his uncle, he expressed his confidence in replacing the Qin Emperor when he, as a juvenile, witnessed the latter's entourage passing in the midst of a huge crowd. In 209 BCE, he killed the provincial governor, raised an army of 8,000, and started the rebellion. His following snowballed to 80,000 and he revived the Chu 楚 state. A couple of years later, he defeated the army of Qin and other revived states, declaring himself "Hegemonic King of Chu 楚霸王" when he was only 25. His military feat at such a young age is a marvel in Chinese history. But, he met his doom at the hands of Liu Bang.

Liu Bang and Xiang Yu rose in rebellion at almost the same place (in present-day Jiangsu) and same time. However, they fought Qin government forces separately. Liu Bang's force was first to enter the Qin capital, Xianyang 咸阳, and overthrow the Qin Dynasty in 207 BCE. He made the famous announcement, which has become a tradition known as "Three items of a new law 约法三章." Actually, he promised residents of the capital (and subjects of the Qin Empire) that all repressive laws of Qin were abolished excluding the death penalty for killing people and imprisonment for hurting others, theft, or robbery. His troops refrained from violent disturbances, but took from the Qin palace all important documents and maps (put to good use later by the Han government). Meanwhile, Xiang Yu also arrived with his overwhelming force. Liu Bang retreated to let Xiang Yu have his way, and Xiang Yu's army looted and burnt many palaces.

Another important figure was Zhang Liang 张良 (250?–185 BCE). After the overthrow of Qin, Xiang Yu's Chu army and Liu Bang's Han army began their contest for supremacy. Liu Bang's emergence as winner was largely due to help from Zhang Liang, whose grandfather and father had been prime ministers of the erstwhile Han state. Zhang Liang was a well-known anti-Qin activist who successfully evaded arrest. He obtained a valuable book about war strategy entitled "Six Strategies 六韬," now internationally famous and translated into many languages including Japanese, Korean, Vietnamese, English, and Russian. Zhang Liang's intelligent strategies helped the initially weaker Han army gain supremacy over the more powerful Chu army of

Xiang Yu. The strategy was essentially to persuade those in the enemy coalition to defect, thus weakening the opponent. In the final battle at Gaixia 垓下 (present-day Lingbi 灵璧 County in Anhui), the Han army besieged 100,000 retreating Chu troops. Han troops sang the folk songs of Chu. Hearing this, Chu troops thought their homeland had fallen under Han domination and lost their fighting spirit. They were eventually wiped out by the Han army. Xiang Yu escaped with a dozen lieutenants who advised him to return to their home in Jiangsu to raise an army and rise again. Xiang Yu said he had lost "face" (honor) to stand before the people who entrusted their sons to him in expectation of a great cause and he had not met that expectation. He committed suicide. With Xiang Yu's death, Liu Bang inaugurated the new Han Dynasty.

One of Zhang Liang's important proposals, accepted by Liu Bang, was to create a new capital in the northwestern interior, Chang'an 长安 (present-day Xi'an 西安) in Shaanxi province. This was a very wise choice, though most important civil and military leaders who lived in eastern China wouldn't have liked it. The double advantage of Chang'an was its strategic position (difficult to attack and easy to defend) and easy access to the rich area of Sichuan. This greatly helped the Han Dynasty strengthen its stability throughout. People in India know that Pataliputra (now Patna in Bihar) was the largest city (population-wise) on earth during the time of Ashoka the Great (it was the capital of the Maurya Dynasty). Chang'an rose as the second largest, and then overtook Pataliputra from the 2nd century BCE onward. During the Sui and Tang dynasties, there truly was the world phenomenon of "all roads lead to Chang'an."

Liu Bang, Han Emperor Gaozu 汉高祖, was a mediocre ruler and modest leader who emerged as head of the victorious rebel army during the civil war in the wake of the great Qin Emperor's death. In 206 BCE, he inaugurated his new imperial career, meekly assuming the title "King of Han 汉王." He was pushed to the

**Chapter 3: A Unified Empire Sans Imperialism**

throne by his followers as the Emperor. His was a short reign of 11 years (206–195 BCE). In 196 BCE, an old and sick Liu Bang (Emperor Gaozu) personally led the army to quell the rebellion of Yingbu 英布 (?-196 BCE). He took the opportunity of being in the east to visit his hometown (Pei County). During a reception, he got drunk and sang the "Song of Gale 大风歌" (a short poem he composed), translated as follows:-

> A gale sweeps with its power
>
> scattering the clouds asunder.
>
> I am home in triumph and glory
>
> after conquering my country.
>
> From where can I get the brave hands
>
> to defend our land so grand?

（大风起兮云飞扬，威加海内兮归故乡，
安得猛士兮守四方！）

The last two lines reveal the worries of the founding emperor of Han, who did not sound very confident.

One episode involving this ruler also indicates the initial difficulty of establishing the common entity of destiny. Lu Jia 陆贾 (240–170 BCE), a leading intellectual well-versed in speech and argument among Liu Bang's early followers, was entrusted by Liu Bang to conclude agreements with Xiang Yu and other contending forces during the process of Liu Bang's rise. After the founding of the Han Dynasty, he repeatedly urged Liu Bang to use the classics (especially the *Book of Odes* 诗经 and *Book of History* 书经) as guides for policymaking. Liu Bang, who was not very cultured, paid no attention to this, even arguing against this advice. He said: "I obtained Tianxia (my kingdom) on horseback 马上得天下." What do the *Book of Odes* and *Book of History* have to do with it? To this, Lu Jia replied: "You can obtain Tianxia on horseback, but you won't be able to rule it on horseback." Finally, Liu Bang conceded to Lu Jia's proposition.

## IV. Good Governance by Emperors Wen and Jing

After the Han founding emperor died, his Queen, whose maiden name was Lu Zhi 吕雉 (241–180 BCE), wielded power in her capacity as Empress Dowager. On the eve of Queen Lu's death, the throne was in danger of leaving Liu Bang's family. The loyal courtiers were in panic and invited Liu Heng 刘恒 (203–157 BCE), surviving son of founding emperor Liu Bang, to ascend the throne. Thus, Han Emperor Wen 汉文帝 (reigned 180–157 BCE) became the supreme ruler of unified China.

Liu Heng (Han Emperor Wen) was the son of a mother who had low status in the palace. Though he was the emperor's son, he learned from boyhood how to be humble, prudent, and lie low. Empress Dowager Lu survived her only imperial son Han Emperor Hui 汉惠帝 (reigned 195–188 BCE) and ill-treated, even murdered, sons of Liu Bang not born by her. Two important veteran courtiers (Liu Bang's trusted lieutenants), Chen Ping 陈平 (?-178 BCE) and Zhou Bo 周勃 (?-169 BCE), instrumental to Emperor Wen's enthronement, further helped the new Emperor destroy Empress Dowager Lu's lobby in the palace immediately after her death. They contributed enormously to Emperor Wen's rule. The Emperor prudently navigated his way to de facto supremacy. He had to show his gratitude to the two courtiers who had helped both his imperial father (Liu Bang) and himself, but took care not to have super courtiers on his watch. It was a delicate task and Emperor Wen handled it well. First, he promoted Chen Ping and Zhou Bo as high as possible while cutting their military ties (both Chen and Zhou were generals). When Zhou Bo was prime minister, the Emperor called him and asked him two questions: How many people did the government execute under death penalty per year? And what is the annual revenue of the government? Zhou Bo answered that he did not know, fearing this could doom his career. But Emperor Wen did not punish him. After this experience, Zhou Bo (Chen Ping died in the third year of the Emperor's reign) and other courtiers realized the Emperor meant business and became loyal and diligent in carrying out their duties.

Emperor Wen presided over the Han Dynasty's transition from infancy to adulthood, from settling of the dust to construction and advancement. China was fortunate to have a ruler like Emperor Wen during this transitional period because he cared for the country's vitality and the people's livelihood. With the goal of "letting the people live in peace 安民," the Emperor implemented *Laozi*'s idea of "quietude leading to orderly society 无为而治" as part of his governing philosophy. His governing style featured light taxation, mild punishment, and minimal government control over economic development. Emperor Wen twice reduced the land tax (on harvests), in 178 BCE and 168 BCE, respectively, from one-fifteenth to one-thirtieth. In 167 BCE, he even exempted the entire land revenue. He introduced the lightest corvée (compulsory labor service for government projects) in China's imperial history, which was once every three years for adult males. He banned corporal punishment and allowed people to mint copper coins, produce salt, open mines, fish, and hunt.

Emperor Wen started his own imperial career with a simple and frugal lifestyle. He liberated all nonpregnant women in the harem to become free citizens and establish their own families and gave them tax-exempt status for life. This policy was later emulated by Liang Emperor Wu, Tang Emperor Taizong, and others. During 23 years as supreme ruler, Emperor Wen always wore coarse silk dresses and never ordered new furniture, carriages, or other living implements. He immediately cancelled a project to build a balcony for his residence when he learned that it would cost 100 catties or about 1,600 ounces of gold, the equivalent of the total assets of ten middle-income families. He refused to accept expensive gifts such as rare jewels. He wanted no fancy tomb for his burial either—all he wanted was a hole for his coffin, in which would be his remains and a few clay pots.

The imperial treasury was hardly touched at all. Few, if any, rulers of China were that frugal.

Throughout history, the governments of China were always known as spendthrifts. During Qin and Han, China started using copper coins as currency. Ancient Chinese copper coins had a square hole in the middle. A thousand coins were strung together by cord (the equivalent of a silver dollar in recent times). The exchequer of Emperor Wen had shelves of copper coin strings that were safely locked up in heavy-duty storage rooms. During Emperor Wen's reign, those rooms were rarely ever opened. Cords that strung the coins together would have rotted, but the money would still be intact.

**Copper coins of the Han Dynasty**

What more do we need to prove the Emperor's frugality! Unfortunately, Emperor Wen's example was seldom emulated by Chinese imperial rulers over two millennia. Whenever this example was emulated, there was a glimmer in China's odyssey along the civilization highway.

Liu Qi 刘启 (188–141 BCE, Emperor Wen's son and successor), known as Han Emperor Jing 汉景帝 (reigned 141 BCE), had a short career. He continued his imperial father's frugal, people-oriented policies. During the first year of his reign, he ordered land revenue reduced by half from one-fifteenth to one-thirtieth

**Chapter 3: A Unified Empire Sans Imperialism**

of the harvest, as Emperor Wen had done. The next year, he announced that only males from age 20 onward would be liable for corvée (compulsory labor service). This meant a male adult had a four-year grace period after reaching adulthood at age 16. He announced amnesty four times during his reign. Also, natural calamities occurred frequently during the Emperor's reign and he immediately reduced the tax burden for victims of disasters. Like his imperial father, Emperor Wen, he led a simple, frugal life.

"Rise of the Han Dynasty began by reducing taxation, which gave people some relief. Then, the reigns of Emperor Wen and Emperor Jing, totaling about 50 years, changed the political trend" (Ban Gu 班固, 32–92 CE). Ban Gu was China's second greatest historian and chronicler of the Han Dynasty. The 41 years of rule by these two good emperors (179–141 BCE) can be regarded as the most genteel and people-friendly period in Chinese history. This was what historical books term as the "good governance of Emperors Wen and Jing 文景之治."

In fact, since the inception of the Han Dynasty, under rules of Emperor Gaozu and Empress Lu, the Han government adopted the policy of "recuperation and accumulation of vitality 休养生息," resembling the trend of "small government and big society" in modern Western politics. The contrast with the luxury-indulgent, arrogant, repressive, and people-unfriendly Qin government was obvious. The Han government was a more true product and representation of Chinese civilization than the Qin Dynasty. We could look at this phenomenon another way and regard the Qin as a transitional period, a moment of growing pains for Chinese civilization in creating the common entity of destiny starting from the Han.

The good governance of Emperors Wen and Jing also encouraged agricultural development, which was a priority in the governance of unified China from its inception. Emperor Wen enunciated the specific policies of "prioritize agriculture 重农" and "the emperor personally participates in agriculture

亲农." In his edict advocating agriculture, the Emperor observed: "Agriculture is the foundation of Tianxia and the lifeline of the people 农，天下之本也，民所恃以生也." He also observed: "Food is the basis of the people while people are the basis of the state 食者民之本，民者国之本." Emperor Wen did farming in his fields and gardens within the palace and held palace rituals of spring tilling and autumn harvesting. His queen also participated in sericulture.

The new picture of the Han Dynasty in contrast with the erstwhile Qin reminds us, again, of the *Qi-Lu-Dao* Confucius adage (from the state of Qi evolved the state of Lu, and from the state of Lu evolved the Dao). We clearly see from this adage how Chinese civilization keeps clear of the "nation-state" development path of war and conquest, even though the Qin Emperor had drawn China close to it. We see in the Han political venture, especially the good governance of Emperors Wen and Jing, the rudiment of a "civilization-state" that was yet unknown to mankind.

## V. The Empire sans Imperialism

In world history, there used to be two kinds of empires: interstate and intrastate. The Roman Empire belonged to the first category, while the Qin–Han Empire belonged to the second. Indian history has witnessed both categories. The Maurya and Gupta "empires" of ancient times and the later Mughal Empire were all intrastate empires although they also had characteristics of a federal structure. By contrast, the British Indian Empire was a typical "imperium in imperio" (state within a state). It had the typical metropole–periphery equation. Before returning to China, Hong Kong belonged to this category of imperialist empire too. People in Hong Kong were divided into three classes: British citizens, British subjects, and Hong Kong residents. After its return to China, Hong Kong gets to keep its special status and the people of Hong Kong are allowed to keep their British identification. While the limited number of British citizens in

Hong Kong are treated as Britons by the British government, British subjects in Hong Kong are treated as foreigners.

People of the Chinese Empire from Qin, Han, to Sui, Tang, Song, and further down to the Ming dynasties, whether rich or poor, privileged or repressed, were all legitimate citizens of China. Liu Bang was neither rich nor privileged, but he could rise to become emperor. This never happened in the Roman or British empires. In the history of the Roman and British empires, there was no emperor like Han Emperor Wen or Emperor Jing, leading a life like an ordinary commoner in China.

Lu Jia's reminder to the founding emperor of Han that he could not rule over Tianxia on horseback underscores the importance of political ideology in the Chinese empire. This political ideology was to have civilization's input into the rule of an empire created through a civil war victory. The afore-mentioned scholar, Jia Yi 贾谊, Emperor Wen's favorite courtier, communicated the ideology in these words "A Critique of Qin" mentioned before:

A sagacious ruler learns from history to plan for the present. He gains insight into personal relationships, analyzes the causes of success and failure, examines development tendencies, follows the rhythm of progress, and carries out timely reform. Thus, his policies are lasting and his society is secure.

He continued

A ruler's establishment of a state should be purported to make Tianxia an orderly place. Prisons should be empty and use of punishment minimal. Prisoners should be condoned for minor offenses and repatriated to their homes. Warehouses should distribute grains and the treasury should give doles to the poor and needy. Light taxation and few levies can help people meet their needs. Simple law and exemption of punishment can encourage behavioral reform, making people of Tianxia more sensitive to renovation and more driven to character cultivation. The world will be at peace when the sage ruler's virtue prevails over Tianxia and the people feel happy and content. When all people within the four seas are happy working, they will shun rebellion.

He went on to say: "The sole purpose of shepherding the people is to make them restful. Restful people can become righteous while restive people may engage in wrongdoing." Such ideas had already prevailed in the Chinese Empire before the founding of the Roman Empire and prior to our Common Era.

Han Emperor Jing was succeeded by his son, Liu Che 刘彻 (157–87 BCE), who reigned 53 years (141–87 BCE). He was the outstanding and world-famous Han Emperor Wu 汉武帝, who firmly established Confucian teaching for China's development with the help of a prominent scholar Dong Zhongshu 董仲舒 (179–104 BCE). The story began in 134 BCE when Emperor Wu invited scholars from all over the country to submit wise, useful suggestions, including an award. Dong Zhongshu's submission impressed the emperor, who called him for private conversations three times. What Dong Zhongshu opined during these conversations became a kind of ideology known as the "three proposals about heaven and humanity 天人三策." But, Dong Zhongshu could not acclimatize himself to the imperial court. He voluntarily retired and stayed home, dedicating himself to research and writing. The emperor continued to consult him by sending emissaries to his house. In this way, he was the academic authority of the Han Dynasty. A well-known publication written by him is entitled *Chunqiu fanlu* 春秋繁露 (literally, "rich dew of spring and autumn") and is now regarded as an important exposition of Confucian philosophy. In Section 16 of this treatise, there is an essay entitled "A Hymn to the Mountains and Rivers 山川颂." I translate a portion of the essay regarding the rivers as follows:

Rivers are made by fountains, flowing day and night without end. Like the strong people, they first fill up before doing work. Like the balancer, they move down with minute observation, bypassing no tiny gap. Like the observer, they flow through the valley with clear orientation. Like the visionary, they reach their goal in a thousand mile journey. Like the sagacious who foretells destiny, they maintain a clean course avoiding the hills and obstacles. Like reformers, they run in with silt but exit crystal clean. Like the brave, they never dawdle before jumping down the cliff. Like warriors, they can conquer terrible things such as fire. Like the virtuous, they sustain life....

A couple of centuries earlier, in *Laozi*, there was a brief discourse on "water is supremely perfect 上善若水," saying:

Water is beneficial to all beings and has no quarrel with anything. It stays in places where no humans like to live, hence, reaching the status of Dao. Water is the symbol of a perfect location to stay, a perfect depth of mind, perfect human love for social behavior, perfect trust for speech, perfect order for governance, perfect ability for enterprise, and perfect timing to make a move. It is faultless because it quarrels with no one.

I mention this discourse on "water is supremely perfect" for a very important reason. Recall the story of China beginning from the two great rivers, Huanghe and Yangtze, which created the Chinese common geographic entity. It was the river-harnessing hero, the Great Yu, who created the Chinese political entity in a hydraulic style. Chinese civilization prospered for millennia on "water and earth 水土," that is, to say, on the intelligent use of water and earth to attain economic prosperity. For thousands of years, when Chinese people found it difficult to acclimatize to the environment of a new place, they have said the "water and earth is not suitable 水土不服." Today, "water and earth" stands for the issue of the environment in Chinese discourse. However, never had Chinese civilization realized that water's home on the globe is the sea, and the sea drowns the virtue of "river/water 水" eulogized in the preceding text by Laozi and Dong Zhongshu. The coup d'état of the sea against Chinese civilization has created great misery for China, which is still felt today.

# CHAPTER 4
## EXTERNAL SECURITY AND INTERNAL STABILITY

Among all Han rulers, Emperor Wu probably has the most stories in Chinese literature. I found two relating to Indian visitors he received. In one story, the Indian visitor presented to him some trappings (ornamental decorations for horses) adorned with marvelous jewels. At night, these jewels shone, making the room as light as daytime. Another story was about the "resurrection fumigation 返魂香" taken seriously in Chinese literature and by traditional pharmacologists. The story goes that when an Indian emissary came to meet the emperor, there was a severe epidemic in the Han capital Chang'an. He presented an egg-shaped perfume to Emperor Wu, who burnt the perfume, as advised by the Indian presenter, and those who had died in the epidemic returned to life. These two stories should not be casually dismissed. Ancient India was famous for jewelry and perfume, so such gifts (obviously dramatized) in China during the 53-year reign (141–87 BCE) of Han Emperor Wu may not be just hearsay. A more famous story is the emperor's rendezvous with the legendary Goddess Xiwangmu/Uma in his Chang'an palace and her presenting a "celestial peach 仙桃" to the emperor. In Chinese legend, Goddess Xiwangmu/Uma met only two Chinese rulers, King Mu of Zhou nearly 3,000 years ago and Han Emperor Wu. These stories, in a way, reflect the wide international dimension of Emperor Wu's personal profile.

We are over a century beyond creation of the common entity of destiny by the Qin Emperor, reaching the most famous and robust period of the Han Dynasty. In Chapter 3, I alluded to people's tendency to see only the majesty of the gigantic Great Wall while missing the scale of effort (including the workers' sweat, blood, and life along with the tears of their families). Similarly, the Chinese common entity of destiny was not only creation of prominent rulers (however overwhelming and authoritarian they may have been): the intellectual elite and the common people also had their share of contribution. There was also a network and infrastructure to keep the entity stable and everlasting. In the opinion of Wittfogel and some other Western

scholars, there existed the essential element of bureaucracy in Chinese history. In comparison to the Roman Empire in which the ruler's personal will was absolutely supreme, there was an invisible "cage of ruling power" in China. Contemporary Chinese authorities today emphasize the importance of "keeping power within the cage." Such a cage existed during the Han, and other subsequent dynasties, in China. I will try to present this picture in this as well as subsequent chapters.

## I. Emperor Wu's Resolution in Driving Away the Xiongnu

Subconsciously, Chinese civilization was trying to carve out the existence of a "civilization-state" in a world of "nation-states." From day one of its existence, the Chinese common entity of destiny realized that the common geographical entity was only good for creation, and not for security protection. The Chinese Empire was encircled by the natural boundaries of the Pacific Ocean, the Himalayan range, and the expanse of the Gobi Desert to the east, south, and west, respectively. But the north, being open, was where the external threat originated. To the north, there was a strong military power called "Xiongnu 匈奴"—a tribe that arose at almost the same time as China was being unified into a huge comity of prosperous, agriculture-hand-industry, socioeconomy. While Xiongnu was a poor, primitive nomadic community, it had a warlike culture with a strong, swift cavalry. As the great Chinese poet Li Bai 李白 (701–762) described in his famous poem "Fighting South of the Town 战城南":

> Xiongnu, the martial tribe,
>
> fondly liked human killing
>
> instead of land tilling.
>
> (匈奴以杀戮为耕作)

Whenever it had sufficient strength, the Xiongnu would invade Northern China, and China was never able to cope with such an aggressor. Qin Emperor Shihuang built the Great Wall, which was extended and fortified during the Han Dynasty precisely to stop the incursion of the Xiongnu cavalry, but to no avail. In 200 BCE, Xiongnu leader Modu Chanyu 冒頓單于 besieged the founder–emperor of Han at Pingcheng 平城 (now Ningwu 宁武 County of Xinzhou 忻州 City in Shanxi province). The Han government had to bribe the Xiongnu queen to rescue the first Han emperor from captivity. In subsequent years, the Han government adopted an appeasement policy toward the Xiongnu by sending money, gifts, goods, and beautiful women to the latter, known as the "Policy of Peace and Affinity 和亲政策" by Chinese historians. During the period of good governance of Emperors Wen and Jing, the Chinese government showed great restraint and tolerance, but could not stop Xiongnu intrusions. Emperor Wen sent General Li Guang 李广 (?-119 BCE) to fight the Xiongnu and gain some brief respite. However, even the ever-victorious General Li Guang ended as a defeated hero. The Xiongnu strategy was not to seriously fight the Chinese expeditionary force during the latter's advance. Instead, when the Chinese force began to withdraw (as their food supply was exhausted), they fiercely attacked from behind, claiming heavy Chinese casualties. Han China was not able to win any campaign against the Xiongnu until the reign of Emperor Wu.

To ensure China's long-term security, Emperor Wu abandoned the appeasement policy and became determined to free China from the Xiongnu tribe forever. He allied with several Central Asian states to jointly fight the Xiongnu, weakening the Xiongnu after a dozen fierce battles. Later, Han Emperor Yuan 汉元帝 (reigned 49–33 BCE) also united with other Central Asian countries to drive the Xiongnu away. It took over a century for China to rid itself of this serious threat and make Northern China secure.

**Stone carving depicting the nomadic scene of the Huns**

In China, people thought the Xiongnu had finally vanished, but that was not the case. The Huns, originating from the Caspian Sea, entered the Caucasus around 150 CE and became a large kingdom within the domain of the Roman Empire from the 4th century onward. The mighty Roman legion could not defeat the Huns. Intrusion of the Huns into Europe was one of the reasons for the downfall of the Roman Empire. Modern French Sinologist Joseph de Guignes (1721–1800) identified this Hun race as descendants of the ancient Xiongnu. This shows that Han Emperor Wu really did a good thing for Chinese civilization and the heavy price he paid was worthwhile. If the Xiongnu (Huns) had remained near China, we can only imagine how insecure China would have been from the Han Dynasty forward.

Emperor Wu was repentant during his final years. In 89 BCE, he established the first instance of a Chinese emperor admitting his own mistakes by issuing the edict *lun tai zui ji zhao* 轮台罪己诏. In this edict, the Emperor revealed how he had demolished the morale and pride of the Xiongnu. They tied their horses and threw them below the wall on the Chinese troop fortifications, saying: "Chinamen, I am a beast! 秦人，我若马！" This shows how devastated and demoralized the

Xiongnu tribe became—a race having enormous self-pride as the masters on horseback now depicting themselves as their steed. The Emperor maintained his position that the "Xiongnu must be decimated and this is the time for it." He blamed himself for "creating trouble for Tianxia instead of doing his utmost for the people." He vowed to change his policies by "stopping tyranny 禁苛暴," "ending excessive taxation 止擅赋," and "vigorously promoting the agricultural base 力本农" while "not slackening armed preparedness 毋乏武备."

When Han Emperor Wu exerted China's utmost energy in fighting the Xiongnu, he sent out quite a number of "Han envoys 汉使" for diplomatic missions and international trade. The most famous Han envoy was Zhang Qian 张骞 (164–114 BCE). Upon returning from his first sojourn in Central Asia, he told the Emperor of his discovery of "Shu cloth 蜀布" (silk fabrics from Sichuan) that he had seen in Daxia 大夏 (present-day Afghanistan) and had been told that it was being reexported by Indian traders. Emperor Wu showed great interest in the report and sent emissaries to Central Asia, as well as from Sichuan to Yunnan, to contact the Indians directly. However, both these efforts failed.

People nowadays refer to Xi'an (ancient Chang'an) as the starting point of the Silk Road. We know Chang'an and Pataliputra were the two greatest cities on earth during the 2nd century BCE, yet did not assume the size of a big metropolitan city (their populations were below a million). Chang'an was still centuries away from being a thriving international trade city (as it was during the Sui and Tang dynasties). During his reign, Indian King Ashoka (304–232 BCE) vigorously spread Buddhism all over the world. This movement of popularizing Buddhist culture created an international highway called *Dharmaratna-Marg* (Road of Buddha-dharma Jewel). This *Dharmaratna-Marg* began from Pataliputra in the Gangetic Plains of the Indus valley and reached Chang'an through Afghanistan, Central Asian states, and Western China. Most eminent Buddhist monks from India and other countries reached China via this road. Indian monks who never carried money (unlike their Chinese fellow believers) were users, not creators, of this international highway. It was constructed by merchants of India, Central Asia, Persia, and other countries (with few, if any, from China). The Road of Buddha-dharma Jewel also carried jewels, perfumes, incense, spices, and high-quality cotton fabrics from India to China. The road was later called the "Silk Road." The *Dharmaratna-Marg* was the Silk Road and the Silk Road was the *Dharmaratna-Marg*. Today's Xi'an was the starting point of the Silk Road and the destination of the *Dharmaratna-Marg*: a two-way highway.

**Wall painting depicting Zhang Qian heading to the west along the Silk Road**

The Silk Road/*Dharmaratna Marg* has been so dearly remembered by Chinese civilization that there have been many gorgeous Chinese paintings about it.

**A Chinese painting of the Silk Road/*Dharmaratna Marg***

The Han Empire was an amalgamation of an emperor, an imperial court, an interest group surrounding the queen that wielded power behind the emperor, a bureaucracy, and the common masses who could demonstrate their power and influence.by organizing armed rebellions. The health and stability of the Han Empire depended on a harmonious relationship and balance of power among all these factions. Overall, it fared well for 200 years until the emergence of Wang Mang 王莽 (45 BCE–23 CE), who became an imperial officer in 22 BCE with backing from his paternal aunt Empress Dowager Wang—the de facto supreme authority. He became a high-ranking officer at age 24 and his popularity in government circles soared as he was diligent, capable, flexible, and skilled in political games. In 6 CE, reigning Han Emperor Ping 汉平帝 (reigned 1 BCE–6 CE) died, while Wang Mang's aunt Empress Wang still wielded power. Wang Mang became the de facto ruler with the title "pseudo-emperor 假皇帝" as the puppet on the throne was a two-year-old baby installed by him. In 7 CE, he proclaimed himself emperor after quelling a revolt and changed the dynastic name from Han to Xin 新, meaning new. In 23 CE, a rebellious peasant army called "Green Forest Army 绿林军" stormed the capital of Chang'an and killed Wang Mang, ending the Xin Dynasty.

There is an episode related to Wang Mang which should have drawn international attention, but never has. In the "geography" section of *Hanshu* 汉书 (annals of the Han Dynasty), there is an account of a foreign country (along the Indian coast) called Huangzhi[1] 黄支 that had an unusual relationship with Wang Mang's regime. In response to Wang Mang's request, the ruler of this Indian Huangzhi sent a live rhinoceros as a gift to boost Wang Mang's reputation. Famous scientist, scholar courtier, Zhang Heng 张衡 (78–139 CE), described, in his composition on Chang'an, that there were rare animals in the imperial park with "huge ears and folding nose 大耳折鼻" (depicting an elephant) and "pointed forehead and short neck 修额短项" (depicting a rhinoceros). China did not have any rhinoceros, so this one must be the gift from Huangzhi to Wang Mang. Imagine how difficult it must have been to transport a rhinoceros from India to China, two millennia ago, by coastal shipping (changing boats from coast to coast in between short distance sea voyages). Unless the bilateral relationship had been very strong, the Huangzhi state would not have taken so much trouble to transport a live rhino to Han China. Unfortunately, we do not have details about this China–Huangzhi relationship.

---

[1]The identity of Huangzhi is in doubt. A conventional theory makes Huangzhi the Chinese speculation of the Indian word *Kanjipuram/Kanjivaram*. This is a guess. From the historical backdrop of Chinese–Indian contacts, Huangzhi should be Bengal, known for elephant teeth and rhinoceros horns. In addition, Huangzhi/Bengal was on the ancient Silk Road.

**Chapter 4: External Security and Internal Stability**

## II. The Eastern Han Dynasty and Beyond

The death of Wang Mang and the end of the Xin Dynasty provided an opportunity for Liu Xiu 刘秀 (5 BCE–57 CE) to demonstrate his statesmanship. He restored the Han Dynasty and extended its existence for another two centuries. During his 33-year reign (25–57 CE) as Han Emperor Guangwu 汉光武帝, he spent four years quelling rebellions before reunifying Tianxia, moving the capital to Luoyang 洛阳, and beginning the new phase of the Han Dynasty—called Eastern Han 东汉 (because Luoyang, the new capital, was to the east of Chang'an, the old capital). But Chang'an was still a political, economic, and cultural center, so Chang'an and Luoyang shared the prominence of being "twin capital cities 二京." Liu Xiu (Emperor Guangwu) inherited the qualities of the founder–emperor of Han for vanquishing all opposition forces, the good governance of Emperor Wen and Emperor Jing for promoting the country's vitality, and Emperor Wu's all-out construction works and propagation of Confucian teachings. He reduced land revenue to the lower rate of one-thirtieth, as Emperor Wen had done. He pardoned convicts and organized them to develop farmland in border areas. He also made troops engage in farmland reclamation. He learned lessons from the erstwhile Western Han 西汉. Though he did not touch the status of existing influential courtiers, he undercut their power. He established a secretariat, under his direct leadership, called *shang shu tai* 尚书台 (literally, ministerial platform) to decide policy and interconnect departments and provinces of the country. He also merged some provinces and counties to reduce expenditure. During the Western Han, those peasants who could not pay their debts became slaves of the usurers. Emperor Guangwu ordered all slaves be emancipated. A large number of classics were destroyed or lost during the reign of Wang Mang. Emperor Guangwu ordered them to be retrieved and preserved in libraries, resulting in a large increase in classics and other books.

Liu Zhuang 刘庄 (28–75 CE), son and successor of Emperor Guangwu, who reigned for 18 years (57–75 CE) as Han Emperor

Ming 汉明帝, was a mediocre ruler. But one episode involving him should be highlighted: It was he who initiated the millennial warm welcome to the advent of Indian civilization in China. This began with the story well known in Chinese tradition as "Han Emperor Ming's Dream of the Golden Deity 汉明帝梦金人."[2] In 65 CE, the Emperor was said to have dreamed of a giant golden deity 16 feet tall with a brilliant halo around his neck flying inside the palace. The next morning, the grand historian of his court Fu Yi 傅毅 (?-90 CE) told him there was such a deity in the West named Buddha. The Emperor immediately sent a party, led by Cai Yin 蔡愔 (dates unknown), to the "Western Regions 西域" (Central Asia and India) in search of the deity. The party brought back to Luoyang two eminent Indian monks, Kasyapa Matanga and Dharmaratna/Dharmaraksa. The Emperor was thrilled and built the now famous Monastery of White Horses 白马寺 (because the two Indian monks had arrived on white horses) to accommodate them and enable them to translate Buddhist scriptures. They completed a book in Chinese entitled *Canon of Forty Two Chapters* 四十二章经 that, unfortunately, is not extant. This episode symbolized the fantastic beginning of Buddhism in China.

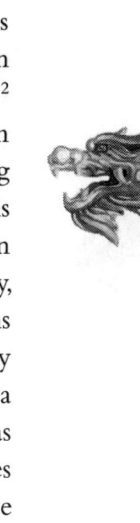

[2] "Han Emperor Ming's Dream of the Golden Deity" is a story, a dream. Thus, we may not question it in detail. For example, the Chinese term "golden deity 金人" was a misnomer. The term originated from the *ji tian jin ren* 祭天 金人 (a metal figurine used to worship heaven), which was a spoil obtained by General Huo Qubing 霍去病 (140–117 BCE) in 121 BCE when he destroyed the Xiongnu headquarters. General Huo later presented it to Han Emperor Wu and it became a famous treasure. This metal figurine was bronze and must have been the idol of the Buddha made in India. While there was no doubt the first *jin ren* 金人 possessed by Han higher-ups was a Buddha statue, it was a bronze figurine and not made of gold. India was a country rich in gold, hence, it had a culture highlighting gold. China was a country poor in gold, but adopted the Indian culture of highlighting gold after dissemination of Buddhism in China, long after Han Emperor Ming's reign. In this story, Han Emperor Ming's dream of a giant golden deity 16 feet tall with a brilliant halo around his neck obviously smacks of gross dramatization. However, this does not mean Han Emperor Ming was not capable of having such an outlandish dream. I have quoted in many of my writings that Emperor Taizong and Empress/Emperor Wu of the Tang Dynasty testified to the truth of this historic dream. It is my opinion that debate of whether this dream is history or fairytale (in Buddhist studies world-wide) serves no good academic purpose.

**Chapter 4: External Security and Internal Stability**

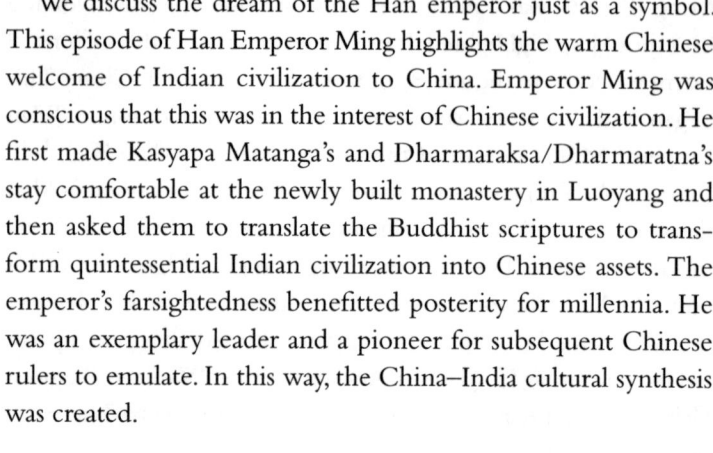

We discuss the dream of the Han emperor just as a symbol. This episode of Han Emperor Ming highlights the warm Chinese welcome of Indian civilization to China. Emperor Ming was conscious that this was in the interest of Chinese civilization. He first made Kasyapa Matanga's and Dharmaraksa/Dharmaratna's stay comfortable at the newly built monastery in Luoyang and then asked them to translate the Buddhist scriptures to transform quintessential Indian civilization into Chinese assets. The emperor's farsightedness benefitted posterity for millennia. He was an exemplary leader and a pioneer for subsequent Chinese rulers to emulate. In this way, the China–India cultural synthesis was created.

The great difference between the ancient Chinese and Indian civilizations lies in India's emphasis on oral tradition and China's emphasis on written tradition (everything must have a written record, and books are made to pass from generation to generation). Today, we see that most Buddhist scriptures are preserved in Chinese documents (much greater in number than in Sanskrit and Pali). We see Chinese Buddhist scriptures in writing and print much earlier than their Sanskrit and Pali versions, preserved on leaves. The earliest Buddhist scriptures preserved on leaves in India are no older than the 7th century, while China has preserved translation of Buddhist scriptures from the 5th century onward. Many Chinese translations of Buddhist scripture were based on recitations by Indian monks. Possibly, some of them never had a written text in ancient India. We see China doing a great service to the historical development of Buddhism by transposing the Indian Buddhist mind from the original oral form to the now preserved written form in Chinese. This is a great event in the history of world civilization and a great Chinese feat initiated by Han Emperor Ming.

Not long after Emperor Ming, a serious problem emerged in that the succeeding emperors' life span drastically declined. Some emperors died without grown sons to succeed them, resulting in successors being enthroned during childhood, even infancy.

There was Liu Long 刘隆 (105–106 CE), who became emperor
when he was only three months old and died eight months later.
He was the youngest Chinese ruler in history and is known
as Han Emperor Shang 殇帝 (literally, the emperor who died
young). The emperor was the crucial element of the Chinese
Empire. The corollary of emperor adolescence was ruling power
falling into the hands of "outside relations 外戚" (meaning
people related to the emperor, but not within the emperor's clan)
or eunuchs (who knew a lot of the secrets inside the palace and
could manipulate imperial persons, especially when they were
juvenile). Han Emperor Ling 汉灵帝 (reigned 156–189 CE) was
enthroned at age 13 and was manipulated by 12 veteran eunuchs.
The juvenile emperor even considered some eunuchs "dad"
and "mom." In 189 CE, the powerful eunuchs assassinated the
decorated General He Jin 何进 (?-189 CE), half brother of
the queen. Subsequently, General Dong Zhuo 董卓 134–192 CE
entered the capital with his troops, killed the queen and eunuchs
in the rival camp, and replaced the emperor. His bigotry virtually
ended the authority of the Han Emperor and plunged the
country into chaos.

In the closing years of Eastern Han, three regional powers
emerged in China vying for supremacy: Wei 魏 (220–265 CE),
Shu 蜀 (221–263 CE), and Wu 吴 (229–280 CE). Some 1,000
years later, Luo Guanzhong 罗贯中 (1280?–1360 CE) wrote a
book in the 14th century about these three kingdoms, now
world famous, entitled *The Romance of the Three Kingdoms*
三国演义. In the first paragraph of the book, Luo Guanzhong
propounded a theory that development of Chinese Tianxia was
governed by the law of "prolonged disintegration leading to
unification 分久必合" and "prolonged unification leading
to disintegration 合久必分." However influential this theory, it
misleads people and results in a wrong reading of the development
of Chinese civilization. The period of the three kingdoms was
not the disintegration of the Chinese entity of destiny. The rise
of the Wu and Shu states symbolized the political awakening of

the Yangtze valley. Under the banner of Wu, a new subculture of *Jiang nan wen hua* 江南文化 (literally, culture south of the Yangtze) began to flourish in the regions of Jiangsu, Zhejiang, and Jiangxi. Similarly, under the banner of Shu, a new subculture of *Bas hu wen hua* 巴蜀文化 (literally, culture of the Ba and Shu states, both in Sichuan) began to flourish, expanding from Sichuan into Hubei and Hunan. This fact was not highlighted in historical books, but is vividly described in great detail in Luo Guangzhong's *Romance of the Three Kingdoms*. Luo's *Romance* is actually fiction, not history. However, it has always been treated as history and the real history, compiled by historian Chen Shou 陈寿 (233–297 CE), has been completely eclipsed. Luo Guanzhong created a fake that has become more genuine than the real thing.

The secret of the success of Luo Guangzhong's "fake-turning-genuine" history of the three kingdoms lies in its inclusion of people's feedback on the historical personalities of the period of the three kingdoms. It further created two new cultural heroes (Guangong 关公 and Kongming 孔明) in Chinese folklore. Guangong was a chief general of Shu. His name was Guan Yu 关羽 (?-220 CE). In history, he was an absconding convict who joined Liu Bei's 刘备 (161–223 CE) rebel force. He was actually an ordinary fighter, twice captured by the enemy and finally put to death by his Wu state captors.[3]

Kongming, whose official name was Zhuge Liang 诸葛亮 (181–234 CE), was an outstanding, talented, and visionary statesman in Chinese history. He was also dramatized by the *Romance*,

---

[3]In the Yangtze valley, there was a long-standing folklore about the "apparition of Guangong." He was, thus, posthumously awarded honorific titles by many subsequent dynasties. He has been a deity among Chinese followers of Confucianism, Daoism, and Buddhism. There have been various kinds of Guangong temples all over China's mainland, Hong Kong, Macau, and Taiwan. The Guangong cult has been popular in South Korea and Japan as well. The cult is spreading worldwide with the proliferation of overseas Chinese. I have seen a Guangong statue in a couple of Chinese restaurants in North America.

but not to the extent of Guangong.[4] The *Romance* rightly highlighted his selfless service to the state and society. He was author of the immortal adage "I dedicate every speck of my energy to the cause until I breathe my last 鞠躬尽瘁，死而后已." This has been the motto of the Chinese elite for nearly two millennia— Zhuge Liang being the model of this spirit. Another notable example of this "dying-in-harness" was the founder–premier of the PRC, Zhou Enlai 周恩来 (1898–1976).

Zhuge Liang left behind two famous essays, entitled "Message Before Expedition 出师表," for the king and courtiers of Shu before he embarked on his northern expeditions in 227 CE and 228 CE. In the first, he wrote: "I was a linen-clad man and farmer at Nanyang 南阳 who led the life of a hermit to survive in a world of turmoil without clamoring for fame." Zhuge Liang was the all-powerful prime minster and de facto ruler of Shu, yet maintained his "linen-clad" (a commoner not wearing silks) simplicity and frugality. He was a good leader and administrator, and the people of Shu state were solidly behind him. He was also a talented strategist. It was Zhuge Liang who created Shu state from scratch. At one point, Shu was the main challenger to the dominant Wei.

The *Romance* is replete with Zhuge Liang's success stories. The most extraordinary episode was his famous "empty-city stratagem 空城计" (known internationally as the "empty fort strategy" today). His favorite general Ma Su 马谡 (190–228 CE) failed him in his second expedition by losing a crucial position to the enemy, and Zhuge Liang was in danger of being overrun by the enemy's counterattack. He was accompanied by only

---

[4]Though the cult of Kongming/Zhuge Liang in China is nowhere near that of Guangong, there are dozens of temples with varying names for worshipping Kongming all over China. The most famous is the "Wuhou Ci 武侯祠" (temple of Lord Wu, Zhuge Liang's posthumous title) in the Wuhou (Lord Wu) District of Chengdu 成都 in Sichuan, built in 223 CE to commemorate Liu Bei and Zhuge Liang. It is also the largest museum of the history of the three-kingdom period, a class-one state-owned museum, and AAAA-class tourist site.

**Chapter 4: External Security and Internal Stability**

5,000 troops and retreated very slowly because of the large number of civilians he had to look after. When he reached the small city of Yangping 阳平, enemy Commander-in-Chief Sima Yi 司马懿 (179–251 CE), who had a huge force of 150,000 men, caught up with him. Sima Yi was also a good strategist, but had great admiration for Zhuge Liang. Zhuge Liang was in imminent danger of being captured by Sima Yi, but knew the latter's admiration and fear for him and decided on a risky strategy. He asked everyone inside the city to remain calm and kept the city gate open when the enemy troops arrived. Alone, he sat on the city wall well composed, playing a musical instrument. When Sima Yi reached the scene, he could not believe his eyes. His initial instinct was that Zhuge Liang had laid a trap to catch him, so he ordered a hasty withdraw of his huge force to safety. The "empty-city stratagem" scared away a victorious enemy and ensured Zhuge Liang's safe retreat. The *Romance* narrates this with vivid descriptions and without fabrication as we know this was

**A portrait of Zhuge Liang**

a true historical episode testified to by a 4th-century historian. Now, the entire world knows this stratagem. In today's world of nation-states, obsessed with competition, Zhuge Liang's "empty-fort strategy" has wide impact in military, political, and even economic life.

Today, a very popular Chinese saying goes: "Combination of the wisdom of three stinking cobblers can match that of Zhuge Liang 三个臭皮匠等于一 个诸葛亮." The saying shows the popularity of Zhuge Liang at China's grassroots. Not only does the name "Zhuge Liang" inspire people to become wise and smart it has also become a synonym of great wisdom, especially in finding solutions to thorny problems. Luo Guanzhong's *Romance of the Three Kingdoms* highlighted great genius rising from common people, while this popular saying expresses the Chinese faith in collective wisdom.

The Eastern Han Dynasty was destroyed by the civil wars among the three kingdoms. In 220 CE, Cao Pi 曹丕 (187–226 CE), ruler of Wei, forced the last Han ruler Emperor Xian 汉献帝 (reigned 189–220 CE) to abdicate and formally established the Wei state, ruled by the Cao 曹 family. Then, Commander-in-chief Sima Yi (who was "defeated" by Zhuge Liang's "empty-fort strategy") stole the show. His grandson Sima Yan 司马炎 (236–290 CE) overthrew Wei and established the Western Jin 西晋 Dynasty (265–316 CE). By then, the independent states of Shu and Wu in the Yangtze valley were vanquished and China was again unified. Then, foreign forces intruded into Northern China and established 16 states at varying times. The native reigning force moved to the south of the Yangtze and ruled the "Eastern Jin 东晋" (317–420 CE) for a century.

## III. Foreign Members into the Chinese "Common Entity"

During the two-millennium period of Chinese empires, there were as many foreigners ruling China as there were natives.

China was under non-Chinese rule for as long as it was under Chinese rule. The Western Jin Dynasty lasted less than a century with Northern China under intrusion and domination by foreign rulers. This is known as the Sixteen States period (304–439 CE).[5] Conventionally, Chinese historians describe it as "five foreign races playing havoc in China 五胡乱华." This description, carrying racist undertones, is historically incorrect. The so-called "five foreign races" were: Xiongnu 匈奴, Xianbei 鲜卑, Jie 羯, Di 氐, and Qiang 羌. They were presented in history books as broad categories, not based on precise identification. For example, to categorize Qiang 羌 as a foreign 胡 race is a little problematic as the Great Yu himself was a Qiang national, and Qin Emperor Shihuang had Qiang DNA. Meanwhile, the Xiongnu 匈奴 race reopened a hitherto closed chapter in that their tribe had been driven away from China's neighborhood and, at this point in time, were creating trouble for the Roman

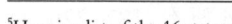

---

[5]Here is a list of the 16 states:

1. Cheng Han 成汉 (304–347 CE), established by the Li 李 family of Di氐 nationality in Sichuan.
2. Former Zhao 前赵 (304–329 CE), established by the Liu 刘 family of Xiongnu nationality.
3. Latter Zhao 后赵 (319–352 CE), established by the Shi 石 family of Jie 羯 nationality.
4. Former Liang 前凉 (301–376 CE), established by the Zhang 张 family of Han nationality in the northwest.
5. Former Yan 前燕 (337–370 CE), established by the Murong 慕容 family of Xianbei 鲜卑 nationality.
6. Former Qin 前秦 (351–394 CE), established by the Fu 苻 family of Di nationality.
7. Latter Yan 后燕 (384–407 CE), established by the Murong family of Xianbei nationality first in Hebei province, then expanding to a large area including Hebei, Liaoning 辽宁, Shandong, Shanxi, and Henan provinces.
8. Latter Qin 后秦 (384–417 CE), established by the Yao 姚 family of Qiang nationality in a vast area of Northern China.
9. Western Qin 西秦 (385–400 CE), established by the Qifu 乞伏 family of Xianbei nationality.
10. Latter Liang 后凉 (386–403 CE), reestablished by the Lu 吕 family of Di nationality.
11. Southern Liang 南凉 (397–414 CE), established by the Toufa 秃发 family of Xianbei nationality in Qinghai 青海.
12. Western Liang 西凉 (400–421 CE), established by the Li 李 family of Han nationality in Gansu and Xinjiang 新疆.
13. Northern Liang 北凉 (397–437 CE), established by the Mengxun 蒙逊 family of Xiongnu nationality in the northwest.
14. Southern Yan 南燕 (398–410 CE), established by the Murong family of Xianbei nationality in eastern China.
15. Northern Yan 北燕 (407–436 CE), established by the Feng 冯 family of Han nationality in Liaoning and Hebei provinces.
16. Xia state 夏国 (407–431 CE), established by the Helian 赫连 family of Xiongnu nationality in Northern China.

Empire. But, there could be political players during this period claiming the ethnic identity of Xiongnu. Moreover, among the 16 states, three were established by the Han race that was supposed to be native Chinese.

Overall, establishment of the 16 states was peaceful and smooth, showing foreign forces joining the Tianxia comity of China to enrich its multiplicity. Though under foreign rule, they existed like autonomous units within the common civilization entity of China. In fact, this was the crucial period when China was connected with the *Dharmaratna-Marg*. Through this *Dharmaratna-Marg*, great Buddhist missionaries started coming into China. One prominent example is Kumarajiva 鸠摩罗什 (344–413 CE).

**A handsome Chinese sculpture of the beloved Kumarajiva**

The son of an Indian (Kashmiri) father and Central Asian (Kuchan) mother, Kumarajiva was regarded as the most precious treasure among the ruling circles of the 16 states. The founder–ruler of the Former Qin Fu Jian 苻坚 (338–385 CE) sent an army contingent to Kuchan to "invite" Kumarajiva to China. When Kumarajiva reached Chang'an, he became the personal property of the Latter Qin ruler Yao Xing 姚兴 (366–416 CE). Yao Xing was a great admirer of Kumarajiva and a farsighted statesman who knew Kumarajiva's cultural value.[6] He established a Scriptures Translation Bureau 译经院, led by Kumarajiva, who had 800 Chinese and foreign scholars and monks at his disposal. Translation of Buddhist scriptures from Sanskrit into Chinese was done through collective effort and open discussion. Each Sanskrit sentence was introduced (recited and explained) by Kumarajiva, with its Chinese translation finalized by him after collective discussion. Emperor Yao Xing sometimes sat in on the discussions as an observer. In this way, the Chinese government maintained the practice initiated by Han Emperor Ming in transforming quintessential Indian wisdom from Indian oral tradition into Chinese written tradition. Kumarajiva had the extraordinary talent of being conversant in both Sanskrit and Chinese, while also having great aptitude for blending Chinese and Indian civilization.

The period of Sixteen States[7] substantially contributed to the development of Chinese civilization. Conventional opinions of "five foreign races playing havoc in China" should instead be "five foreign races creating prosperity in China."

---

[6]Emperor Yao Xing was concerned that the seed of Kumarajiva's talent would vanish from humankind when the monk passed away. Thus, he accommodated Kumarajiva in luxurious living circumstances attended by pretty maids. Kumarajiva could not resist the temptations and violated the religious discipline. He fathered many children born of these maids and the seeds of Kumarajiva's talent were left in China. This is an extraordinary, memorable episode in the history of Sino-Indian cultural intercourse.

[7]The period of Sixteen States was chiefly a phenomenon of political development north of the Yangtze river. South of the Yangtze remained under native Chinese rule called the "Eastern Jin 东晋" (317–420 CE). This south–north division in China further developed the "two-China" phenomenon known in history as the period of "Southern and Northern Dynasties 南北朝." South of the Yangtze was the period of "Southern Dynasties 南朝," having four successive dynasties of Song 宋 (420–479 CE), Qi 齐 (479–502 CE), Liang 梁 (502–557 CE), and Chen 陈 (557–589 CE). North of the Yangtze was the period of "Northern Dynasties 北朝," having the Northern Wei 北魏 (386–534 CE), Northern Qi 北齐 (550–577 CE), and Northern Zhou 北周 (557–581 CE).

Today, we see the tragedy of partitions of states. When Great Britain was about to withdraw from India, it created the partition of the Indian subcontinent into India and Pakistan. Subsequently, Pakistan was partitioned and Bangladesh established. The Korean Peninsula has been partitioned into North Korea and South Korea from the end of World War II to this day. The erstwhile Berlin Wall was the symbol of partition of Germany and the division between the Communist Bloc and "free world" (today, it has disappeared). During the late 1940s civil war period in China, the United States and USSR attempted to partition China along the Yangtze (with "Communist China" in the North and "Guomindang China" in the South). Mao Zedong vehemently resisted. "We won't make the Southern and Northern Dynasties," he said. A million PLA troops crossed the Yangtze and unified Chin's mainland. Had Mao Zedong not defied Stalin, there would be "two Chinas" today and China would have fallen into an unprecedented trap of partition. Look at the partition of India and the enmity between North and South Korea. How miserable would China have been had the great Yangtze river been the permanent boundary between the Communist North and Guomindang South!

The historical period of the Southern and Northern Dynasties was far different from the India–Pakistan equation or the current North–South Korean division. The Southern and Northern Dynasties maintained the unified status of Chinese civilization, with each ruled by the Chinese political system and the Chinese intellectual elite manning administration on both sides of the Yangtze. Cross-Yangtze movement by traders and other travelers was freely open as usual. Luoyang and Chang'an were still the political, economic, and cultural centers of China, though under non-native rulers. The main stage of China's interaction with other countries lay in the foreign-ruled Northern Dynasties. More importantly, forces that reunified China during the Sui and Tang dynasties emerged from the foreign-ruled Northern Dynasties, not native-ruled Southern Dynasties. Chinese history books have treated the Northern Dynasties as an integral part of Chinese development.[8]

Like the Sixteen States, the Southern and Northern Dynasties were also a period crucial to development of Chinese civilization, contributing to the stability and maturity of the Chinese common entity of destiny. The main highlight was the face-lift given to Chinese spiritual and material life by the vibrant influence of Buddhist culture. People on both shores of the Yangtze vied to erect Buddhist temples and worship Buddha and Bodhisattvas. Most of the famous Buddhist shrines throughout China were initially established during this period. Buddhist preachers from India and Central Asia thronged China. The most famous was Bodhidharma 菩提达摩 (?-535 CE), a former prince from an ancient South Indian state (who had to become a monk if he was not in the line of succession). While studying, Bodhidharma's guru, Prajñātāra, told him that the most important country on earth was China and he should go there to disseminate Buddha dharma. Bodhidharma went to China from South India by sea, arriving in Guangzhou 广州 (Canton) before 478 CE. That means that he landed in one of the Southern Dynasties of China. From Guangzhou, he went to Nanjing, capital of the Liang Dynasty. He arrived there during Liang Emperor Wu's 梁武帝 (Xiao Yan 萧衍 464–549 CE) reign. The Emperor was a "disciple of the *Bodhisattva-sila*" (he was called the "Bodhisattva Emperor 菩萨皇帝"), patronizing and participating in the movement to disseminate Buddhism. Strangely, Bodhidharma did not stay in Nanjing for long. There was a story that his

---

[8]The major portion of the history of the Northern Dynasties (386–581 CE) was written by the Northern Wei 北魏. It was established by the Toba 拓跋 family of Xianbei nationality; hence, it was also known as Toba Wei 拓跋魏 or Yuan Wei 元魏. It lasted 148 years (386–557 CE) and had 20 emperors. In 534 CE, the Northern Wei split into the Eastern Wei 东魏 and Western Wei 西魏. In 550 CE, the Eastern Wei was overthrown by its powerful courtier Gao Yang 高洋 (526–559 CE) who established the Northern Qi 北齐. In 557 CE, the Western Wei was overthrown by the powerful Yuwen 宇文 family, which established the Northern Zhou 北周. In 577 CE, Northern Zhou vanquished Northern Qi.

meeting with Liang Emperor Wu ended unpleasantly, but many, even Buddhist historians, don't believe the story. Bodhidharma moved on to the domain of the Northern Dynasties, settling in the Shaolin Monastery 少林寺 near Luo-yang. There he was famous for meditating nine years before a rock using great concentration.

**A portrait of Bodhidharma**

After his death, Bodhidharma was revered as the founding patriarch of the Chan 禅 sect of Chinese Buddhism. Chan Buddhism is a Chinese invention and is very popular in Japan (禅 is pronounced "Zen" in Japanese), and the overwhelming majority of Chinese Buddhists are Chan Buddhists. Chan (transliteration of Sanskrit "dhyana/meditation") spirit blends the Indian belief of gods residing inside the *hridaya-guha* (cave of the heart) and the Chinese/Confucian tradition of *zheng xin cheng yi* 正心诚意 (the heart being in the righteous position with all intentions focused and sincere) to create a Chinese way of devotion to Buddha, the Enlightened One, by paying greater attention to self-cultivation of spiritual consciousness than chanting scriptures and worshipping idols. Chan spirit has made the Chinese populace compassionate and helped Chinese poets create a Chan poetic vision to produce masterpieces. Bodhidharma also linked Indian civilization with its Chinese counterpart. In India, he was the 28th patriarch succeeding the Buddha according to Chinese Buddhist historiography (there is no such counting in India). Then, he was the founding patriarch of Chinese Chan Buddhism. Later, he was the sixth patriarch of Chan Buddhism with Reverend Huineng 慧能 (638–713 CE) as founding patriarch of the "Southern Sect 南宗" of Chan. Then, the sixth patriarch of the "Southern Sect," Reverend Yixuan 义玄 (?–867 CE), created the "Linji Sect 临济宗." Today, Reverend Xingyun 星云 of Foguangshan/Fo-Kuang-shan 佛光山 in Kaohsiung 高雄 City of Taiwan is the 48th successor of Patriarch Yixuan. This succession of Buddhist patriarchs makes Reverend Xingyun the 86th successor of the Buddha. We can see two scenarios from such a calculation. First, the Chinese and Indian civilizations are like two melons on the same vine within the Himalaya Sphere. Second, China has carried forward Indian Buddhism to become a modern religious culture as a Chinese redemption for the benefit it has received from India. Bodhidharma had a great impact on the development of Chinese civilization. For instance, he contributed to the development of martial arts at the Shaolin Monastery. He was also the deity of the anti-Christian Boxers at the end of the 19th century (discussed in Chapter 8).

Geographically, the seat of the Chinese Empire remained in the eastern end of Eurasia, but, culturally, Chinese civilization was progressively interconnecting Central Asia and South Asia via Central Asia. The energy released by the *Dharmaratna Marg/* Silk Road contributed greatly to the vibrant cultural development of China from the 6th century onward. An important manifestation of this vibrancy was popularization of Buddhism in China, as stories of Kumarajiva and Bodhidharma epitomize. Chinese civilization was on the move. Buddhism (the incarnation of Indian civilization) was also on the move. The two movements

converged on Chinese soil to open a new page of Chinese civilization.

We have now reached the end of the period we may regard as Version 1 of the Chinese common entity of destiny. This Version 1 was full of difficulties, tensions, strains, and actions, presenting a picture of robust existence and powerful dynamics.

# CHAPTER 5

# THE PROSPEROUS TANG DYNASTY AND ITS GOLDEN CULTURE

In Chinese history, we treat the dynasties of Qin and Han as a cluster. The cluster of the Sui and Tang dynasties is the subject of this chapter. This "cluster" phenomenon doesn't mean there was a smooth extension from the preceding to the succeeding dynasty. We know there was war between Qin and Han, and the Han army, led by Liu Bang, stormed the Qin capital, Xianyang (near present-day Xi'an), to overthrow the Qin Dynasty. When we conceive of the idea of a Qin–Han cluster, we view it from a holistic perspective to see that the Han Empire was basically the same Chinese Empire after changing its name from Qin to Han. We can also regard the Han Dynasty as an improved version of the Qin Dynasty. It is in this same sense that we think of the Sui–Tang cluster. There was, however, a little difference. The uprising of the Tang army did not need to overthrow the Sui Dynasty, which had ended on its own. The rise of Tang just restored order to the country and became a successful successor of the erstwhile Sui.

## I. China's Reunification under the Sui Dynasty

At the end of Chapter 4, I underscored the contribution of Buddhism to the development of Chinese civilization. It was a good sign that a baby born in a Buddhist temple (the Prajñā Monastery 般若寺 in Dali 大荔 County of Shaanxi) grew into an architect of the reunification of China and creator of the Sui Dynasty. He was Yang Jian 杨坚 (541–604 CE), son of Yang Zhong 杨忠 (507–568 CE), who's Xianbei name was Puliuru, given by the emperor of Western Wei. Yang Jian 杨坚, the son, also had a Xianbei name of "Narayan," which is the name of the Hindu God Vishnu. Thus, the Chinese avatar (reincarnation) of the Indian deity is Sui Emperor Wen 隋文帝 (reigned 581–604 CE), who was the most devout Buddhist ruler, after Liang Emperor Wu, during the period of Southern and Northern Dynasties.

"Thriving Era of Kaihuang 开皇盛世" was a historic term used to compliment Sui Emperor Wen's reign with "Opening

Emperor 开皇" as its reign title. It was comparable to the good governance of Han Emperors Wen and Jing. Sui Emperor Wen imposed light taxation. He proclaimed the "opening emperor's law," which reinforced the rule of law to authorities at all levels. He alleviated the punishment of former governments. He strengthened population registration, resulting in the discovery of 1.65 million unregistered citizens and increased government revenue. He paid attention to land ownership and seriously implemented the "equitable land system 均田制" introduced by the Northern Wei. He also discouraged land amalgamation. He abolished governmental monopolies in the trade of salt and liquor. He established the "government granary" to ensure food security. He also established the "charity granary" to provide food grains to the poor and calamity victims. He simplified local administration to a two-tiered *zhou* 州 (province) and *xian* 县 (county) system, saving a lot in revenue. He punished corruption and dismissed incompetent officials. He abolished the post-Han system of "nine gradations of the social talents" (into A1 上上, A2 上中, A3 上下, B1 中上, B2 中中, B3 中下, C1 下上, C2 下中, C3 下下) for government recruitment and replaced it with the world-famous Imperial Examination System to promote meritocracy. During his reign, people became rich or well to do, and the granaries were full. The emperor himself led a frugal life. He demoted his luxury-addicted eldest son Yang Yong 杨勇 (568–604 CE) from crown prince to ordinary citizen.

There were numerous stories about this devout Buddhist Emperor's infusion in the holy relics of the Buddha (called *sheli* 舍利 in Chinese and being the transliteration of the Sanskrit *sari*). It was said that after cremation of the Buddha, his bones were transformed into *sari* (shining, bean-like particles), which would bring fortune and happiness to the human world. A mysterious Brahmanic monk 婆罗门僧人 was said to have placed such *sari* relics in the Emperor's residence. *Sari* appeared in the emperor's dinner plates and it appeared when he was combing his hair. In 601, the emperor ordered that a magnificent reliquary pagoda be built in the capital of all 30 *zhou*/provinces.

Chapter 5: The Prosperous Tang Dynasty and Its Golden Culture

He sent 30 delegations, each carrying a reliquary box (with *sari*, and gold and silver ornaments inside), to the state capitals to be installed in the pagodas. At noon on the 15th day of the 10th month of that year (601), a ceremony for completion of the reliquary pagoda was simultaneously held in the imperial capital Chang'an and all provincial capitals, and the entire country refrained from animal slaughter and nonvegetarian food. Hundreds of thousands of people participated in this country-wide ceremony. The festivity was repeated the next year. The *sari* relics fever in China lasted until the end of Emperor Wen's reign in 604. This episode was a precursor to the all-China fever of royal reception to "Buddha's bone 佛骨" in 873, during the Tang Dynasty.

Emperor Yang Guang 杨广 (569–618 CE; reigned 604–618 CE), the second and final ruler of Sui, 隋炀帝 was even more outstanding and famous than his imperial father. He started the project of the famous Grand Canal of China, linking the north with the south. While all major rivers in interior China flow west to east, this river flowed from north to south. He reinforced the Great Wall and expanded Luoyang. He led an expeditionary force against the "Tuguhun 吐谷浑" (a kingdom established by the Murong tribe of the Xianbei race around Qinghai). He fought a war with "Koguryo/Korea 高句丽", a powerful kingdom on the Korean peninsula. He formally instituted the Imperial Examination System for recruiting high-ranking government officials. He was fond of touring the country and building makeshift palaces in various places, enjoying a luxurious lifestyle, in the company of beautiful women. He emulated Yao Xing of Latter Qin in establishing a sutra-translation institution. He sent envoys to "Western foreign countries 西蕃," reaching the Gangetic Plains of India and modern Uzbekistan. He pursued a pro-foreign trade policy, ordering restaurants in the border area to provide foreign traders with food and drinks free of charge.

The Turkic tribe who had subjected themselves to the reign of Sui Emperor Wen grew into a powerful force under the

leadership of Shibi Khan (Guitar Ashina). In 615, when Emperor Yang was inspecting Northern China with 17,000 guards, he was suddenly surrounded, in a blitzkrieg attack, by Shibi Khan's cavalry of several hundred thousand men. Emperor Yang retreated into the walled city of Yanmen 雁门 (in present-day Xidai 西代 County of Shanxi province). Shibi Khan's troops besieged the city, but failed to break into it. Emperor Yang fearlessly supervised the defense on the rampart with enemy arrows falling before his feet. Chinese reinforcements quickly arrived from all over and lifted the siege. This episode was similar to the founder–emperor of Han being besieged at Pingcheng (also in present-day Shanxi) in 200 BCE, but Emperor Yang was not in imminent danger of captivity. The Chinese common entity was certainly more mature and stable, though still vulnerable to invasion from neighbors.

Sui Emperor Yang was comparable to Han Emperor Wu in exhausting the country's vitality that accumulated during the thriving era of Kaihuang. However, he did not weaken China (as Han Emperor Wu had done). He made Luoyang a huge metropolitan center and moved his capital there. The Grand Canal linked the two great rivers of Yangtze and Huanghe, closely interconnecting the political center in Northern China with the economically prosperous Jiangnan (south of the Yangtze) area. It was Emperor Yang who created the most prosperous belt of Eastern China in modern Jiangsu and Zhejiang that remains so to this day.

The shining star of this belt was the new city of Yangzhou 扬州 (north of Nanjing), perhaps the richest commercial center in the world until it was ransacked by Nurchen invaders half a millennium later. While Europe was spell cast within doors (as outdoors was "pagandom") during the Dark Ages, Yangzhou did not sleep at night. Night markets and entertainment buzzed with life from dusk to dawn. It was in Yangzhou that Sui Emperor Yang was killed by his soldiers as he lay in the embrace of women. The central attraction of Yangzhou was the "Twenty-fourth Bridge 二十四桥" downtown. For centuries, beautiful actresses danced on the bridge on moonlit nights watched by a huge riverside crowd, who felt that they were angels from heaven.

**Chapter 5: The Prosperous Tang Dynasty and Its Golden Culture**

## II. Two Great Tang Emperors

The 290 years of the Tang Dynasty 唐朝 (618–907 CE) pushed prosperity of China even higher than during the reign of Sui Emperor Yang. This period produced perhaps the greatest ruler in Chinese history Li Shimin 李世民 (598–649 CE) who became Tang Emperor Taizong 唐太宗 (reigned 626–649 CE). His 24-year reign has been affectionately praised as "good governance of Zhenguan 贞观之治," highlighting his reign title of Zhenguan. Li Shimin joined the army in 615 at age 18. He fought against the Turkic force that besieged Sui Emperor Yang at Yanmen in Shanxi. When China was in turmoil following the death of Emperor Yang, his father Li Yuan 李渊 (566–635 CE) rose in rebellion. Li Shimin was commander-in-chief of this rebel army. After establishment of the Tang Dynasty under his father, who became Tang Emperor Gaozu 唐高祖 (reigning 618–626 CE), Li Shimin was actually the administrative chief. However, his father made Li Jiancheng 李建成 (589–626 CE), his eldest son, crown prince, virtually barring Li Shimin from imperial succession. Li Shimin's talent and ambition would not reconcile with his fate. In 626, he staged the "Incident at the Xuanwu Gate

**Yangzhou, the city did not sleep during Sui–Tang**

玄武门政变," killing his eldest brother (the crown prince) and another younger brother. In the same year, Li Shimin forced his imperial father to abdicate the throne in his favor. Confucian norms that a gentleman should be loyal to the king, obedient to his father, and affectionate to his brother were palpably violated by Li Shimin. But Chinese civilization has condoned his misbehavior and recognized him as an outstanding ruler and brilliant statesman.

Emperor Taizong is considered to be a role model for good governance in China. Some commentators describe his administration as "honest and enlightened governance." He adopted policy prioritizing agriculture, advocated frugality, accumulated vitality for the country, rejuvenated culture and education, perfected the Imperial Examination System, and thus created a peaceful and restful society. He vigorously dealt with external threats, showing respect to cultures of surrounding nationalities and ensuring stability of border areas. The miracle of his reign was that he presided over a country that he made virtually free of corruption without resorting to stringent anti-corruption measures. The emperor set an example of honesty and led officials throughout China in devoting themselves to public interest. Cases of officials abusing their power for private gain were fewer than at any other time in Chinese history. He created a smooth government structure called the "Three Divisions and Six Ministries 三省六部制," somewhat resembling the triple divisions of power of a modern democracy. He was unprecedentedly democratic in that he subjected his own edicts to the scrutiny of a division called *menxiasheng* 门下省 (literally, ministry below the gate) specifically established to do the job. No edict would be issued in his name without endorsement of this Ministry: This eliminated the chance of the emperor issuing orders when he was impulsive or in bad mood.

The Indian King Shiladitya Harshavardhana hosted the famous Chinese pilgrim Xuanzang 玄奘 (602–664 CE) in India and had heard of Chinese music titled "The Music of Prince

Qin's Victory in Battle 秦王破阵乐." He asked Xuanzang who the prince of Qin was and was told he was the reigning Tang Emperor. King Harsha immediately sent an ambassador to Tang China. His knowledge of the music praising the Tang Emperor testifies to the emperor's international fame.

Emperor Taizong shared his brilliant governance ideas through his writings, which have served as valuable advice to subsequent Chinese rulers to this day. He authored two treatises entitled *The Exemplary Emperor* 帝范 and *The Golden Mirror* 金镜书. He likened the ruler to a vessel and the people to water, propounding the theory that the shape of water changes according to its container, thus arguing that it was the ruler, and not the people, who is responsible for the shape that a country took. He quoted Confucius: "As civilization is deeply penetrating, so is military power widely prevalent. As virtue has a wide influence, so has deterrence a wide impact." According to Emperor Taizong, Confucius also said: "We must rely on civilization and virtue to make people restful, and rely on military deterrence to fortify border defense 安民必以文德，防边必以武功." His argument was that virtuous rule and military power were indispensable in governing the Chinese common entity of destiny. The Tang Dynasty benefited enormously by this balanced policy guaranteeing prosperity and security.

The emperor was highly perceptive in observing: "To make people happy, officials must suffer. If officials are happy, people suffer 民乐则官苦，官乐则 民劳." China would have been a perfect civilization-state if these remarks were always observed by ruling authorities. He also said a monarch was meant "to make people live happily 乐民之君" and should "sacrifice all personal desires to make everyone live happily within the four seas 屈一身之欲，乐四海之民." He further said:

If you block the avenue of sincere and frank submissions, you will have few loyal subordinates. If you open the avenue for flattery and sweet reports, you'll surround yourself with sycophants and dishonest subordinates. A muddleheaded ruler is perpetually foolish in defending his shortcomings while an enlightened ruler constantly does well by thinking of his shortcomings.[1]

The most often quoted saying of Emperor Taizong is: "The ruler is like a boat while the people are like water. Water can support the boat or capsize it 君，舟也，人，水也；水能载舟，亦能覆舟." All these sagacious words outlined a political ideology contributing to the golden period of Tang.

Chinese historians describe the era of Emperor Taizong as "Beginning Tang 初唐," while the period of "Thriving Tang 盛唐" began with Emperor Taizong's great-grandson, Li Longji 李隆基 (685–762 CE), who reigned 44 years (712–756 CE) as Tang Emperor Xuanzong 唐玄宗, the longest reign during the Tang Dynasty. Emperor Xuanzong was the most romantic and talented musician the Chinese common entity had ever seen. His reign was divided into two eras: the Kaiyuan 开元 Era (713–741 CE) and Tianbao 天宝 Era (742–756 CE). The Kaiyuan Era is generally regarded by Chinese historians as the most thriving period, surpassing any thriving era of the past.

The cream of Tang poets, China's greatest, such as Li Bai, Du Fu, and Wang Wei lived during the era of Emperor Xuanzong. Du Fu 杜甫 (712–770 CE) wrote these words 20 years after the Kaiyuan Era:

> I remember the thriving Era of Kaiyuan
>
> millionaires lived in many a small lane.
>
> White rice and yellow millet overflowed
>
> the public and private granaries both.

---

[1]Even to Emperor Taizong, these wise words were more easily said than done. Once, he became furious when a veteran courtier Wei Zheng 魏征 (580–643 CE) openly criticized his misrule in court. Afterward, he was comforted by the queen's opinion that such a candid and loyal courtier like Wei Zheng emerged only under a great ruler. The queen's remark awakened the Emperor's statesmanship. He awarded Wei Zheng for his sharp critique afterward and encouraged other courtiers to emulate Wei Zheng.

**Chapter 5: The Prosperous Tang Dynasty and Its Golden Culture**

No more wolves on roads in the land,

no more wait for an auspicious day,

it was safe to travel far away.

Best silks in brisk passages

moved by boats and carriages.

Men worked on the farmland,

wives busy with yarn in hand.

A musician in palace was our emperor

thus friendship in Tianxia grew stronger.

No natural and man-made calamity

for a period more than a century.

In society, there was the rule of law.

A country of bliss as people saw.

Du Fu was 52 when he wrote these words summarizing what he saw 20 plus years earlier during the prime of his life. These words are the most authoritative depiction of the thriving Era of Kaiyuan and thriving Tang. "No natural and man-made calamity for more than a century" is weighty testimony to a good time of peace, security, and stability in Chinese history. This is a great compliment for the 28-year Kaiyuan Era and the entire early period of Tang, including the rule of emperors Gaozu, Taizong, Gaozong, and Empress/Emperor Wu. It is interesting to note that during the Kaiyuan Era, there were "millionaires living on street corners and lanes," thus indicating widespread prosperity. Du Fu led a lower middle class life and his poems show a realistic picture of contemporary life. He wrote in a poem around 751 (at the end of the Tianbao Era):

How people regret having sons

and suffer great misfortune at once.

Had they known, it would have been

far better to have only daughters.

Daughters marry neighbors,

sons die in god-forsaken places

their skeletons unable to trace.

In another poem, written in 755, Du Fu wrote these immortal lines.

Liquor and meat go to waste

inside the red gates.

On the road skeletons lie,

those who die of frostbite.

(朱门酒肉臭，路有冻死骨。)

Before ascending the throne, our musician-in-chief, Emperor Xuanzong, spent a lot of time in the musical department of the palace called "Pear Garden 梨园" learning from musicians and conducting musical performances. A famous topic of gossip in China from the time of Emperor Xuanzong until now is the Emperor's romance with the most renowned and enchanting Lady Yang 杨贵妃.

She smiled, turning her eyes

toward the romantic Emperor,

beauties in the palace on all sides,

lost their charm and color.

(回眸一笑百媚生，六宫粉黛无颜色。)

This is how the famous Tang poet Bai Juyi 白居易 (772–846 CE) depicted the enchanting power of Lady Yang, with the romance ruining Emperor Xuanzong's reign and ending the period of Thriving Tang.

Chapter 5: The Prosperous Tang Dynasty and Its Golden Culture

The combination of brisk trade and travel along the Silk Road between Emperor Xuanzong's capital of Chang'an and Central Asia with Emperor Xuanzong's passion for music and dance attracted many pretty Central Asian dancers to perform in his palace. Among them was a Sogdian lady from the Uzbekistan area named Yana 曹野那 who was taken into Emperor Xuanzong's harem as one of his darlings. These Central Asian dancers were known in Chinese books as "foreign ladies of the revolving dance 胡旋女." They performed in the Tang palace for over a century from the Kaiyuan Era onward. Bai Juyi, being a high-ranking imperial officer, saw the performances and wrote a poem entitled "Foreign Lady of the Revolving Dance 胡旋女" in which he described:

Raising her sleeves in both hands,

her moves tuned to musical strands

Body pliant revolving

like a snowflake flying,

turning left and right tirelessly,

thousands of rounds look so easy.

These lines remind me of the Kathak dance I saw in India, introduced from Afghanistan and its surrounding areas during the Mughal Dynasty (16–19th centuries). The same dance reached China almost 1,000 years earlier than it reached India.

## III. The Golden Tang Culture

At the outset of this chapter, I described the founder–emperor of the Sui Dynasty as an avatar (reincarnation) of Indian civilization because he had been given the name of a Hindu god. It is important to see the openness of China even at that time, which garnered additional energy for development of the Sui culture. Now, we see the extraordinary energy of Tang culture, which was, to an even greater extent, due to such openness. The Tang ruling family was even more of an avatar of foreign civilizations as the first three Tang emperors were born of foreign mothers. The third Tang ruler, Emperor Gaozong, was the son of Emperor Taizong and grandson of Emperor Taizu. His grandfather was only half Chinese as he was born to a foreign mother. His father was only one-quarter Chinese as he was born to a foreign mother and half-Chinese father. He, himself, was only one-sixteenth Chinese as he was born to a foreign mother and quarter-Chinese father. Li Bai, the greatest Tang poet, was a foreign descendant born outside China. Do you think such an alien affinity could make China fertile soil for Sinocentrism? Chinese scholars refer to this as the dominant influence of the "culture of the steppe 草原文化" on Tang China.

"Steppe 草原" refers to the "Great Steppe" or the Eurasian Steppe. This "culture of the steppe" influence indicates input from a vast variety of cultures from China's immediate west to the depths of Central Asia, even Persia, Arabia, and India. The influence of the "culture of the steppe" manifested in Chinese language, costumes, food habits, and other aspects of Chinese lifestyle. An example is included further to show the exotic fashion of Tang women as reflected by the famous "tri-color pottery of Tang 唐三彩". This influence injected fresh blood into the Chinese cultural body and increased the energy of Chinese culture to create the Tang "golden period." Thus, both

**Exotic fashion of Tang women**

Chapter 5: The Prosperous Tang Dynasty and Its Golden Culture

physically and spiritually, Tang China expanded beyond the common geographical entity created by the Yangtze and Huanghe valleys. I will go a step further and describe the thriving Tang culture as Eurasian-Chinese. It was a xenophilic culture, not xenophobic, with no trace of the Zhongguo-versus-barbarian prejudice that Sinocentrism wants you to believe.

Tang Emperor Taizong, serious about learning the experiences and lessons of previous dynasties, set up institutions to sort historical records. Eight of the 24 orthodox chronological dynastic annals of Chinese history (completed in the 18th century) were compiled during the Tang Dynasty. The 10-volume reference series called *Ten Encyclopedias to Master History* 十通 was a millennial academic endeavor beginning from the Tang Dynasty. As a matter of fact, the Tang Dynasty earned its reputation as the "golden age" of Chinese history because of its magnificent achievements in culture and literature. Tang Dynasty literature and art is best known for exceptional poets such as Li Bai, Du Fu, and Bai Juyi, and accomplished painters such as Wu Daozi 吴道子 (680–759 CE).

Wang Wei 王维 (692–761 CE), who had a very successful career as an imperial officer, was a great poet and painter. A well-known compliment to him says: "There is painting in his poetry, and poetry in his painting 诗中有画，画中有诗." It is not unusual that a Chinese painting has a poem written on it. Thus, a poem in the painting can be done, but a painting in the poem is a rare achievement. Wang Wei's mastery of this has not been rivaled. If you are conversant in Chinese, you can enjoy his rare talent of creating a "painting in his poetry." Let me try to show this by translating a portion of Wang Wei's poem "Autumn Evening at My Country Resort 山居秋暝."

> The hill looks spotless after a shower,
>
> an evening of autumn's tint and color.
>
> Glint of the moon through pine needles.
>
> Clean stream flows on murmuring pebbles.

A group of washer women home going

through the bamboo chatting and giggling.

A fishing boat sails in the pond

pushing the lotus around.

(空山新雨后，天气晚来秋。明月松间照，
清泉石上流。竹喧归浣女，莲动下渔舟。)

The poem consists of 40 syllables/characters, and I have translated 30 of them. Many Chinese artists have tried in vain to create a verisimilar painting out of this picturesque poem.

*Snow and River*, by **Wang Wei (reputedly)**

Tang China produced two marvelous, matchless stone sculpture Buddha statues. One is the Vairocana Buddha of the Fengxian Monastery 奉先寺 in the Longmen Grottoes 龙门石窟, made under Empress/Emperor Wu's special patronage and guidance. Perhaps we cannot find anywhere another Buddha statue so perfectly and beautifully carved, and a Buddha image so noble, graceful, compassionate, and handsome.

**Chapter 5: The Prosperous Tang Dynasty and Its Golden Culture**

The other is the world's largest Buddha statue in Leshan (乐山), Sichuan province, which was carved out of a rock hill. It is a sitting Maitreya Buddha, 71 meters tall. It has a head width

**World's most graceful Buddha at the Longmen Grottoes**

**World's largest Buddha statue at Leshan**

of 10 meters, an ear length of 7 meters, eye and mouth widths both of 3.3 meters, a neck width of 3 meters, a shoulder width of 24 meters, and a foot length of 11 meters. These two statues have survived over a millennium and will be the symbols of Chinese civilization for thousands of years to come.

Tang painter Wu Daozi created a new heaven and new earth of landscape and human figure painting. For that, he earned the fame of "sage painter 画圣." Tang sculptor Yang Huizhi 杨惠之 (8th century) was famous for making the statue of Avalokitesvara with a thousand arms and eyes, and is revered as "sage sculptor  塑圣." Tang Empress/Emperor Wu was a music lover who went to great lengths to compose music for palace ceremonies. Of all imperial rulers worldwide, Tang Emperor Xuanzong was probably the most outstanding musician. He created the popular mood of art-loving and merrymaking pacifism in China. The Tang imperial court collected famous musical pieces from China and foreign countries and compiled the "Ten-volume Music 十部乐" of which the "Heavenly India Music 天竺乐" was a part. At that time, the Indian subcontinent remained divided and there was no collection like the Chinese "Heavenly India Music," meaning the first volume of Indian music was compiled by the Chinese palace. Regrettably, the music is now lost. The Tang Dynasty featured two great pilgrims to India, Xuanzang and Yijing 义净 (635–713 CE). Xuanzang's *Da-Tang xi yu ji* 大唐西域记 (*Accounts on the Western Regions* compiled during the Great Tang Dynasty) and Yijing's *Nanhai ji gui nei fa zhuan* 南海寄归内法传 (*Dharma in Buddhist Countries Sent from the South Sea*) have become required reading reference books for modern scholars studying ancient India. The Tang Dynasty produced maximum achievements in translating Buddhist scriptures from Sanskrit to Chinese. Xuanzang and Yijing were prolific translators. There were many productive translators among the foreign monk scholars during this period, including Amoghavajra (705–774 CE), Dipankara (613–687 CE), Sangha (?–710 CE), Bodhiruci (?–727 CE), and many others. They produced several hundred fascicles of Chinese translations.

Chapter 5: The Prosperous Tang Dynasty and Its Golden Culture

Pilgrim Xuanzang included an important observation in his *Accounts on the Western Regions*, which I translate as follows:

About the name of Heavenly India, there are controversies. In the past, it was called Shen/Juan Du, or Xiandou. In correct definition, it should be called Yindu.... The (Indian) name *Yindu/Indu* is what we call the moon in Tang. Indians have various names for the moon, and the aforesaid is one of them. It symbolizes endless transmigration of all beings. The world is an eternal dark night without dawn. It is like the sun having gone into hiding and people living by candle-light. Though the stars are twinkling, nothing can match the brilliance of the bright moon. All this is because the land features a succession of sages and prophets who guide the common people and things like the moonshine. Therefore, we name the land Yindu/Indu.

I have a hunch that the modern word "India" is the European name for Xuanzang's "Yindu/Indu," and not the Indian native word "Hindu" or the Arabic word "Sindhu." If true, Xuanzang, a Chinese pilgrim, was the name giver of India just as Kautilya/Chanakya was for China. It is also my firm belief that Li Bai's world-famous masterpiece "Reflections on a Quiet Night 静夜思" was greatly inspired by Xuanzang's "Yindu/Indu," depicting a "country of bright moonshine of the Buddha" (in Indian—*Buddha-prabha-bhumi*). Following is my translation of Li Bai's "Reflections on a Quiet Night."

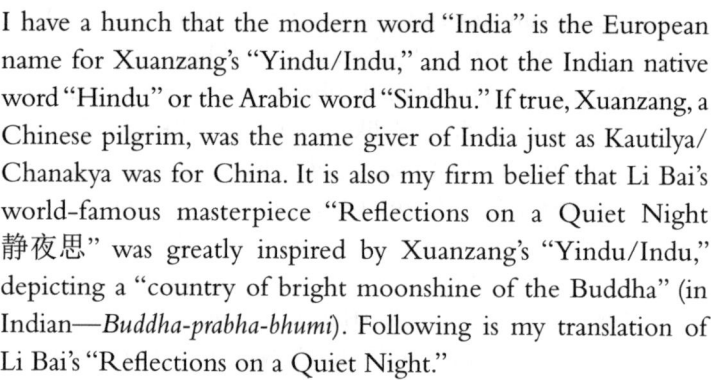

I lie in bed,

the moon shines bright.

Frost on the ground, am I right?

I raise my head,

the moon shines bright.

I miss my home sweet.

I hang my head,

folks I can't greet!

(床前明月光，疑是地上霜。举头望明月，

低头思故乡。)

These are the words of a wanderer far away from home and loved ones. In the shortest poem, only 20 characters, Li Bai skillfully repeated the compound "ming yue 明月/bright moon" to create a cogent narrative showing a Tianxia common entity of destiny under the blessings of Buddha light/*Buddha-prabha*.

To this masterpiece of Li Bai, we can add Meng Jiao's 孟郊 (751–814 CE) "Song of the Wandering Son 游子吟."

Mom's needle and thread

make the wandering son's dress.

Dense strands and stitches

my passage blessed by her bliss.

A tiny blade the life I own

mindful for my mom so kind.

Mom, you are my sunshine

in the spring of many a moon.

(慈母手中线，游子身上衣。临行密密缝，

意恐迟迟归。谁言寸草心，报得三春晖。)

This poem has added the element of "compassionate mother 慈母" to the Chinese common entity of destiny. It was Buddhism that introduced the Indian concept of "karuna/compassion" to China. Thus, the Chinese people began to realize their gratitude for the "compassionate mother." Previously, there had been the erstwhile Chinese term "lenient father 慈父" criticizing people's laxity in teaching their children. Meng Jiao likened himself to "a tiny blade" in blissful Chinese Tianxia. His Chan environment

**Chapter 5: The Prosperous Tang Dynasty and Its Golden Culture**

was daytime life, in contrast to Li Bai's night scene. The two poets jointly opened the vista of China during both day and night.

A poetess and housewife Lady Du Qiu (杜秋娘), born in 791, left behind a famous masterpiece called "Golden Thread Dress 金缕衣."

Listen, my dear,

a golden-thread dress

is somewhat worthless

not the match and peer

to your youthful minute and hour.

Pluck the pretty flower

when it's radiant today,

don't you muck about,

and bear the twig away,

too late to regret.

(劝君莫惜金缕衣，劝君惜取少年时。
花开堪折直须折，莫待无花空折枝。)

Meng Jiao's "Song of the Wandering Son" documents the gratitude of a son for his compassionate mother, but did not show her face. Lady Du Qiu's "Golden Thread Dress"[2] is the dialogue of China's "good wife and good mother 贤妻良母" with youthful Chinese. It shows the face of Meng Jiao's compassionate mother.

---

[2]Du Qiu's poem created the Chinese vogue of treasuring the "priceless minutes and hours" of golden youth sustained by billions of Chinese for over 1,000 years. Today, wherever the Chinese people go, they carry this vogue along with them. The overseas Chinese community, especially in the United States, made news by showing it. There are innumerable modern reincarnations of Du Qiu among the overseas Chinese. In recent years, some earned the reputation of "tiger mom." The January 8, 2011, edition of the *Wall Street Journal* carried an article titled "Why Chinese Mothers Are Superior." We see the millennial influence of Lady Du Qiu's poem "Golden Thread Dress."

Following is my favorite poem of Luo Yin 罗隐 (833–910 CE), entitled "Self Amusement 自遣."

In success I sing my song,

I suck it up when things go wrong.

Tons of fret and regret,

I am not upset.

Wine plentiful and I hollow,

I am a jolly good fellow.

Tomorrow, if there is worry,

let me worry tomorrow.

(得即高歌失即休，多愁多恨亦悠悠；
今朝有酒今朝醉，明日愁来明日愁。)

This poem is my life's companion although I have hardly taken 800 drops of wine in my octogenarian life. For me, it has been "Sanguine spirit plentiful and I hollow, I am a jolly good fellow." This sanguine spirit, I think, is the survivability and adaptability of Chinese people, coping with vicissitudes and maintaining their smile through their trouble.

Anyone who cares to read Tang poetry can discover the tremendous energy in Chinese civilization. But, space does not allow me to provide the rich flavor of the literary feast of Tang poetry that is really the "golden treasury" of thousands of masterpieces, each like the few I quoted. While I must leave them alone, I cannot leave the "Song of Liangzhou 凉州词," written by Wang Han 王翰 (8th century).

Shining jade cup with tasteful wine

'tis what I've longed for:

this joyous drinking round.

But, there the bugles sound,

**Chapter 5: The Prosperous Tang Dynasty and Its Golden Culture**

my wine cup, should I leave?

How about a drunkard goes to sleep

on the battleground?

O, Please don't snicker,

tell me, how many warriors

returned home, my dear,

during the last thousand years?

(葡萄美酒夜光杯，欲饮琵琶马上催。
醉卧沙场君莫笑，古来征战几人回？！)

This poem has been recited by as many Chinese as Li Bai's "Reflections on a Quiet Night" and Lady Du Qiu's "Golden Thread Dress." There are numerous illustrations as well. Liangzhou (near present-day Wuwei 武威 in Gansu province) was the border area during the Tang Dynasty. The poem reflects war fatigue

**A portrait of Li Bai**

among the Tang garrison troops. This is, perhaps, the world's earliest anti-war poem. Wang Han did not like killing for the sake of victory, lamenting that few victors had returned home from time immemorial. With this sentiment, China would not deviate from its odyssey along the civilization highway.

## IV. The "Common Civilization Entity" of Asia

Tang China was, indeed, blessed by Buddha light, and there emerged a new star, Wu Zetian 武则天 (624–705 CE), the most remarkable woman in Chinese history. She began her career as a low-ranking *cairen* 才人 (literally, "talented person") of Emperor Taizong's harem to become a trusted friend and lover of Emperor Taizong's son and successor Li Zhi 李治 (628–683 CE). After Li Zhi ascended the throne as Tang Emperor Gaozong 唐高宗 (reigned 649–683 CE), Wu Zetian became his Queen and wielded political power when the Emperor's health faltered. In 674, Emperor Gaozong proclaimed himself "celestial emperor 天帝" and Wu Zetian "celestial queen 天后." Wu Zetian attended the imperial court behind the curtain. After Emperor Gaozong died in 683, Wu Zetian ultimately changed her status from "empress

**A portrait of Empress/Emperor Wu Zetian**

Chapter 5: The Prosperous Tang Dynasty and Its Golden Culture

Dowager" to "son of heaven" (emperor). She even arrogated to herself the title *Cishi yue gu jin lun shen sheng huang di* 慈氏越古金轮神圣皇帝 (literally, "Maitreya, surpassing history, Golden Cakravartin, Sacred Emperor").[3] With this title, she monopolized the symbols of preeminence of both India and China.

Emperor Taizong wrote the Preface for the Tripitaka Master Xuanzang's translations. Empress–Emperor Wu emulated this example by writing the Preface for the Tripitaka Master Yijing's translations in an essay entitled "Preface to the Tripitaka Master's Sacred Teachings 三藏圣教序." In the essay, the Empress/Emperor said she "was a follower of Sakyamuni's teachings from childhood 幼崇释教" and "cherished the desire to carry humanity aboard the Buddha's compassionate boat to sail away from the sea of sorrow 欲运六道于慈舟，迥超苦海." Anyone who hears these words would not be wrong in thinking that the speaker is an Indian idealist. By writing this, I feel that during the Tang Dynasty, boundaries of nation-states in Asia were fading, and there was neither China, nor India, but only "Chindia," the English word invented by my good Indian friend Jairam Ramesh (former union minister and presently member of parliament), who would not mind my abusing his intellectual property.

Empress/Emperor Wu was one of the 20 emperors of Tang Dynasty and a prominent ruler. But, orthodox Chinese history books do not recognize it, portraying male chauvinist prejudice.

---

[3]The first two syllables *Cishi* 慈氏 was the Chinese name for the Indian bodhisattva Maitreya, who became the "future Buddha" of Chinese legend. The fifth and sixth syllables *jinlun* 金轮 (golden cakra/wheel) refer to the Indian Buddhist ideal of "Chakravartin" (universal ruler). "Chakravartin" is an Indian ideal, and people with "Chakrabarti/Chakravarti" as their family name (said to be the crème-dela-crème of Bengalis) are only found in eastern India. But, the lone "Cakravartin" (universal ruler), albeit self-proclaimed, existed only in Tang China—Empress/Emperor Wu Zetian.

There is, indeed, the puzzle of emergence of Emperor Wu Zetian in male chauvinist China just as another historical puzzle of the Indian bodhisattva Avalokitesvara had his (bodhisattvas are male) gender metamorphosis to become "Goddess of Mercy," that is, bodhisattva Guanyin 观音in China.

Recall the *Laozi* quote in Chapter 2 that "The Chinese universe creates Yin and Yang: Yin and Yang create Heaven, Earth, and Humanity." The concept of Yin and Yang embrace both male and female as the pair of intertwined fish, shown in the picture of Taiji/Taichi. The picture also reflects the affection between men and women. The ancient Chinese legend of Goddess Xiwangmu/Uma also testifies to Chinese civilization's respect and affection for femininity, as does the concept of "compassionate mother 慈母." All this indicates that Chinese civilization is capable of featuring a female "son of heaven" and transforming an India bodhisattva into a goddess of mercy.

**The "Goddess of Mercy" image of Avalokitesvara**

**Chapter 5: The Prosperous Tang Dynasty and Its Golden Culture**

No one in China is sure when Avalokitesvara's gender metamorphosis occurred. The Longmen Grottoes, expanded and renovated by Empress/Emperor Wu, did not feature the female Guanyin/Avalokitesvara. Images of Guanyin/Avalokitesvara in the Tang caves of the Mogao Grottoes 莫高窟 in Dunhuang 敦煌 often have a mustache. We can safely conclude that until the time of Wu Zetian, Avalokitesvara was still a male deity. Did the reign of Empress/Emperor Wu have any intention to change the gender of Avalokitesvara? The answer could be yes. In all her edicts, Empress/Emperor Wu used the phrase "I, the Emperor on the Phoenix Dais 鸾台朕." In 683, in her obituary for her imperial husband, Wu Zetian wrote: "The court of bird opens the scene, and the virtue of dragon shines on the system 鸟庭开象，龙德含章." This "court of bird 鸟庭" is the same as "phoenix court 凤庭." All imperial appointments made by the Empress/Emperor were prefixed with "phoenix pavilion 凤阁" and "phoenix dais 鸾台" in their titles. We know the Tang Dynasty vigorously advocated the dragon image as a sign of imperial power. The emperor and his courtiers wore the dragon robes. The imperial capital was called "Dragon City 龙城." During the reign of Empress/Emperor Wu, poets tended to replace "dragon 龙" with "phoenix 凤." Empress/Emperor Wu's imperial palanquin became the "phoenix palanquin 凤辇" instead of Tang's conventional "dragon palanquin 龙辇." Empress/Emperor Wu's vigorous propagation of phoenix culture injected feminine affection and softness into Chinese civilization. Her effort created the "Dragon–Phoenix culture 龙凤文化" in China. But for the efforts of Wu Zetian and others, there would be no Goddess of Mercy/Guanyin image in China.[4]

---

[4]Empress/Emperor Wu started the enthusiastic Guanyin/Avalokitesvara cult in China. She ordered creation of an altar inside the Guangzhai Monastery 光宅寺 in the capital, Chang'an, in 703. It consisted of exquisite stone sculptures of a number of idols with an 11-face Guanyin/ Avalokitesvara statue as the main figure. Most statues of this altar are now preserved in Japan and the United States. In sum, the phenomenon of Empress/Emperor Wu, the cult of Guanyin/ Avalokitesvara, Xuanzang's offering the name "Indu/Yindu" for India, and India and China's being regarded as the land blessed by Buddha light, created a common civilization entity uniting China and India.

Traveling so far with me in a geo-civilization paradigm and leaving the nation-state geopolitical paradigm far behind enables us to conceive present South Asia and East Asia as an identical civilization sphere during the Tang Dynasty. There was one Chinese translation from Sanskrit of a sutra entitled *Sutra of the King of Human Love* 仁王经 or *Prajñā pāramitā Sutra of the King of Human Love Protecting the Country* 仁王护国般若波罗蜜多经, which cannot be traced to its Indian origin. The earliest translation of this scripture was by Kumarajiva (or more specifically, the translation bureau under his leadership). Then, there was a retranslation by the Indian/Sri Lankan monk Amoghavajra 不空 (705–774 CE) who was very influential in Tang China, having baptized Emperors Xuanzong and his two immediate successors, Emperor Suzong 唐肃宗 (reigned 756–761 CE) and Emperor Daizong 唐代宗 (reigned 762–779 CE). Amoghavajra held many public meetings chanting and expounding the Sutra when China faced external aggression. These meetings allegedly helped China repel the enemies. This translated sutra has been very popular in Korea and Japan, as well as China, for over a millennium.

From the Indian perspective, this Sutra is somewhat of a myth. The Chinese word *ren* 仁 (human love) is China's special

**Indian "Mahacina-tara"**
**(Goddess of Great China)**

Chapter 5: The Prosperous Tang Dynasty and Its Golden Culture

Confucian value without Indian connection. How would a Buddhist scripture of Indian origin contain such an exclusively Chinese word in its title? We know this scripture was a Tantric text, generally differentiated from orthodox (or pure) Buddhist faith in India. Buddhist Tantra has had popular following in eastern India as well. There is an Indian Tantric goddess Mahacina-tara (Goddess of Great China), who has innumerable images. Here is one whose national identity is obscure.

If someone identifies the goddess in the center of the picture (Mahacina-tara) as the Chinese Guanyin/Avalokitesvara, or even Tang Empress/Emperor Wu, we will not be surprised. In geo-civilizational paradigm, Asian cultural phenomena do resonate with one another.

I think we have sufficient evidence to conceive of China and India as being in the same common civilization entity during the Tang Dynasty. This scenario can be extended to all of East Asia. Japan had no script and used Chinese script to develop its civilization. This probably began in the 5th century CE when Japanese Buddhist monks in Baekje (South Korea) returned with Chinese Buddhist scriptures in "kanji/Chinese script 汉字" during the Baiji period of Japanese history. During the subsequent Nara period (710–794 CE), as many Japanese scholars returned after completing their studies in China, kanji script was officially adopted with proper Chinese pronunciation. Chinese script helped develop Japanese civilization. Korea adopted Chinese script prior to the Tang Dynasty, by which time China, Korea, and Japan shared a common script.

There are different theories about the ancestry of the Japanese race. In 1973, historians at Tokyo and Kyoto universities unanimously told me the earliest residents of Japan were from China's mainland. They were called "Wa" people (written in Chinese as "和"). Early Chinese translation of the Japanese "Wa" was *wo* 倭. The *Latter Annals of Han*, in its account on "Eastern Foreigners 东夷," informs us that Han Emperor Guangwu appointed the "King of Wa 倭王." Chinese and Japanese both fit the description of "common language/script and ethnicity 同文同种." The only problem is not many people know about it.

Chinese and Koreans also fit the description of "common language/script and ethnicity." The two earliest Chinese dynastic annals give us information that the *Jizi* 箕子 people came from China to establish the earliest country in Korea. Throwing aside the "nation-state" prism, we clearly see very intimate intercourse between residents on the Korean Peninsula, Liaodong Peninsula 辽东半岛, and Shandong Peninsula 山东半岛. Generally speaking, the three peninsulas share a common living environment and could easily be one socioeconomic entity if political boundaries didn't exist. It is easy to conceive of China and Korea in the same common civilization entity during the Tang Dynasty.

Japan started sending missions to China during the Sui Dynasty and their numbers grew greatly during the Tang Dynasty. These missions consisted of officials and young students. Officials had to return after some time, but young students could stay. There were a total of 13 Japanese missions to Tang China, with as many as 600 people in a single mission. The Tang government arranged for the young Japanese students to study at the imperial academy called *guozi jian* 国子监 (literally, "campus of the state's sons"). Many stayed for several decades. After returning to Japan, they became a major force for developing Japanese culture. There was Abe Nakamaro (698–770 CE), whose Chinese name was Zhaoheng 晁衡. He qualified for the imperial examination and became an officer of the Tang government during the thriving Kaiyuan Era. Unfortunately, he drowned while sailing back to Japan. Li Bai, a good friend of Nakamaro, wrote a poem to mourn the tragedy which I translate as follows.

**Chapter 5: The Prosperous Tang Dynasty and Its Golden Culture**

Dear Officer Zhao of Japan

going home from Chang'an.

Boat after boat,

island after island.

Alas,

Never reaches home the bright moon,

sinking to sea bottom one afternoon.

Sad mood of the white cloud

troubles my thoughts throughout.

(日本晁卿辞帝都，征帆一片绕蓬壶。
明月不归沉碧海，白云愁色满苍梧。)

This poem has lived forever binding the hearts of the people of China and Japan.

An even greater link between China and Japan was the Chinese Buddhist monk Jianzhen 鉴真 (688–763 CE) known as the endeared "Ganjin" in Japan. After several failed attempts, the Japanese succeeded in escorting him to Japan in 753. He played a great role in helping Japan rejuvenate its culture and has been revered as the "national guru" of Japan. In 1973, I visited the "Toshodai Temple 唐招提寺" of Nara, built by Jianzhen/Ganjin in typical Tang Chinese style. All of Jianzhen/Ganjin's personal effects on exhibition at the temple were marked "national treasure." Today, the entire temple is regarded as a national treasure and recognized by UNESCO as a world heritage site.

China, India, Korea, and Japan formed a "common civilization entity" during the Tang Dynasty. It is a historical fact, but the

pious wish is also important. It is built on historical reality, not imagination. Today, in our much troubled world, East Asia and South Asia are productive and vibrant, with great potential to contribute to a new order of humanity.

# CHAPTER 6

# THE GLORIOUS AND PATHETIC SONG DYNASTY

The Tang Dynasty was a dynamic transitional period. Song, the major dynasty established on the foundation of Tang, consolidated the changes and reforms of Tang to advance further afield. Seen from this perspective, we can understand why many Chinese and international scholars feel the Song Dynasty was even greater than the Tang Dynasty.

## I. Prosperity of Song China

The Song Dynasty 宋朝, lasting 319 years (960–1279), was marked by a thriving economy, booming culture, advanced technology, and overall development of an urban market economy. Song administration improved upon that of Tang. During Tang, the relatively equitable system of land ownership (called *juntian* 均田) collapsed, leading to serious land amalgamation detrimental to agricultural development. Also, the urban commerce and industry of Tang China was constricted by excessive governmental regulation. The Song government reformed and improved both rural and urban development. The Song economic system was the most advanced of the contemporary world. Its land policy promoted agricultural development, while its industrial and commercial policy stimulated trade and transportation. Water channels were more navigable and the quality of boats was improved, resulting in unprecedented development of water-borne transportation in China. There was also a quite developed iron and steel industry. Currency (copper coins and paper money) circulated well and loans were easily available. All this gave economic development a powerful boost.

China has always had labor-intensive farming, achieving the highest per acre yield in the world during proto-scientific times. Chinese agriculture kept improving—the Tang standard was higher than Qin–Han, and the Song standard was even higher than Tang. The substantial improvement of Song agriculture was largely due to the introduction of high yield seeds from Champa 占城 (present-day central and southern Vietnam). Wheat production was not a major crop before Tang, but it rapidly developed

during Tang (attracting the Tang government to levy tax on it). During Song, wheat production spread from Northern China to south of the Yangtze, greatly increasing its production.

After tea evolved as an elegant beverage during Tang, tea production became the leading commercial crop during Song. There were over 200 tea producing counties in Song China, a great leap above that of Tang China. The Tang government prohibited private tea trade, while the Song government was more liberal. Song China began to trade internationally with Chinese tea exchanged for foreign horses. There were three tea–horse routes from Chang'an to export tea to Central Asia, West Asia, and South Asia. The millennial "tea culture" of Kashmir was instilled by the ancient "tea–horse route." Sichuan tea was exported to Nepal and India through Tibet. British colonizers found that Indians had already been drinking tea during pre-British times. Tea in Indian vernacular was called "chai," close to its Chinese name of *cha* 茶, but not close to the English name "tea" (earlier spelled as *the*), which originated from a Fujian dialect.

There was another important Song commercial crop, namely, sugarcane. Improvement in living standards and cuisine among Song people resulted in the increasing consumption of sugar. Indians invented a form of sugar that was jaggery and common in the Indian market for millennia, called gur, which is still liked by common Indians. Ancient Indian missions used to present jaggery to Chinese rulers, called "stone honey 石蜜" by ancient Chinese. Since ancient China could not produce it, it was treated as a precious luxury. Tang Emperor Taizong invited eight monks and two technicians from the Nalanda Monastery to Yangzhou to teach Chinese workers how to make it, marking the beginning of sugar production in China. During the middle of the 8th century, a poor girl in Suining 遂宁 County of Sichuan province accidently invented the making of white sand sugar, and Suining became the home of sand sugar production. During the Song Dynasty, China suddenly became the world's major sugar

producing country, exporting it to Southeast Asian and South Asian countries, including India. Today, in all Indian vernaculars, sugar is called *chini*, homonymous to the Indian word for Chinese people. Kautilya/Chanakya coined the Indian term *cina/ chin* for China because it was the silk producing country. A thousand years later, Indians began using this term for China, being the sugar producing country. Today, many Indians still believe China was the inventor of sugar making, not knowing that sugar (including sugar making) was originally an Indian gift to China. The sugar industry of Song was booming, producing a variety of goods such as "sugar frost 糖霜," "stone honey 石蜜," "semi-liquid sugar 乳糖," "sugar sand 沙糖," and "box sugar 合子糖."

Francis Bacon (1561–1626), English philosopher, statesman, and scientist, wrote in his *Instauratio Magna*/The Great Instauration that three great Chinese inventions (printing, gunpowder, and the mariner's compass) "have altered the face and state of the world." Gunpowder and printing were invented in China during Tang, but went into substantial industrial production from Song onward. Gunpowder was popularly used in circus shows in Song China to create the effect of an explosion, fireworks, and smoke. The mariner's compass is an instrument to tell people about the "four cardinal directions" of north, east, south, and west. The Chinese people used a similar instrument during the Warring States period before the Qin Dynasty. The instrument was known as "the needle pointing to the south 指南针." During the Song Dynasty, such an instrument was easily available and popularly called "a fish pointing to the south 指南鱼." Song China virtually began the popular orientation of the cardinal directions. Printing was actually first invented in India. From the archaeological site of Mohenjo Daro, an ancient Indian city (now in Pakistan) around 4,500 years ago, it was discovered that people had already been making seals for printing for 1,000 years. The Indian practice of printing Buddha images on fabrics spread to China, and the first printed books of the world were Buddhist scriptures in Chinese produced by Chinese

Buddhist temples during the Tang Dynasty. Bi Sheng 毕昇, a Song intellectual, invented movable printing blocks during the Qingli 庆历 Era (1041–1048) of Song Emperor Renzong's 宋仁宗 (reigned 1022–1063) time. Each movable block was a separate seal, like that of Mohenjo Daro, but Bi Sheng transformed them into a device for printing books. This was a great improvement over the Tang printing method that carved text on a wooden plate that could not be reused to print other materials. Bi Sheng's movable blocks were made of baked clay with a Chinese character carved on it. Blocks were uniform in size and could be combined to print a text or rearranged to print other texts. This technique lasted over 1,000 years until invention of photoset printing in modern times.

It is important for the world to know that the Song Dynasty was a prolonged victim of foreign aggression, yet Song Chinese never thought of using gunpowder for national defense. Had they done so, history would have been rewritten. It was during the 13th century that Mongol troops used gunpowder to attack European cities, ushering in modern warfare. Should we consider the Song Chinese so dumb and the Mongols so smart? Absolutely not! These two had just the opposite orientations and cultures. Pacifism was the DNA of Song culture. There was a Chinese saying: "Like a good piece of iron won't be turned into nails, a good man never becomes a soldier 好铁不打钉，好男不当兵." This defined Song ethos. The Song Dynasty marked a new phase in China's odyssey along the civilization highway in which people would not stoop so low as to apply their mind to war and weaponry, even if at the expense of their security and existence.

A renowned German philosopher G. W. F. Hegel (1770–1831) tried to support his contempt for the "incompetent, backward, and incapable" Chinese in his *Philosophy of History* by pointing out that the inventors of gunpowder (the Chinese) had to wait many centuries for the European Jesuits to make "their first cannon." Hegel thought Westerners, Europeans, and Germans were far superior to Chinese as civilized human beings. His

prejudice has been very commonly shared in the Western world for centuries, even today. I think China can yield to Hegel's bigotry and concede to the Western world as a backward entity in the scramble for superiority and hegemony in the "nation-state" world. But, in China's odyssey along the civilization highway, gunpowder was for fireworks in happy festivals, not wars. What Hegel thought was "incompetent, backward, and incapable" was a sign of wisdom and civilization. If people want to say gunpowder is the ancestor of bombs and improvised explosive devices (IEDs; which terrorize life in our contemporary world), they should leave out China. China never contributed to this kind of development of so-called "civilization."

It is not China's own assessment that they had three or four great inventions (including paper making). These were Western opinions imposed on China. Like India, China has had innumerable great inventions, such as rice culture, sericulture, tea culture, book culture, hydraulic culture, urban culture, highway culture, and many more. In my opinion, porcelain should be regarded as the greatest Chinese invention that has, indeed, changed the world's outlook. Based on a foundation of Tang industrial development, Song China reached the zenith of porcelain production. Song porcelain combines the finest art and precision technology and is a smart synthesis of harmonious civilization with popular culture. There were famous porcelain kilns in various places producing large quantities of porcelain not only for the royal family, aristocrats, officers, and scholars but also for the common folks.

Today, porcelain has reached nearly every family on earth. Every rich household has a collection of elegant porcelain (along with a substantial quantity of other Chinese products) as decoration. This is the contribution of Chinese civilization! Porcelain always has two main functions—both as a household tea set and dinner set and as brilliant decoration pieces in the drawing rooms of ordinary homes and in corporate offices or conference rooms. They make excellent vases and flower pots as well. The decorative function of porcelain surpasses that of glass and metal, and can be bought for a wide range of prices. Porcelain insulates heat, is waterproof, and not easily stained. It is easy to clean and its color is permanent. If there were no porcelain, the modern world would look dull and its living standard would suffer. There is no other Chinese invention that has "altered the face and state of the world" as much as porcelain.

There were five great kilns during the Song Dynasty producing porcelain decoration pieces, and tea and dinner wares (so exquisite and marvelous that even the tea sets and dinner sets have become priceless treasures). These were the "Ru Kiln 汝窑," "Official Kiln 官窑," "Jun Kiln 钧窑," "Ge Kiln 哥窑," and "Ding Kiln 定窑." All have disappeared without a trace. Even more incredible is that 1,000 years of Chinese and international effort has failed to replicate the Song products. The blue-color porcelain produced by the Ru Kiln has had great influence on later porcelain production. Less than 100 pieces of Ru Kiln blue-color porcelain remain in the world today. Any museum in the world possessing a piece of it is immensely proud. The site of the Official Kiln is not traceable as the Northern Song capital, Bianjing 汴京, has sunk underground. Many Southern Song Official Kiln products have been passed down to become rare treasures. Products of the Jun Kiln are described as "gems of the

**One of the priceless treasures; a Ru Kiln product**

**One of the priceless treasures; a Jun Kiln product**

Chapter 6: The Glorious and Pathetic Song Dynasty

country 国之瑰宝," bringing \$1 million each at international auctions. Restoration of Song glory is the passion of the Chinese porcelain industry today. In 1991, Yuzhou 禹州 City in Henan province established a special research institute to study the secret of the Jun Kiln, in addition to a Jun Kiln museum and public square of Jun Kiln porcelain. These places seek to retrieve cultural heritage as well as develop tourism and modern industry. This is evidence of the far-reaching influence of Song porcelain.

The Song Dynasty created the "Porcelain Capital 瓷都" of China at Jingdezhen 景德镇, a city in Jiangxi province. This city began producing pottery even during the Warring States period. During Tang, it was already an important porcelain producing center. Zhao Heng 赵恒 (968–1022), who was Song Emperor Zhenzong 宋真宗 (reigned 997–1022), ordered all products of this city for use of the palace and named it "Jingdezhen 景德镇" in 1004, the first year of the Jingde 景德 Era. Since then, it has been the leading center of porcelain production in China, with half a dozen equally famous porcelain centers elsewhere in competition. Today, the city has a porcelain college and research institute. It is the center of China's porcelain culture. Its products, especially the tea and dinner sets marked by the four Chinese characters *wan shou wu jiang* 万寿无疆 (thousands of years of long life without end), are seen the world over, becoming a symbol of Chinese culture.

## II. Market Economy and New Lifestyle

A brewery industry also illustrates the affluence of Song economy. Wine brewing was prohibited during the Qin and Han dynasties when food grain yield was low. The government wanted to ensure that grain would sustain the masses instead of being converted into alcohol to satisfy the exclusive desire of the privileged for luxury. But, brewing and drinking among the rich could hardly be prohibited in China. The Tang economy produced plentiful grain to feed the people, thus wine brewing

and drinking became popular. Du Fu described Li Bai as "drinking gallons of wine to produce hundreds of poems 李白斗酒诗百篇." Tang poetry smelled heavily of alcohol. There was no severe famine during Tang China, so alcohol addiction was not much of a curse. Song China enjoyed even greater affluence than Tang. The Song government initially monopolized liquor brewing and trade, but gradually opened them.

Su Dongpo 苏东坡 (1037–1101), the greatest of the Song poets, went a step further than the alcoholic Tang poets. He was not only a connoisseur of wine but also the maker of his own precious drink. He rhymed:

> Drinking for three rounds
>
> of this wine I've made
>
> gives a pleasure so profound
>
> like formal banquet at state.

Song commercial prosperity ushered in an unprecedented era of thriving communication and transportation. Famous Song poet Liu Yong 柳永 (987–1053) wrote the following descriptions in his poem "Happy to Go Home 归朝欢."

> Everywhere the traveling laborers
>
> line up distant roads and rivers.
>
> So many travelers to and fro
>
> by the single wheel and pairs of oar.
>
> Their goals are the same
>
> some for profit others for fame.
>
> (路遥川远多行役，往来人，只轮双桨，
> 尽是利名客。)

**Chapter 6: The Glorious and Pathetic Song Dynasty**

We see from this poem people on the roads accompanied by their "traveling laborers 行役"—porters who, in India and many Asian countries, are called "coolies." There were merchants whose goal was profit. There were also scholars who wanted to qualify for imperial exams and government careers for fame. The poem highlights *zhilun* 只轮 (single wheel—a wheelbarrow) and *shuangjiang* 双桨 (pairs of oars, indicating boats). The rugged terrain of Southern China suited the ancient Chinese invention of the wheelbarrow, which became popular transport during Song, carrying both goods and passengers on hilly roads and mountain passes. The poem displays the brisk land and water traffic in Song China. Travelers took wheelbarrows and boats as transport that had to be manned by transport workers. Song literature is replete with the term "traveling laborers," which is even the title of a couple of poems.

Chinese laborers servicing transportation on water has been a common sight since the Song Dynasty. In Southern China, transportation via waterways was quite developed. There was also a Chinese invention internationally known as the "Chinese noria 筒车" or "Persian wheel." It was a huge revolving wheel installed at the shore of small rivers with buckets on it. When the wheel

**Picture of the "Chinese noria"**

was pushed by the force of water currents, it started moving and the buckets took water from the river and poured it into the fields many meters higher than the river. This device was invented during Sui, but popularly used during Song.

I grew up beside the Lian River 涟水, in Hunan, and was familiar with this "Chinese noria," popularly used for irrigation in Southern China from the Song Dynasty onward. It automatically revolved day and night for the benefit of landowners and farmers, but was torment for China's traveling laborers working on the boats. There had to be sufficient water force to operate the wheel, so people dammed the river, leaving only a narrow opening in the middle for only one boat to pass through. Boats sailing downstream had easy passage, but boats sailing upstream had a lot of trouble. At this mid-river passage, the current was too rapid and forceful for boatmen with bamboo poles to overcome. Boatmen had to go onshore to pull the boat through with a thick rope. There was a term for such boatmen, *qianfu* 纤夫 (boat trackers). One end of the rope was tied to the boat while the other end was tied to the back of the boat tracker, who bent forward and walked steadily (at times even crawling). There had to be a team of boat trackers to pull a boat upstream through the opening of the river dam. I was very familiar with this sight of sheer human force used to defeat the force of nature.

**Chinese boat trackers at the Three Gorges**

Chapter 6: The Glorious and Pathetic Song Dynasty

Of course, what I saw beside the Lian River was no comparison to the boat trackers of the Three Gorges 三峡 (now disappearing) of the Yangtze. It was no comparison with the scene in the world-famous painting *Barge Haulers on the Volga* by the renowned Russian painter Ilya Repin (1844–1930) and the depiction of the world-famous "Song of the Volga Boatmen."

Song China had a thriving economy and culture, and the information about people's lives was recorded, particularly in two important books. The first, written by Meng Yuanlao 孟元老 in the 12th century, was entitled *Records of the Dream of Flowers in the Eastern Capital* 东京梦华录. The second, written by Wu Zimu 吴自牧, who lived around the 13th century, was entitled *Records of the Dream of Millet* 梦粱录. These two books described the Northern Song capital of Bianjing 汴京 (now Kaifeng 开封 in Henan province) and the Southern Song capital of Lin'an 临安 (now Hangzhou 杭州), respectively. In Bianjing, people did not prepare breakfast at home, but instead ate snacks in the markets or on street corners. Some people spent time in the tea houses eating breakfast and enjoying games. After the day's work was finished, people went to various entertainment centers to see wrestling, puppet shows, shadow plays, drama performances, cross talk shows, or to participate in riddle-guessing games.

"Talk shows 说话" were story-telling entertainment. They provided a boost to the development of popular literature in China and were the precursor to Chinese fiction. There were four types of Song talk shows. The first was popularly known as "talking history 讲史," which was a narration of historical anecdotes. The second type was called "small talk 小说," which talked about love stories, popular heroes, and fairytales. The third type, telling Buddhist stories, was a continuation of what Tang China had started, mainly organized by Buddhist temples. The fourth type was called "joint shows 合生" and included two storytellers to make the show more attractive. During the Song

Dynasty, many talk show hosts emerged, but the text of their talk was written by others. Such texts were called "huaben 话本" (script for the talk show). All subsequent famous Chinese novels were improved versions of Song "huaben" scripts. The Song huaben scripts were virtually the predecessors of fiction in world literature. However, huaben scripts were sold to the talk show hosts and became their intellectual property. Authors of these scripts have been forgotten. They missed the opportunity to become the earliest novelists in the world.

Night curfew was imposed in China from Qin–Han through Tang, but was completely lifted during the Song.[1] Thus, nightlife became a Song rage. A common sight was lanterns hanging everywhere in cities. Pedestrians walked with lantern in hand. The Song palace was like a "lantern mountain 灯山" at night. Lanterns had special designs such as "bodhisattva Manjusri riding the lion," "white elephant," and so on. Southern Song writer Xin Qiji 辛棄疾 (1140–1207) wrote the following lines in his poem "First Night of the Year 元夕."

> Trees of a thousand flowers
>
> greet the east wind at night,
>
> a million stars in the sky
>
> as if twinkling showers.
>
> Fragrant carved carriage
>
> drawn by gem-adorned steeds
>
> to and fro through the streets.
>
> Flutes spread musical sound,

---

[1] There were places for commoners to eat, listen to music, and watch shows. Night markets for eating, entertainment, and tourism were booming. Some night markets were permanent, while others were makeshift, moving from place to place. The capital of Northern Song, Bianjing, and Southern Song, Lin'an, were most famous for these.

**Chapter 6: The Glorious and Pathetic Song Dynasty**

jade wine pots pass around.

Fish and dragons throng

from dusk to dawn.

(东风夜放花千树，更吹落、星如雨。宝马雕车香满路。
凤箫声动，玉壶光转，一夜鱼龙舞。)

There is ample information in this brief description about the hedonistic, luxurious merrymaking of Song society. China was poor in precious stones and jewelry, most of which was imported. Yet here we see "fragrant carved carriages drawn by gem-adorned steeds." In the first paragraph of Chapter 4, I alluded to Han Emperor Wu's receiving an Indian gift of trappings (ornamental decorations for the horse) adorned with rare jewels. This was said to have put into vogue jewel-adorned saddles and bridles among China's elite. In this poem, there is *baoma diaoche xiang man lu* 宝马雕车香满路, translated as "gem-adorned horse, carved carriage, with fragrance all along the road." This line reminds me of the common marriage procession scene in India in which the bridegroom's party parades on the street, while the bridegroom rides a horse that appears adorned with jewelry. China was poor in the production of aromatic wood, and Song China set a record for importing perfume from India and other South and Southeast Asian countries. Thus, it was foreign, especially Indian, perfume that permeated the air of the Song capital from carriages drawn by horses decorated with Indian, or other foreign, jewels.

In this poem, there is also a description of *hua qian shu* 花千树 (trees of a thousand flowers), meaning bundles of thousands of lanterns. The description *xing ru yu* 星如雨 (stars falling like twinkling showers) is that of fireworks. The description *yu long wu* 鱼龙舞 (fish and dragons dance together) means royalty celebrating the festival along with commoners. This poem described how Southern Song China celebrated *yuanxi* 元夕 (first night of the year), as its title indicates. This celebration of the first night of the year is now called *yuan xiao jie* 元宵节 (first evening/night festival, universally known as the Lantern Festival). This important festival has been celebrated for over 1,000 years, but few Chinese know about its origin. It was Tang Emperor Xuanzong who started the celebration after accepting suggestions from the Buddhists. He lifted night curfew for three nights on the 15th of the first moon and the entire country heartily celebrated it. It was called *shangyuanjie* 上元节 (His Majesty's first night festival). The Tang and Song communities set the tone and for over 1,000 years the Chinese New Year holiday has lasted 15 days from the "First Day 元日" or "First Morning 元旦" until the "First Night 元宵." Why is there a 15-day gap separating the first day/morning from the first night? As just mentioned, this celebration was started by Tang Emperor Xuanzong according to suggestions of the Buddhists. The original aim of the festival was to celebrate the new year of the "country of the Buddha 佛国"—India. In India, a month begins on the full moon day, that is, the 15th day of the month according to the Chinese lunar calendar. This means the original aim of the *yuanxiao* 元宵 (Lantern Festival) was to celebrate the New Year of India, the "country of the Buddha." While the Tang celebration of the Indian New Year was for three days and nights, the Song celebration increased to five days and nights. From the description in Xin Qiji's poem, the Song celebration surpassed the sensational inception of it by Tang Emperor Xuanzong.

"Chinese chess 象棋" (its Chinese name literally means "elephant chess") was created and began to become popular during the Song Dynasty. It is an adaptation of the international chess invented by India. In addition, the cruel Chinese custom of foot-binding (tightly binding the feet of a young girl with thick cloth to prevent the foot growing until adulthood, causing immense suffering) of high-class women began during the Song Dynasty (low-class women, who had to work in the field, could not have bound feet). There was a connection between Chinese chess and foot-binding. From the Song Dynasty onward, the so-called "four skills 四艺," namely, playing the harp 琴, playing

**Chapter 6: The Glorious and Pathetic Song Dynasty**

chess 棋, calligraphy 书, and painting 画 began to become popular among the elite. When women joined in this, they stayed mostly at home because their big feet weren't appealing. So the idea of foot-binding for the sake of beauty (just like women slimming in modern times) emerged. Foot-binding was vehemently condemned by the "New Culture Movement" in China during the 1920s and 1930s (by that time, the practice had virtually disappeared) as a crime committed by Chinese tradition. We can see that this evil practice was connected to the hedonistic pacifism that was the rage in Song China.

**The bound feet of traditional Chinese high-class women**

Foreign trade, especially overseas trade, thrived in Song China. Song ships were equipped with the mariner's compass (spreading it into the Arab world and Europe) and were capable of long voyages. Song ships were large, capable of carrying 500–600 passengers. They anchored on the western coast of India, and traders had to change to smaller boats to enter the Persian Gulf. Song China traded overseas with Korea, Japan, Southeast Asia, South Asia, and Africa, reaching as far as Egypt. Song scholar Zhou Qufei 周去非 (1135–1189) wrote *Answering Queries about Foreign Lands* 岭外代答 and Zhao Rushi 赵汝适 (1170–1228) wrote *Accounts of Foreign Countries* 诸蕃志 as pioneering accounts in Chinese about foreign countries. Song

China had over 20 foreign trade ports, led by Guangzhou, Quanzhou 泉州, Mingzhou 明州 (present-day Ningbo 宁波 in Zhejiang province), and Mizhou 密州 (present-day Zhucheng 诸城 in Shandong province). Joining this prosperous trade were merchants from Persia, Arabia, and India, many of whom lived in Guangzhou and Quanzhou. In Guangzhou, foreigners lived in *fanfang* 蕃坊 (foreign settlements). The earliest Arab mosque in Guangzhou, *huai sheng si* 怀圣寺 (Huaisheng/prophet-remembering mosque), was a very popular shrine for Muslims during the Tang and Song dynasties. There was a Hindu temple in Quanzhou, which is gone today, but statues of Hindu gods can be seen in the Quanzhou Museum. Some Arab and Indian descendants qualified for the Song imperial exams and became Chinese officers. The Song practice of importing *xiangyao* 香药 (literally, fragrant materials and medicines) from India and Southeast Asia was internationally famous. The so-called *xiang yao* 香药 included perfumes, spices, and incense. Chinese also used them for medicinal purposes; hence, the word *yao* 药 (medicine) was added.

## III. Academic Achievements During Song Dynasty

Song China was also a great period for poetry, especially the *ci* 词 form (as distinguishable from the *shi* 诗 form). The *shi* form of poetry reached its zenith during the Tang Dynasty, while the Song Dynasty was virtually the cradle of *ci* poetry. Both the Tang *shi* form and Song *ci* form have rigid rules for the number of lines, words, words in each line, and rhyming scheme, as well as the "tone" rhythm. The difference lies in the latter's irregular length of lines versus the former's regular length of lines (either five or seven characters). With irregular line length, Song *ci* has a flavor of informal conversation and is more expressive of emotion. As an example, the following is my translation of renowned Song poetess Li Qingzhao's 李清照 (1084–1155) masterpiece of *ci* poetry entitled "Spring of Wu-ling 武陵春."

**Chapter 6: The Glorious and Pathetic Song Dynasty**

Good for the gale to disappear,

fragrant is the air,

flowers blown off everywhere.

I'm tardy to begin the day,

won't do my hair,

it's too late!

I live in the same residence,

but there's a difference,

my dear one is no more,

nothing to look for.

My cheeks soaked in tears

here I wish to murmur my fears.

I hear Shuangxi is good for outing.

Should I go for boating

to make myself happy?

O, no,

I won't go!

The boat might not carry

the load of my sorrow.

(风住尘香花已尽，日晚倦梳头。物是人非事事休，
欲语泪先流。闻说双溪春尚好，也拟泛轻舟。
只恐双溪舴艋舟，载不动许多愁。)

Song China did not have a ruler with high academic accomplishments like Tang Emperor Taizong, but Tang China did not have as many renowned academicians and theoreticians as Song China. During Northern Song, there were great masters such as Shao Yong 邵雍 (1011–1077), Zhou Dunyi 周敦颐

(1017–1073), Zhang Zai 张载 (1020–1077), Cheng Hao 程颢 (1032–1085), and Cheng Yi 程颐 (1033–1107), while Zhu Xi 朱熹 (1130–1200) and Lu Jiuyuan 陆九渊 (1139–1193) dominated Southern Song. The two new schools of *lixue* 理学 (literally, study of reasoning) and *xinxue* 心学 (literally, study of heart/mind) rose in Song China.

In my opinion, the best sayings about Chinese civilization came from the mouths of two Song scholars. The first scholar was Fan Zhongyan 范仲淹 (989–1052), who said in his famous essay "Notes on the Yueyang Tower" 岳阳楼记: "Be the first to worry the worries of Tianxia and the last to enjoy the enjoyment of Tianxia 先天下之忧而忧，后天下之乐而乐" and "Worry about the masses from the apex of the ruling dais and worry about the ruler from the most remote corners of the country 居庙堂之高则忧其民，处江湖之远则忧其君." The second scholar was Zhang Zai 张载, whose words I have translated as follows.

> Establish the heart for Heaven and Earth,
>
> establish the life for the living people,
>
> carry forward the forgotten teachings of past sages,
>
> create grand equality/harmony for posterity eternally.
>
> (为天地立心，为生民立命，为往圣继绝学，
> 为万世开太平。)

In Song China, there was already a popular saying that "All good words of humankind have been said by the Buddha 世上好言佛说尽." However, for those Chinese who could not, or would not, read Buddhist scripture and listen to sermons of Buddhist preachers, they would not get the "good words" of the Buddha. The "good words" of Fan Zhongyan, especially "Be the first to worry the worries of Tianxia and the last to enjoy the enjoyment of Tianxia," advocated the "bodhisattva spirit" of Mahayana Buddhism, hence, it was a part of the "good words" said by the Buddha. What Fan Zhongyan said has become a household saying in China.

From the Southern and Northern Dynasties to Song, Buddhism had already popularized the Indian concept of "bodhicitta" ("enlightened mind," which means in Chinese "enlightened heart 菩提心.") While this Indian concept of bodhicitta focused on the "mind of enlightenment," in ancient China, people had no idea about the brain/mind and believed all ideas, sentiments, and emotions were generated from the heart 心. In fact, the Indian concept of bodhicitta was rather similar to Confucian ideas of "human love" and "righteousness." I think Zhang Zai used the expression *li xin* 立心 to mean *li pu ti xin* 立菩提心 (to establish the "bodhicitta/enlightened heart") because to him it was coterminous with Confucian "human love and righteousness." If we interpret the first line with such a *Chindia* perspective, the other three lines are easy to decipher. Indian tradition believes there is only one holistic "life" shared by all living beings. Zhang Zai's second line of "establish the life for the living people" resonates exactly with this Indian tradition: He felt the need to protect and perfect the common "life 命" of humankind. His third line "carry forward the forgotten teachings of past sages" would, obviously, include the teachings of Confucius and Mencius, as well as that of the Buddha and other world sages. Thus, he highlighted the term "forgotten teachings 绝学" to reiterate that good teachings should not be neglected and forgotten. The final line "create grand harmony for posterity eternally" highlights the ideal of *taiping* 太平/grand equality. We should not confuse it with the conventional Chinese concept of "everything under control 太平无事." A quintessential Indian value that Buddhism introduced to China was "equality 平等." In fact, one of Buddha's Chinese titles was "The King of Equality 平等王."

An important advancement in philosophical thinking in Song China was the discourse on *taiji* 太极 (literally, "the ultimate end"), including *wuji* 无极 (literally, endlessness). Zhou Dunyi

wrote in *A Note on the Picture of Taiji/Taichi* 太极图说: "The ultimate end is development of endlessness." It was Zhou Dunyi who popularized this, now world famous, picture of Taiji/Taichi. In the famous Zhu Xi–Lu Jiuyuan debate at the Ehu 鹅湖 Monastery in 1175, just a century after Zhou Dunyi passed away, Lu Jiuyuan disagreed with the proposition of "endlessness." We know that Confucius and Mencius never talked about the universe, and Laozi and Zhuangzi made only random comments, which does not form a definite worldview. Evidently, Song worldview developed far beyond the ancient Chinese philosophers. We also note that the Song worldview definitely had the input of the Indian "Brahman/ultimate reality." From ancient times until today, Indians have regarded it as the "highest universal principle." Song discourse on the "*Taiji/Taichi* Ultimate End" and "endlessness" sounds very similar to Indian discourse on "Brahman." Zhu Xi agreed with Shao Yong that "Xin/heart is Taiji/Taichi 心为太极" and added: "Human love is heart 仁即心也." How did Song philosophers come to know the Indian philosophy about Brahman and thus fuse it into the Chinese value system? "Mahayana" is the special variety of Buddhist philosophy that has prevailed in China throughout history. Literally, "Mahayana" means "the great vehicle." True to its name, the Mahayana/great vehicle has carried quintessential Indian culture to China across religious boundaries. For example, pre-Buddhist ancient Indians already had the concept of "paramatman/supreme soul/spirit" prevailing over the individual existence that was "atman." Buddhism propagated this concept in China and created the Chinese concepts of "macro-self 大我" and "micro-self 小我." Chinese Buddhism even went a step further to advise people to rid themselves of "*atmagraha*/ego-clinging 我执" and replace it with "dharmagraha/truth clinging 法执" so humans could attain enlightenment and enter the realm of "selflessness 无我." Zhu Xi (as well as other Song philosophers) had deep connection to the Buddhist movement. When he went to the Southern Song capital, Lin'an (Hangzhou), for the imperial exams, he carried in his bag the quotations of Chan Master Reverend Dahui 大慧禅师, not Confucius. Zhu Xi was fond

of quoting Reverend Dahui's words that "Every person has a Taiji/Taichi, and everything has a Taiji/Taichi."

**The picture of Taiji/Taichi**

## IV. Vulnerable China Ravaged by Nation-states

We have progressed through the development of the Chinese common entity of destiny from Qin–Han to Sui–Tang and Song. Sui–Tang China was more progressive, civilized, and prosperous than Qin–Han China, but relatively weaker. Song China was even more progressive, civilized, and prosperous, but yet weaker than Sui–Tang China. These two aspects are both contradictory and noncontradictory. If China could have developed by closing its door free of external influence, such a contradiction would not have arisen. Unfortunately, not following the nation–state line did not make China free from external interference. As the Chinese proverb says: "The wind blows nonstop, not allowing the tree to rest 树欲静而风不息." China may be likened to an oasis in the nation–state's desert, potentially engulfed by the desert at any moment. The Han Empire was aware of this danger and did its best to drive the Xiongnu away. For 130 years (626–756) during Tang, from Emperor Taizong to Emperor Xuanzong, the Chinese government vigilantly adopted measures to address potential external danger. This ability declined during the middle and sunset periods of Tang; thus, China had a difficult time dealing with external challenges and aggression. Song China did not do enough to strengthen defenses when unprecedentedly

strong and intelligent armies, including those at its northern border, had emerged. Had China been poor and backward in economy, science, and technology, it would have gone under long before the Song Dynasty actually ended. In fact, early Song rulers, including Emperor Taizu 宋太祖 (reigned 960–976), Emperor Taizong 宋太宗 (reigned 976–997), Emperor Zhenzong 宋真宗 (reigned 997–1022), and Emperor Shenzong 宋神宗 (reigned 1067–1085) did seriously resist the aggression of Khitan 契丹 (Liao 辽). Song emperors Taizong and Zhenzong led expeditions to fight Khitan. Emperor Zhenzong and his successors firmly resisted the strong lobby for moving the Song capital to the south. There was a lack of solidarity within the Song government from the inception of the dynasty. A large portion of Song defense forces had to be deployed to address internal dissension, thus undermining wholehearted dedication to fighting external enemies. Another obstacle was created by the independence of the vassal state Dangxiang 党项, which declared itself, in 1038, the Dynasty of "Great Xia 大夏"—Chinese history books call it "Western Xia 西夏." From 1040 onward, the Northern Song government fought five wars with the Western Xia, without attaining decisive victory. Western Xia survived the Northern Song government, which collapsed in 1127. Northern Song's wars with Western Xia increased its vulnerability to the northern aggressors.

In its final phase, Tang China was devastated by regionalism and excessive power in the hands of garrison generals. This led the Song government to adopt a policy of "strong trunk and weak branches 強干弱枝" and an orientation of "prioritizing civilians over the military 重文轻武," making regional military forces weak while maintaining an elite army in the center. It subjected army generals to the control of civilian officers. Such measures prevented Song China from creating a strong force for national defense. No brilliant general could emerge from such a system. It was due to such policies that Northern Song could not quell the independence of the Western Xia. Northern Song also could not prevent Khitan from establishing the "Great Liao

大辽国," with its capital in Beijing from 916 to 1125. Then, Nurchen 女真, subordinate to the Great Liao, declared its independence in 1115 and established the "Great Jin 大金国." The Northern Song government allied with Great Jin to destroy Great Liao, causing Song China to face an even worse external enemy. Great Jin (1115–1234) moved its capital from Heilongjiang 黑龙江 province to Beijing and stormed the Northern Song capital of Bianjing in 1127, taking away Song ruler Emperor Qinzong 宋钦宗 (reigned 1126–1127), his imperial father Song Emperor Huizong 宋徽宗 (reigned 1100–1126), the queen, other ladies of the harem, members of the royal family, imperial officers, and common people, totaling 100,000 people and treasures of uncountable value. This was the well-known "National Shame of the Jingkang Era 靖康耻" and the end of the Northern Song Dynasty. Subsequently, Zhao Gou 赵构 (1107–1187), younger brother of Emperor Qinzong, was enthroned as Song Emperor Gaozong 宋高宗 (reigned 1127–1162) and Song China retreated south of the Yangtze River with Lin'an (Hangzhou) as its imperial capital, relying on the Yangtze River as the wall of national defense.

Meanwhile, there emerged a talented general named Yue Fei 岳飞 (1103–1142), a hard-liner patriot and a smart general who had three-fifths of the country's army, nicknamed the "Army of Yue 岳家军," under his control. His reputation evoked terror within Nurchen Jin political and military circles and there was a chance he could rejuvenate Song China if the Emperor trusted him. Unfortunately, this was not the case. He was recalled from the battlefront while he was winning victory after victory and put to death on a treason charge. For centuries, Yue Fei has been regarded as a patriotic hero and even revered as a deity in Zhejiang and other places (including Taiwan).

Though Yue Fei died young, his patriotic and fighting spirit has lived eternally through the *ci* poem he left behind entitled "Red is the Entire River 满江红." I have translated this masterpiece as follows.

I stoop over the railing,

within me my blood is boiling.

The drip, drip rain is gone.

I raise high my head,

eyes searching ahead,

I let out loud cries on and on,

emotion surging high

like the turbulent tide.

Fame with awards for thirty years

I treat them as dust and earth.

There's still thousands of miles to cover

marching with the moon and clouds together.

Lying idle to see my head turning gray,

in frustration and dismay?

Nay, that's not my way!

The Great Shame of Jingkang

yet to be washed away,

a patriot's regret is never so strong!

Let us ride and drive and dash

over the Helan mountain pass.

Eat the enemy's flesh we don't feel hungry,

drink his blood to quench our mouth's thirst.

We shall regain and recover

every mountain and river

that belongs to our country.

Then we report to His Majesty.

**Chapter 6: The Glorious and Pathetic Song Dynasty**

This was not only Yue Fei speaking but the voice of Chinese civilization to urge Song China to resolve the crisis. Unfortunately, it fell on deaf ears!

How the Southern Song (1127–1279) lived after the "National Shame of the Jingkang Era" and death of Yue Fei is testified to in another famous poem by Lin Sheng 林升 (dates unknown) entitled "Writing at My House in Lin'an/Hangzhou 题临安邸." The following is my translation.

> Hill after hill a green vision
>
> lofty mansion after mansion.
>
> Song and dance at the West Lake,
>
> night and day without any break.
>
> Revelers enchanted by warm breeze
>
> everyone is drunk and feels at ease.
>
> Hangzhou is no new place,
>
> old Bianjing has set the pace.

> (山外青山楼外楼，西湖歌舞几时休？
> 暖风熏得游人醉，直把杭州作汴州。)

Now we have seen the path trodden by three dynasties—Sui, Tang, and Song—which opened a new page of development in Chinese civilization. A new vision of a big fishbowl emerged before us. We see millions of fish swimming smoothly, freely, and happily inside the harmonious atmosphere of the fishbowl. But gluttonous cats were waiting by its side, ready to jump in. Chinese civilization embarking on its odyssey along the civilization highway was severely threatened. Meanwhile, Genghis Khan and his mighty cavalry rose from the north to shake the world, making all of Eurasia weep, while the Southern Song capital was still "enchanted by warm breeze." People awoke only after the

Mongols overthrew the Great Jin and reached the northern shore of the Yangtze River and Sichuan. Alas, it was too late.

In 1279, Mongol troops were about to occupy all of Southern Song. The last Song emperor Zhao Bing 赵昺 (1272–1279) was only eight years old. Over 100,000 Song civilians and soldiers escorted him to the sea with several hundred boats joined together to form living quarters off the Guangdong coast (near present-day Jiangmen 江门). The resistance could not last. Courtier Lu Xiufu 陆秀夫 (1236–1279) received an incorrect signal and thought Mongol troops were on board. He did not want the "National Shame of the Jingkang Era" to repeat and jumped into the sea with the child emperor, both in full ceremonial attire. Seeing this, all the Song civilians and military on board jumped into the sea. The commander-in-chief of Southern Song Zhang Shijie 张世杰 (?–1279) was not at the scene. When he heard the Emperor was gone, he also jumped into the sea. Such was the end of the final war fought by Song China. The result was over 100,000 corpses (including that of the Song Emperor) floating at the seaside too pathetic to witness. Had Song China reduced, even by 1 percent, its hedonistic pleasure to increase national defense, the end would not have been so tragic.

# CHAPTER 7

# CIVILIZATION HIGHWAY DAMAGED BUT EXTENDED

CHINA: A 5,000-YEAR ODYSSEY

The Sui–Tang–Song new version of the Chinese common entity of destiny ended tragically. The big fishbowl was broken and the merrymaking fish got devoured by the nation-state cats. But, the odyssey of Chinese civilization along the civilization highway did not stop. There was an upside to the downside: Chinese civilization resurrected itself after a brief coma. In the new Mongol Yuan Dynasty, Chinese civilization and the Chinese common entity came back to life. It marched ahead with wounds all over its body.

Over 100,000 Song civilians and military personnel who did not expect the worst to happen to them drowned themselves in the sea. There were the "three heroes during the demise of Song 宋亡三杰." Two of them, Lu Xiufu and Zhang Shijie, committed suicide by jumping into the sea. The third, Wen Tianxiang 文天祥 (1236–1283), unsuccessfully attempted suicide in an effort to escape captivity. He was captured and escorted to the Mongol Yuan capital, Beijing. He declined an offer from Kublai Khan (1215–1294), founder of the Yuan Dynasty 元朝 (1271–1368), to serve in the Yuan government. Kublai Khan met with him several times in the imperial palace to discuss Chinese civilization. These discussions had an impact on Khan. To uphold the authority and dignity of the new dynasty, Kublai Khan had to concede to the will of his subordinates to put Wen Tianxiang (who refused to surrender) to death. Wen wrote a unique, long poem entitled "Song of Righteous Spirit 正气歌" while in prison, regarded as "the ultimate heroic song of the millennium 千古绝唱." In the song, he wrote:

> With the righteous spirit
>
> Earth would not alter.
>
> With the righteous spirit
>
> Heaven would not falter.

It is the soul of human society

and the root of morality.

(地维赖以立，天柱赖以尊。三纲实系命，

道义为之根。)

In this poem, the "righteous spirit" symbolizes Chinese civilization, which would stand firm like "Heaven would not falter" and "Earth would not alter."

## I. Chinese Civilization Hijacked by the Nation-state

In 1206, Genghis Khan Temüjin (1162–1227) established his Mongol Empire and led the most powerful army the world had ever seen during the prescientific era to conquer the world. From 1211 to 1214, his cavalry defeated the 400,000 strong army of Nurchen Jin and marched into Hebei and Shandong. In 1214, the Jin government moved its capital from Beijing to Bianjing. Genghis Khan immediately occupied Beijing and the territory north of the Huanghe (Yellow river). In 1219, Genghis Khan led an army of 100,000 Mongol soldiers, in addition to 50,000 Turkic soldiers, to invade the Khwarezmian Empire and defeat the latter's 400,000-man army. The Khwarezmian ruler Alā al-Dīn Muḥammad fled to Europe and the Mongol army pursued him. In this Eurasian expedition, Genghis Khan organized the previously captured Chinese technicians into a special task force to make missiles filled with gunpowder, stone-throwing devices, and carriages for scaling city walls, all of which greatly helped his horsemen win battles. The effect of gunpowder was terrifying. The people of Song China should have used it to terrify Genghis Khan's horses. Instead, they handed it to the latter to conquer Eurasia and revolutionize warfare of the nation-state world. After Genghis Khan died, his third son Ögedei (1186–1241) succeeded him. Ögedei's death in 1241 ignited a crisis of succession. Möngke (the trusted lieutenant and adopted son of Ögedei) gained prominence. Möngke died in 1259 in

Sichuan. His younger brother Kublai Khan annexed the Chinese domain and established the Yuan Dynasty. Meanwhile, there were four separate Mongol khanates independent of Kublai Khan's empire: The Ögedei Khanate in present-day Xinjiang; Chagatai Khanate in present-day Xinjiang from Turpan to Ili; Qipchaq ulisi Khanate in present-day Russia and Eastern Europe; and Il Khanate in the southern part of Central Asia and Iran. A large part of Eurasia became a Mongol colony, with China forming a part of it.

Kublai Khan defeated his brother Ariq Böke to become supreme ruler of China. He took from the Chinese classic *Yijing* 易经 (Book of Change) the word *yuan* 元 to name his new dynasty. The concept of *yuan* 元 denotes "first." Kublai Khan's choice of it reminds us of the Qin Emperor's proclaiming himself as "Qin Shihuang" (Beginning Emperor of Qin). Kublai Khan vanquished Southern Song in 1279 and reunified China, but failed to bring all four Mongol khanates in Eurasia under his control. The four Mongol khanates existed in isolation from each other, disappearing over the course of time. The last of them, the Qipchaq ulisi, was overthrown by the Russians toward the end of the 15th century.

When Genghis Khan was overpowering a large tract of Eurasia, he had a fast-moving cavalry aided by the engineers. The Mongol army of Yuan China absorbed large numbers of Nurchen and Chinese soldiers (including recruits from Southern Song). The size of the army was greatly enlarged, but the fighting power was not. In 1277, Myanmar was in chaos and Mongol troops went there to control the situation. However, they had to withdraw due to the heat and other unfavorable climatic conditions. In 1287, Myanmar was again gripped by disorder and the Mongol Governor of Yunnan sent troops to control Myanmar. However, they again had to retreat since timely food supplies failed to reach the frontline.

Mongol troops thrice failed to conquer Annam (present-day northern Vietnam). In 1257–1258, Mongol General Uriyanqadai

led 30,000 troops to invade Annam immediately after he conquered Yunnan. But he could not maintain his momentum in the wake of a few quick victories. The Trànruling family of Annam was prepared to fight a long, drawn-out war, but Uriyanqadai had no patience and retreated. In 1282, a huge contingent of 500,000 Mongol troops entered Annam under the pretext of gaining passage to Champa (now southern Vietnam and Cambodia/Kampuchea). The Annamese were not fooled. They were ready to fight to the end and Annamese fighters had the words "kill Tartar" engraved on their arms in Annamese language. There also arrived Song Chinese immigrants, wearing Chinese costumes, to join the Annamese resistance. Thinking a big reinforcement had arrived from China to fight them, the Mongol army became panic-stricken. The Annam troops counterattacked and many Mongol soldiers surrendered. The weather was too hot for the Mongols, an epidemic broke out, and the invasion ended. In 1287, Kublai Khan launched the third and final invasion of Annam, dispatching 300,000 troops and 300 ships by land and sea. The Annamese allowed the Mongol warships to pass, but attacked the supply ships in the rear and seized a huge quantity of grains and weapons, cutting off supplies to Mongol troops in the front. Before the tide arrived, the Annamese drove logs into the shallow water along the coast. Mongol warships arrived with the tide. After the water receded, the Mongol warships were locked up by the logs and could not move. Soldiers onboard were either drowned or captured. Only 50,000 of the 600,000 Mongol troops in the second and third invasions returned to base.

Mongol invasions against Japan in 1274 and 1281 were equally unsuccessful. In the 1274 invasion, a 30,000 strong naval force composed of Mongols, Koreans, and Chinese sailed from the eastern coast of present-day South Korea and reached Kyushu in Japan. A severe hurricane helped the Japanese defenders, causing heavy casualty to the invaders. Only 13,000 Mongol troops, along with 200 Japanese captives, returned. The 1281 expedition consisted of 150,000 men who sailed separately to Nokonoshima

Chapter 7: Civilization Highway Damaged but Extended

Island and Fukuoka Island in Kyushu to join forces. However, the voyage was tough and encountered a storm. The Mongol commander fled, leaving behind an exhausted army on the islands to be butchered by the Japanese. Only 20,000–30,000 soldiers returned.

Chinese civilization did not join the Mongol conquest of Eurasia. Yet there was an international impression of a "yellow peril," with the image of China implicated. Similarly, from Qin–Han to Sui–Tang–Song, Chinese troops never seriously threatened the security of Vietnam or invaded the country as the Mongol Yuan did. But, there is an international impression today that China was always an aggressive and repressive big brother to Vietnam. It was the Mongol Yuan who caused a lot of damage to the international image of Chinese civilization.

Inside China, the Mongol Yuan virtually created hell with all the evils of the nation-state. Yuan Chinese society was divided into four classes. The highest class was the Mongols and the second highest was called "Semu People 色目人," a generic term for non-Mongol and non-Chinese people of various ethnic origins. Native Chinese were placed into the two lower classes. The third class was "Han People 汉人," which included subjects of the erstwhile Nurchen Jin Dynasty as well as native Chinese in Sichuan and Yunnan areas which fell under Mongol control before the end of Southern Song. Southern Song Chinese were in the fourth and lowest class designated as "Southerners 南人." The local administration of the Mongol Yuan was called "Daruyaci" and was headed by a Mongol and assisted by a Semu and Han. Common people of the third and fourth classes, namely, Han and Southerners, were not allowed to keep weapons (even iron agricultural implements were banned). They were also not allowed to have religious ceremonies or entitled to keep eagles and dogs as pets. This four-class social hierarchy also determined prioritization in government recruitment policy. Mongols were invariably the first choice for any government appointment with Semu next. If a suitable candidate from these two classes was not

available, Han would be considered. Southerners had virtually no chance to become a Mongol Yuan officer. In government taxation, Mongols were totally exempt, Semu received a two-thirds exemption, and Han and Southerners shouldered the brunt of the tax burden. Mongol Yuan law basically targeted Han and Southerners. Mongols were above the law. A small number of rich natives close to the regime could share this privilege by bribing the law enforcing authorities. Imperial exams were not held until near the end of the Yuan Dynasty, with Chinese intellectuals in virtual hibernation.

No account of how people lived during Mongol Yuan was written. It was said that 30–50 families of Han and Southerners were subject to the supervision of a single Mongol soldier who could do anything he wanted from taking their money to raping their women. Such Mongol soldiers were abhorred by the people. It was said that when Zhu Yuanzhang rose in rebellion, people communicated with each other by hiding a chit inside a moon cake. On the chit, it was written "kill the Tartar 杀鞑子." On the night of Mid-Autumn Festival, every family was feasting and eating moon cakes. Upon seeing these chits, they did what the chit had called for, and supervising Mongol soldiers all over China were killed at the same time. All this information is hearsay. China was so vast with so many people, it would be impossible for Mongol Yuan to post a soldier to rule and watch all Chinese families in this manner. This "kill the Tartar" story may be true in some localities. It symbolically reflects the truth of national repression begetting national rebellion.

There were all kinds of rebellions at the end of Mongol Yuan. There was the force called the "Incense Army 香军" led by Han Shantong 韩山童 and his son Han Lin'er 韩林儿. Other forces included the "Red Scarf Army 红巾军" led by Liu Futong 刘福通 and Xu Shouhui 徐寿辉, the "Han Army 汉军" led by Chen Youliang 陈友谅, and the most important force was led by Zhu Yuanzhang, whom I will highlight later. The rebel army of Han Shantong consisted of Buddhist followers who regularly

burnt incense to worship the Buddha, hence earning the name "Incense Army." According to Indian tradition, burning incense was a way to communicate with deities. Thus, Han Shantong's Incense Army popularized Indian religious tradition in Chinese political life. The Yuan Dynasty began with the most powerful military force on earth, but it could not last even 100 years. It was brought down by semiliterate and illiterate Chinese rebels.

## II. Yuan Contributions to Chinese Civilization

There is no denying the fact that the Mongol Empire was a Mongol empire. There is also no denying the fact that the Mongol Yuan Dynasty was within the realm of Chinese civilization. In 1271, Kublai Khan issued his "Edict on the Title of the State 建国号诏" in which he said: "We go according to the noble laws of the sages and fixed systems of previous dynasties 稽列圣之洪规，讲前代之定制." The edict observed: "We implement the spirit of Tianxia for one family. We emulate the proper beginning of *Spring and Autumn*. We inaugurate the 'Great First' of the *Book of Change*." These words reinvigorated the energy of Chinese civilization, not Mongolian tradition. All 10 successors of Kublai Khan adhered to this new tradition. Kublai Khan advocated "implementing Han governance 行汉法," which was strongly opposed by rulers of the four Mongol Khanates. All his fellow Mongol detractors sank into oblivion, but Kublai Khan's Yuan Dynasty has survived as part of the history of Chinese civilization. In other words, Kublai Khan led the Mongol ruling family on the Chinese odyssey along the civilization highway to enable Chinese civilization to extend further afield.

Beijing became the great capital of Mongol Yuan and its population greatly increased, requiring increased supply of food grains from the south. Kublai Khan decided to expand the Grand Canal of Sui–Tang–Song into a real grand canal linking Beijing with Hangzhou via inland navigation. After completion of the project, there was a straight-line waterway running 1,700–plus kilometers between Beijing and Hangzhou, reducing the previous water transportation route via Luoyang by 900 kilometers. This benefitted Yuan and post-Yuan economic development in China.

India is the home of cotton and inventor of the cotton textile industry, spanning 5,000 years of history. Liang Emperor Wu of the Southern Dynasties received a mission from the Indian Gupta Dynasty with gifts. Among these gifts was an item called *gubei* 古贝 in Chinese historical records. *Gubei*, along with its synonym *jibei* 吉贝, were Chinese pronunciation of the Sanskrit word "karpasa/cotton." The Liang Emperor liked the *gubei* gift from India, a gown made of cotton. He continued to wear it for years, even with patches. The cotton plantation and cotton textile industry gradually moved to China through Central Asia, reaching Shaanxi prior to Mongol Yuan. However, the cotton plantation and cotton textile industry began to thrive during the Yuan Dynasty in Songjiang 松江 (present-day Shanghai). The pioneer was a lady named Huang Daopo 黄道婆 (Grandma Huang Dao).

When we discuss the arrival of cotton textiles in China, we must recall Du Fu's famous lines quoted in Chapter 5: "Liquor and meat go to waste inside the red gates, on the road skeletons lie, those who die of frostbite." Du Fu emphasizes people dying of frostbite (not hunger), an indication of the serious Chinese problem during Tang (and earlier periods too) of protecting the poor from severe cold during winter. For the rich, there was no problem because of silk and fur. However, for the majority of people who could not afford silk and fur, there was no effective protection against the cold. The arrival of cotton and cotton fabrics solved this problem. Ordinary Chinese could warm up with cotton-quilted clothes. Mongol Yuan became the beginning of Chinese people getting warm 温, just as important as their getting enough to eat 饱. People greatly welcomed this revolutionary change. The Yuan Chinese intellectual Xie Fangde 谢枋得 (1226–1289) repeatedly wrote about it. He left behind a poem praising cotton, from which I translate a few lines as follows.

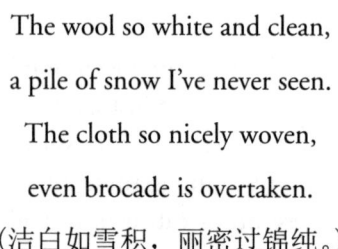

> The wool so white and clean,
>
> a pile of snow I've never seen.
>
> The cloth so nicely woven,
>
> even brocade is overtaken.
>
> （洁白如雪积，丽密过锦纯。）

This was the first time Chinese literature described cotton and marveled at how the snow-like stuff could become brocade-like fabric. Again, in Xie Fangde's poem:

> It is so much better
>
> than the coat of sheep skin.
>
> Its great merits altogether
>
> that fox fur can't win.
>
> （羔缝不足责，狐腋难拟伦。）

There was no exaggeration in such comparisons. Coats made of sheep skin and fox fur were coarsely made in those days. They were heavy and smelly as compared with the light, soft, and clean-quilted cotton coat. The poem goes on to say:

> I'll make a big coat
>
> with this cloth and wool,
>
> miserable winter I promote
>
> to spring in the Third Moon so beautiful.
>
> （剪裁为大裘，穷冬胜三春。）

The Mongol Yuan Dynasty brought the people of Tibet into the Chinese common entity. Human activity began at the

foothills of the Himalayas. Sichuan, in southwestern China, was one such place. It was in Sichuan that the Wushan Ape Man, Sanxingdui civilization, and ancient Qiang race (including the Great Yu) emerged. We know Qiang people were the ancestors of Tibetan people. We don't know when they started settling on top of the Himalayas. It was during the Tang Dynasty that the importance of the Tibetan people began to be recognized as Emperor Taizong presented a royal lady Princess Wencheng 文成公主 (called "rGya Mo bZa" in Tibet) to Tibetan ruler Songtsen Gampo. After him, there was the prolonged period of the "Era of Fragmentation in Tibetan history." When the Mongol Empire rose, the Sakya government of Tibet sent reverend pandita Gonggar Gyaltsen to Liangzhou 凉州 (present-day Wuwei 武威 in Gansu province) to negotiate with Mongol Prince Gotan to subject Tibet to the Mongol Empire in 1247. Kublai Khan appointed reverend Chögyal Phagpa (Chinese name 八思巴), nephew of Tibet's Sakya ruler, as "state preceptor 国师." In 1260, reverend Phagpa was further revered as the "Maharatna Dharmaraja 大宝法王" and "imperial preceptor 帝师." Kublai Khan appointed all Tibetan government administrators through the recommendation of Phagpa. In 1290, there was turmoil in Tibet. Kublai Khan sent troops to Lhasa to restore order and strengthen the authority of the Sakya government. It was the Mongol Yuan central government that helped Tibet maintain stability. It was also from this time that China had the entire courses of the two great rivers within its common entity.

Buddhism, especially Tibetan Buddhism, boomed during the Yuan Dynasty. *Yuanshi* 元史 (Annals of the Yuan Dynasty) records in its chapter on "Religious Ceremonies 祭祀" that Kublai Khan, in 1270, erected a white silk canopy on the imperial throne with the Sanskrit word *maravijiya* "victory over the demons" written on top in gold. Each year, on the 15th day of the second moon, reverend Chögyal Phagpa, the "imperial preceptor," led a group of *fanseng* 梵僧 (literally, Brahman priests, but actually Indian and other foreign Buddhists) to perform a religious ceremony around the canopy.

The Buddhist tradition had eight bodhisattvas. One of them, Maitreya, became the "future Buddha 未来佛" of China. Another bodhisattva Bhaisajyaguru was regarded as *yaoshifo* 药师佛 (literally, "Buddha, the medicine guru"). Four of the eight bodhisattvas, very popular among Chinese worshippers, gradually settled at four famous shrines in China: Avalokitesvara (Chinese name "Guanyin 观音") at Mount Putuo 普陀山 in Zhejiang province; Manjusri (Chinese name "Wenshu 文殊") at Mount Wutai 五台山 in Shanxi province; Samantabhadra (Chinese name "Puxian 普贤") at Mount Emei 峨眉山 in Sichuan province; and Kṣitigarbha (Chinese name "Dizang 地藏") at Mount Jiuhua 九华山 in Anhui province. Kublai Khan officially confirmed these four Buddhist shrines through his edict in 1214. The Mongol Yuan Emperor Sidibala (reigned 1302–1323) went to Mount Wutai on pilgrimage.

**Chinese "Future Buddha" Maitreya in Mogao Grottoes**

In Indian Buddhist legend, Maitreya is the bodhisattva who lives in the Tusita Heaven (residence of the Buddha from where he arrived in the human world to start the Buddhist movement). Chinese Buddhist tradition has firmly established the theory that he will be the future Buddha to succeed the present Buddha, Sakyamuni. Through China, this theory has spread to Japan, Korea, Vietnam, and other Asian countries. Today, the Maitreya/ future Buddha image one sees throughout the world is distinct from the image of Buddha. The latter is essentially Indian, while the former (Maitreya/future Buddha) is essentially Chinese in features and style. The image of Maitreya/future Buddha is obese and exposing his bump belly. He is always smiling and at ease (people call him the "laughing Buddha"). Such an image symbolizes the ardent aspiration for harmony and tension-free life sans struggle. Recall the image of the world's largest Buddha statue in Leshan in Chapter 5, which is a statue of Maitreya/ future Buddha, created during the Tang Dynasty. During the Song Dynasty, the smiling/easy Buddha image was firmly established. I believe the energy of optimism created by this image helped Chinese people survive the challenge of Mongol Yuan nation-state rule.

Kublai Khan's 1214 edict officially confirming the permanent resting place on earth for the four Indian bodhisattvas, namely, Avalokitesvara, Manjusri, Samantabhadra, and Ksitigarbha in China is culturally very important in world history. First, the world vindicated the Mongol ruler's decision (there is no dispute, unlike that of Jerusalem). Second, as the great Indian poet Rabindranath Tagore (1861–1941) said, "India has two aspects— in one, there is a householder, in the other, a wandering ascetic."[1] Indian civilization introduced the spirit of "wandering ascetic" to China, where the spirit of "householder" stood supreme. Buddha, bodhisattvas, and all the Indian pilgrims to China were "wandering ascetics," while the Chinese "householders" never stopped building homes for them. Thus, Kublai Khan declared, on behalf of Chinese civilization, this *Chindia* affection and friendship. One may tour Mount Putuo in Zhejiang, Mount Wutai in Shanxi, Mount Emei in Sichuan, and Mount Jiuhua in Anhui to see how

---

[1] Uma Dasgupta, *Rabindranath Tagore: My Life in My Words* (New Delhi: Penguin Viking, 2006), 309.

Chapter 7: Civilization Highway Damaged but Extended

happily the four Indian bodhisattvas are enjoying the hospitality from their Chinese worshippers. Third, at these four holy shrines, Kublai Khan's name is repeated daily by innumerable guides to Chinese and international tourists, showing the deep footprint of the founder–ruler of the Yuan Dynasty in Chinese life.

## III. Ming China Returned to the Civilization Highway

Zhu Yuanzhang 朱元璋 (1328–1398), the Chinese hero who overthrew the repressive Mongol Yuan regime, was a real proletariat who had no property besides the figurative oppressor's chain on his body. He had begged for food and is the real hero of the "from-beggar-to-emperor" miracle of Chinese history. Like Li Shimin, Zhu Yuanzhang was good at fighting and winning wars. In him, the warlike Mongols met their nemesis. Born into the family of a poor peasant in Anhui, he grazed cattle for the landlord when he was a boy. His parents and elder siblings all passed away when he was young. He joined the local Buddhist temple as a servant. After some time, the temple closed and Zhu

**A portrait of Zhu Yuanzhang**

Yuanzhang became a beggar. The anti-Mongol uprising offered a chance to exhibit his talent. He gathered his own army and joined the force of Han Lin'er for a while. His force outgrew others and he stormed Beijing to overthrow Mongol Yuan. He established the Ming Dynasty, returned to the south, and made Nanjing the Ming capital to show that "Southerners" could not be humiliated. This was the first time that the political center of China moved to the Yangtze valley.

The Ming Dynasty 明朝 (1368–1644) established by Zhu Yuanzhang was sandwiched between the two powerful nation-state movements of Mongol Yuan and Manchu Qing. Ming China was an intermission that could not revive the Tang–Song version of the Chinese common entity of destiny, much less the reemergence of the big fishbowl of merrymaking pacifism. As founding Ming Emperor Taizu 明太祖 (reigned 1368–1398), Zhu Yuanzhang was outstanding for transforming the severely damaged Chinese common entity into a new dynasty of com-mendable political administration, prosperous economy, and a strong military. He maintained a strong standing army, even during peacetime. He ordered the army to reclaim virgin land in order to become economically self-sufficient. He vigorously dealt with corruption, leading to the deaths of many of his former loyal and meritorious lieutenants. While he invited bad commentary in public opinion, there is unanimous praise for his frugal lifestyle. His imperial palace lacked a flower garden, unlike all previous imperial palaces in Chinese history. But there was a vegetable garden to make his palace self-sufficient in vegetable consumption.

Doubtlessly, the originator of the idea, and person in charge, of this palace vegetable garden, was the Queen, Lady Ma 马氏, who distinguished herself in Ming history. She was the foster-daughter of one of the uprising leaders, Guo Zixing 郭子兴 (1312–1355), who was the patron of Zhu Yuanzhang when the latter made his debut. It was Guo Zixing who discovered the military talent of Zhu Yuanzhang and gave the latter an opportunity to exhibit his fighting talent. Guo also arranged the marriage of Zhu and his adopted daughter. Lady Ma was very affectionate to her husband, and they stuck together for decades through thick and thin. As soon as he became Emperor, Zhu Yuanzhang made Lady Ma his queen. It was a bright spot in Chinese civilization that such a peasant couple reigned over an empire. As previously mentioned, foot-binding of high-class women became popular from the Song Dynasty onward. However, Lady Ma, like all other female peasants who had to work in the field, did not bind her feet. She was ridiculed in the imperial capital as "Ma the big feet 马大脚." In the beginning, she was fond of sauntering out of the palace. As she became a public mockery, she confined herself indoors. She brought her frugal habits into the palace and refrained from politics, never patronizing any of her own relatives. This automatically freed her husband from the usual trouble of interference in state affairs by the queen's family. Though she did not involve herself in politics, she did save the lives of a good number of courtiers through her entreaties to her husband for leniency. Only after her death did the Emperor put to death many eminent courtiers. People sang songs to remember her, eulogizing her as the "sage and compassionate lady 圣慈."

It's a little ironic that the new Ming regime, the success story of a pious and patriotic peasant uprising, continued to have anti-establishment peasant uprisings. This shows that Zhu Yuanzhang's symbolic peasants' regime did not help peasants throughout China be liberated from landlord repression and exploitation. On the contrary, the success story of Zhu Yuanzhang emboldened repressed peasants to take up arms. The Hongwu 洪武 Era of Zhu Yuanzhang had the most peasant uprisings in Chinese history. Uprisings were isolated and scattered, some as large as several hundred thousand, others as small as several hundred participants. They did not occur simultaneously, but were instead spread over the provinces of Guangdong, Guangxi, Fujian, Jiangxi, Hunan, Sichuan, Shaanxi, Shandong, and Zhejiang. The well-known secret society, the "White Lotus Society 白莲教,"

which had been behind the anti-Mongol Incense Army and Red Scarf Army, was now behind a number of uprisings. Such uprisings survived Zhu Yuanzhang's reign by decades. The most famous was the one led by Tang Sai'er 唐赛儿 (1399-?), the female leader of Shandong's White Lotus Society in 1420. This coincided with Ming Emperor Chengzu 明成祖 (reigned 1402–1424) moving the capital from Nanjing to Beijing, in addition to employing hundreds of thousands of workers to renovate the palace, repair the Grand Canal, transport grain from the south to the north, and impose heavy tax on the people.

Emperor Chengzu was one of the outstanding rulers of imperial China, and his reigning era was called the "thriving era of Yongle 永乐盛世" (1402–1424). The Emperor's personal name was Zhu Di 朱棣 (1360–1424) and his situation was like that of Li Shimin (Tang Emperor Taizong). Zhu Di, the youngest son of Zhu Yuanzhang, had helped his father fight for, and established the new dynasty, and was in the prominent position of "Prince of Yan 燕王." Being the fourth son of the Emperor, he was out of the line of succession. However, fortune suddenly turned in his favor as all his elder brothers had passed away by the time his imperial father died. Zhu Di had a strong claim to the throne, but the imperial harem, in collusion with some courtiers, selected the son of the late crown prince to succeed Zhu Yuanzhang as Ming Emperor Hui 明惠帝. Once Emperor Hui was enthroned, Zhu Di rebelled. He marched to Nanjing from Beijing with a huge force. Seeing that everything was over, Emperor Hui ordered the palace be set on fire. Afterwards, Zhu Di carefully searched the charred corpses but could not find the body of Emperor Hui, who must have fled the palace during the chaos. After Zhu Di became the new Emperor, he launched a failed countrywide search to find his missing rival.

Ming Emperor Chengzu's "thriving era of Yongle" was a distant echo of Tang Emperor Taizong's "thriving era of Zhenguan," and the Chinese common entity of destiny gradually returned to its old course of odyssey along the civilization highway. An outstanding

**Chapter 7: Civilization Highway Damaged but Extended**

feat of the "thriving era of Yongle" was production of the most voluminous encyclopedia in the world: A collection of 370 million Chinese characters in 22,937 fascicles in 11,095 volumes. Emperor Chengzu personally supervised hundreds of courtiers and scholars to compile *The Great Compendium*. It was a comprehensive collection of all the information of astronomy, geography, philosophy (Yin and Yang 阴阳), medicine, religion (*sengdao* 僧道, namely, Buddhism and Daoism), technology, skills from all Chinese books, and written materials for his personal reference. At first, only one written copy of this Yongle Compendium was produced. The Emperor carried it wherever he went and was its only reader. Later, a second copy was produced and kept in the palace. One copy was kept in Beijing and another in Nanjing. Chinese civilization was a cultural treasury, and this Yongle Compendium was the most treasured of the Chinese cultural treasury. For millennia, Chinese civilization had created an enormous treasury of materials in writing and using the Chinese inventions of paper, ink, and printing to preserve knowledge and wisdom for all time. Then, immeasurable time and energy was spent to distill the most treasured information from all these materials and convert them into *The Yongle Compendium*. Unfortunately, only 4 percent of it (800 fascicles) exists today. Loss of the larger portion of *The Yongle Compendium* means loss of priceless and treasured information on Chinese civilization. Also, the time and energy spent to create this treasure were washed away. This is, indeed, a great misfortune. Today, the surviving 800 fascicles of this great *Yongle Compendium* are scattered among the National Library of China in Beijing (161 volumes), National Palace Museum in Taipei (62 volumes), and various libraries and museums in Britain, the United States, Germany, and Japan. These fragments of the great *Yongle Compendium* have become cultural treasures of the world.

The government of Emperor Chengzu was famous for its "cabinet system 内阁制," created by the Emperor. He selected learned scholars to be members of the cabinet and regularly discussed state affairs with them. Cabinet members did not have official responsibility in government departments and were not allowed to interfere with the functioning of the administration. They did not receive reports of the petitions of courtiers and officers. Emperor Chengzu reduced taxes and established institutions for disaster relief. He asked officers to go to the grassroots level to understand how people lived and truthfully report the suffering of the people to him. Violators would be punished. In 1412, 500 officers from local governments throughout China came to the capital to see the Emperor. He asked everyone to give him details of people's living conditions, promising that he would not punish those who spoke out about the miseries of the common people. The Yongle Era enjoyed the highest revenue of Ming China, indirectly reflecting the moderate prosperity of the people.

All major Chinese rivers flow east. It was through the great effort of Chinese people that there was the Grand Canal linking the north and south. The Grand Canal and the Great Wall are the two gigantic monuments of historical China. The Beijing–Hangzhou Grand Canal, created during Mongol Yuan, was often choked with silt due to neglect, resulting in disuse of the canal and use of sea coastal shipping as an alternative. The sea alternative was not ideal due to hurricanes. When Emperor Chengzu moved the capital to Beijing, he first adopted a policy of using the Canal and sea transportation in tandem. Later, he devoted all effort to dredging the Canal and ceasing coastal shipping, which was beneficial for economic development.

Tibet voluntarily joined the Chinese common entity of destiny during Mongol Yuan, while the Yuan Chinese army went to Tibet to quell rebellions. The Ming Dynasty did not continue the practice, but Tibet continued as a part of the Chinese common entity. Tibetans were keen to enjoy the Ming government's warm hospitality and traveled to the capital of Nanjing, later Beijing, to see the Ming emperors. Local governments of Ming China, along the route of Tibetan tours, were obliged to provide hospitality as well. As the number and size of Tibetan tour groups increased, this became increasingly burdensome for local governments. Thus,

Emperor Chengzu and his successors had to create regulations to address this situation. They classified the elite of Tibet into seven categories: (a) king and head of Tibetan religion 教王; (b) the posterity of the Buddha of Western heaven 西天佛子 (living Buddhas); (c) the great state preceptor 大国师; (d) the state preceptors 国师; (e) Chan masters 禅师; (f) lord abbots 都纲; and (g) lamas 喇嘛. Emperor Xianzong 明宪宗 (reigning 1464–1487), in 1465, issued an edict that only people in the state preceptors category and above were entitled to official visits to see the Ming Empire, and delegations should not exceed 150 people. This restriction continued throughout Ming.

The cordial China–Japan relationship established during Tang and Song ended abruptly during Mongol Yuan due to the Mongol invasions of Japan. However, Japan did want to trade with Yuan China, which was much more prosperous than Japan. The Ming government maintained normal diplomatic contact, but was lukewarm in welcoming Japanese "tributary delegations." On a nonofficial level, trade contacts between the two countries were brisk. From the 16th century onward, maritime activity in East Asia entered a new era with the arrival of Europeans. Saint Francis Xavier (1506–1552), cofounder of the Society of Jesus, first went to India, then to Japan. In Japan, he discovered the prevailing influence of China and decided to go there to disseminate the message of Jesus Christ. In 1552, he arrived on Shangchuan Island 上川岛, near Taishan 台山 in Guangdong off the coast. His plan to use the island as a base to conduct his China program ended due to his untimely death.

## IV. Zheng He's Seven Expeditions to the Indian Ocean

The Ming government generally prohibited coastal people from undertaking overseas trade, but official contacts with foreign countries were not hampered. The most outstanding maritime event was Emperor Chengzu's initiative to launch unprecedented expeditions, led by Zheng He 郑和 (1371–1433), starting in

1406 and ending in 1433. Zheng He was a eunuch and confidant of Emperor Chengzu. In 1406, he led a huge mission of over 28,000 officials, Buddhist monks, scholars, soldiers, and sailors with a fleet of 240 ships (including 62 large ships of about 120 meters long and over 60 meters wide) to visit the countries of the Indian Ocean. The mission returned and reported its experience to Emperor Chengzu, who would order five subsequent voyages. During the reign of Emperor Xuanzong 明宣宗 (reigned 1425–1435), the Zheng He mission was sent, for the final time, to the same destinations: Zheng He passed away during the voyage.

**A portrait of Zheng He**

People often like to compare the seven voyages of Zheng He with that of Christopher Columbus' (1451–1506) to the New Continent just a few decades later. Zheng He's voyages were earlier with many more ships, much longer distances (his seven trips covered over 70,000 nautical miles, equal to traveling around the earth three times), and many more contacts with other people than the Columbus voyage from Europe to America. However, the Columbus voyage resulted in the European discovery of the "New Continent" and expansion of the new movement of colonialism, while Zheng He's did not bring any change to the world situation. Columbus has been forever remembered by various people of the world. Many countries of the American continent celebrate "Columbus Day." Zheng He has, long ago, been virtually forgotten in China.

**Chapter 7: Civilization Highway Damaged but Extended**

What made these Zheng He expeditions of 600 years ago unusual was a combination of diplomatic intercourse and trade transactions. These expeditions warmed up China's relations with many states on the Indian peninsula. These states not only warmly received officials of Zheng He's mission but also sent direct missions to the Ming court in Beijing. I list these states according to Chinese records: Banggela 榜葛拉 (Bengal), Guli 古里 (Kozhikode/Calicut), Kezhi 柯枝 (Kochi/Cochin), Xiao Gelan 小葛兰 (Quilon), Gambali 甘巴里 (Coimbatore), Zhaonapuer 沼纳朴儿 (Jaunpur), Suoli 琐里 (Chola), Jayile 加异勒 (Kayal), Xialabi 夏剌比 (Cambay), Ewa 阿哇 (Ahmedabad), Kuchani 窟察泥 (Kutch), Bakeyi 八可意 (Broach), Dahui 打回 (Diu), Wushalati 乌沙剌踢 (a state in Gujarat), and Lani 剌尼 (another state in Gujarat). This list reveals that the Ming Dynasty had maximum official contacts with the Indian continent.

I must highlight Ming China's relations with Bengal. Ming records clearly mention *Banggela guo* 榜葛拉国 (country of "Bangla"), unmistakably Bangladesh. Today, the entire world thinks Bangladesh is a new state born of the "War of Independence" in 1971, and that there is no earlier history for it. This is an incorrect impression. In my opinion, there was a prominent Bangladesh during the dawn of our Common Era which was in close contact with China.[2] In any case, in the context of Zheng He's voyages, we have seen the name "Bangladesh" with vivid description of it. While space does not allow me to go into detail, I want to highlight a special gift the government of Bangladesh presented to China, creating a great sensation in Ming China. The Ming named the gift *qi lin* 麒麟

---

[2]Refer to what I alluded to in Chapter 4 regarding China's contacts with the Indian Ocean state of "Huangzhi" in Chinese records. I firmly believe this state has been wrongly identified as Kanjipuram/Kanjivaram, which did not have such ancient prominence. There is no other ancient state that could fit the Chinese description of "Huangzhi," except one located in present-day Bangladesh. I expect future research by other scholars to vindicate my proposition.

(unicorn), a famed mythical animal that has never been seen on Earth. Chinese history books confirmed that Bangladesh presented a unicorn to China in 1414. The Ming palace created a painting of it, while a poem praising the animal was written by the grand academician of the imperial court, Shen Du 沈度 (1357–1434), entitled "Tribute to the Unicorn that Brings Auspicious Omen 瑞应麒麟赞颂." This painting is preserved in the Palace Museum of Taipei and can be seen online (as well as many imitations). However, the so-called "unicorn that brings auspicious omen" was actually an ordinary African giraffe![3] As the Chinese had never seen a giraffe before, they believed it was a real unicorn. As the appearance of a unicorn was considered to be an auspicious omen, and the augury for appearance of a sage, the Bangladesh gift arrived in Ming China with a bang, giving the Emperor a tremendous boost in reputation because the "sage" to appear would be none other than Emperor Chengzu himself.

In international circles, Zheng He often gained the title "Admiral" and his seven voyages were described as "the rise of the Chinese navy," neither of which are historically true. The ships were not warships, not fitted with cannons (China was not making cannons at that time, as pointed out by Hegel). A large portion of those on board, apart from the sailors, were civilians, including Buddhist monks and scholars. During his 23-year reign, Emperor Chengzu had two major military war fronts: Annam and Mongolia. The Ming–Annam conflict had a complicated background, initially caused by north–south fighting within the Indochina peninsula. Emperor Chengzu sent an officer whose name was Li Qi 李錡 (dates unknown) to

---

[3]This episode tells us that a Bangladesh existed a long time ago and it was a prominent Muslim country. Bengal never produced any giraffes, but the Bangladesh of the 15th century thrived with foreign trade and could have easily imported a couple of giraffes from Africa, which was not far away. Why would Bangladesh make such a presentation? Was 15th century Bangladesh aware that the Chinese fancied the unicorn and did they resolve to make the Chinese believe the giraffe was the legendary unicorn?

**Chapter 7: Civilization Highway Damaged but Extended**

188

fact-find as the Annam government (established by a usurper) was deceiving him while people were arriving from the peninsula

with conflicting reports. The Annam government attacked Li Qi's mission and tried to kill him. Li Qi survived the attack and returned to report to Emperor Chengzu who was infuriated and sent a large force of 800,000 soldiers to vanquish the Annam usurper regime in 1407–1408. The Ming Emperor personally led five expeditions against Mongolia from 1409 to 1424. The last two expeditions occurred after Zheng He returned from his sixth voyage. Emperor Chengzu's Mongolian expeditions and Zheng He's voyages were in opposite directions, but what the Emperor spent on war with Mongolia far exceeded that of Zheng He's voyages.

**The 15th century Bangladesh gift to China (an imitation of the Ming court painting)**

The Emperor had a close confidant named Yao Guangxiao 姚广孝 (1335–1418), who was a Buddhist monk (dharma name—Daoyan 道衍) and had become the think tank of the Emperor in Beijing even before Emperor Chengzu was enthroned. Reverend Daoyan (or Yao Guangxiao) played a decisive role in encouraging the Prince of Yan, Zhu Di, to revolt and march on the imperial capital of Nanjing. After Zhu Di succeeded and became Emperor Chengzu, he liked the monk so much that he gave him a lay name and imperial costumes to sit in the court to deliberate important state affairs and policies. However, Reverend Daoyan insisted on remaining a monk and lived in the temple after his imperial duties were finished. Zheng He was the offspring of the ruling family of Bokhara (present-day Uzbekistan). His great great grandfather served in the Mongol Yuan Dynasty as governor of Yunnan.

CHINA: A 5,000-YEAR ODYSSEY

During childhood, Zheng He's name was Hajji Mahmud Shamsuddin. When Zhu Yuanzhang's forces recovered Yunnan, Shamsuddin became a captive and was taken to Zhu Yuanzhang's palace as a eunuch with the new Chinese name Zheng He. Reverend Daoyan converted him into a Buddhist follower with the dharma name Fujixiang 福吉祥. It must have been at the suggestion of Reverend Daoyan that the Emperor appointed Zheng He as commanding officer of the voyages, meaning there was a Buddhist motivation behind the Zheng He expeditions. On Zheng He's missions, there was also an Arabic and Persian language interpreter named Ma Huan 马欢 (1380–1460). The surname "Ma" was usually an abbreviation for "Mohamed," indicating he was Muslim. Ma left behind a famous account briefly introducing some of the countries contacted by the mission. This account was entitled *Yingya shenglan* 瀛涯胜览.[4] In Ma Huan's account introducing the "State of Guli 古里国" (Kozhikode/Calicut), he wrote that there were five castes in Kozhikode: Muslims 回回, Nankun 南昆 (the Nairs), chiti 哲地 (the rich), Geling 革令 (Kling), and Mugua 木瓜 (the Mukkuwar/Mukkuwa outcaste). This account is very informative, constituting the earliest history of the Kerala society in southern India. Ma Huan also made an interesting, but somewhat erroneous, narration, which I translate as follows.

> The king is a Nair and a follower of Buddhism…. The king and the people of the state refrain from eating beef. The great chiefs are Muslims who refrain from eating pork. The king entered into an agreement with the Muslims: You refrain from eating beef, and we shall refrain from eating pork. We respect each other's interdict. This is how they live today. The king made a bronze Buddha statue called "Nainar 乃纳儿." He built a Buddha temple. The Buddha's altar is made of bronze tiles. There is a well beside the temple. At daybreak, the king goes there and draws water from the well to wash the Buddha statue.

---

[4] The English translation of this account has been widely circulated and was published in 1970 under the title *The Overall Survey of the Ocean's Shores*.

**Chapter 7: Civilization Highway Damaged but Extended**

This account is, indeed, a valuable record of life in Kerala in the 15th century. But, Ma Huan mistakenly identifies Hinduism as Buddhism. There is an important revelation in this mistake, namely, Ma Huan, Zheng He, the Ming rulers, and the Ming Chinese still thought of India as the land of Buddha. We know Emperor Chengzu was a Buddhist and had a Buddhist monk, Reverend Daoyan/Yao Guangxiao, as his imperial courtier and right-hand man. This "land of Buddha" confusion must have boosted the enthusiasm behind Zheng He's expeditions to the Indian Ocean. I think this point has been overlooked by many Chinese and international historians who studied the Zheng He episode.

In short, the seven expeditions of Zheng He were very unusual events in Ming China and should not be construed as a Chinese attempt to dominate the Indian Ocean. We see no follow-up activities after the death of Zheng He, which marked the end of this unusual episode. During a period when maritime activities were prohibited, the Ming Dynasty was not in tune with the global trend of maritime exploration. The two great navigators of the 15th century, Zheng He and Christopher Columbus, symbolized the two different development roads of Chinese civilization vis-à-vis the Western Brave New World. While the latter rode the sea waves to reach all shores on Earth (including the Chinese coast), the former remained a continental common entity of destiny and turned its back toward the Pacific Ocean. Though the Ming Dynasty was replaced by the Manchu Qing Dynasty in the 17th century, this "turning-the-back-toward-the-sea" Chinese mood did not change until the 19th century, by which time it was too late.

The Chinese common entity of destiny of the Ming Dynasty ended in a strange and perplexing way. The final Ming emperor Zhu Youjian 朱由检 (1611–1644) ascended the throne at the age of 18 and had potential to become a great ruler. He led a frugal life, refraining from sexual indulgence, working extremely hard, and improving in administration. By that time, China had discovered an effective strategy in defending against the northern invaders. The Great Wall was renovated and fortified from Beijing toward the sea coast, and a kind of "Gate of China" was built at Shanhaiguan 山海关 (now under jurisdiction of Qinhuangdao in Hebei province). The name "Shanhaiguan" denotes the "pass through mountains and sea." With a strong force stationed there, China's northern security was more or less ensured. The last Ming emperor appointed an able general, with a huge army, to station there.

However, two powerful peasant uprisings arose, one led by Li Zicheng 李自成 (1606–1645) in Shaanxi province and the other led by Zhang Xianzhong 张献忠 (1606–1647) in Sichuan province. The Ming government virtually collapsed under the weight of these two rebellions. Li Zicheng occupied Xi'an 西安, proclaiming himself "great successful king 大顺王," and led his "great successful army 大顺军" of 500,000 men to march on Beijing. After three months of fierce fighting, Li Zicheng's force occupied Beijing in 1644. The last Ming emperor committed suicide, hanging himself on a tree within the palace compound in Beijing. At that juncture, the crucial Ming general for China's security, Wu Sangui 吴三桂 (1612–1678), who commanded a huge army stationed at Shanhaiguan, and whose duty was to defend China against the likely invasion of the Manchu force from the northeast, chose neither to protect the Ming Emperor from Li Zicheng's rebel force nor continue to defend China against Manchu invasion. Instead, after the Emperor's death, he opened the gate of Shanhaiguan to invite the Manchu army to invade China. This baffling episode led to the demise of the Ming Dynasty.

# CHAPTER 8

# MANCHU CHINA AND THE CHALLENGE OF THE SEA

We now enter the 17th century, a crucial juncture in world history. The European continent, including Britain, was rising and expanding its influence worldwide. The Industrial Revolution was gathering momentum. China, supposed to be the "center of the world" according to the theory of Sinocentrism, curiously could not survive under its native administration, but instead had to invite a foreign nation-state (Manchu) to lead its odyssey along the civilization highway. The Manchu Qing Dynasty 清朝 (1644–1911) was the second time (the first being Mongol Yuan) China was ruled by non-natives, with inevitable national repression. One of its most hated rules was to force every man in China to shave his head and keep a long queue in the back. If "kill the Tartar" was the universal Chinese revolt mantra against the Mongol Yuan during the mid-14th century, patriotic Chinese revolted against the Manchu Empire at the end of the 19th century by cutting the queues on their heads, which were to them symbols of slavery.

**The Manchu hairstyle for men**

However, Manchu Qing was different from Mongol Yuan in many respects. Mongols forced their way into China on horseback with bows and arrows, but Manchus (also on horseback with bows and arrows) were invited into Beijing and interior China by Ming generals Wu Sangui, Shang Kexi 尚可喜 (1604–1676), and Geng Zhongming 耿仲明 (1604–1649). The trio virtually paved the way for Manchu conquest. Furthermore,

while Mongol Yuan ruled China in a distinct alien style, Manchu Qing completely integrated itself into the Chinese common entity.

## I. The Thriving Period from Kangxi to Qianlong

It is noticeable that Chinese intellectuals and common people refer to Manchu rulers by their era name rather than their posthumous title, unlike with all previous dynasties. "Kangxi 康熙" was the reign title of Emperor Aisin Gioro Xuanye (1654–1722) and his posthumous title was "Shengzu 圣祖" (sacred patriarch). People call him "Emperor Kangxi 康熙皇帝" to show more intimacy, if not affection. He reigned 61 years (1661–1722), the longest reign in Chinese history. His grandson Aisin Gioro Hongli (1711–1799) could have broken this record, but refrained from doing so out of filial piety to his grandfather. Called "Emperor Qianlong 乾隆皇帝," he abdicated after completing his 60th year (reigned 1735–1795) and survived four more years as imperial father (Chinese term, "super emperor 太上皇"). What is called the "thriving period from Emperor Kangxi to Emperor Qianlong 康乾盛世" is the reign of these two, most long lived, Chinese emperors with Emperor Yongzheng 雍正皇帝 (reigned 1722–1735) in between. There had never been such a long (134 years) "thriving period" in Chinese history.

During the Kangxi Era (1661–1722), the Chinese population exceeded 100 million for the first time. During the Qianlong Era (1735–1795), the Chinese population increased to over 300 million, one-third of humanity. Both the size of China's national economy and its labor skill (including per acre yield) during the "thriving period from Kangxi to Qianlong" surpassed all previous times. China's economic volume was approximately one quarter of the world, making it the world's greatest economic power. Liang Qichao 梁启超 (1873–1929), famous modern Chinese scholar and failed reformer of 1898, called this period the "Renaissance of China." New books created include: *kangxi zidian* 康熙字典 (the Kangxi Dictionary) and the

world-famous Kangxi Encyclopedia, the Chinese title of which is *gujin tushu jicheng* 古今图书集成 (literally, a collection of information from all books of all time)—an emulation of the *Great Compendium of Yongle*. During this period, we see publication of important history canons such as *The 24 Dynastic Annals* 二十四史 and *shitong* 十通 (literally, 10 general reference books).[1] Publication of books in China during the "thriving period from Kangxi to Qianlong" exceeded the total number of books published in all other countries. Manchu Qing emperors, especially Emperor Qianlong, made the "great civilization-state" of China world-famous.

Emperor Kangxi had many eminent Catholic missionaries of the Society of Jesus (the Jesuits) around him. Since the renowned Reverend Matteo Ricci (1552–1610) of Italy distinguished himself as the first Jesuit in China during the Ming Dynasty, many European Jesuits had followed him. The French Jesuit Reverend Joachim Bouvet (1656–1730) arrived at the court of Emperor Kangxi and became a conduit between the Manchu Emperor and King Louis XIV of France. On Bouvet's second visit to China in 1698, he brought another French Jesuit father,

---

[1]During the Qianlong Era, the imperial court published the "three general reference books" (三通), that is, *tongdian* 通典 (general reference book of historical institutions and regulations), *tongzhi* 通志 (general reference book of historical events), and *wenxian tongkao* 文献通考 (general reference book of historical documents), and the supplementary volumes to them, that is, *xu tongdian* 续通典 (supplementary volume of the general reference book of historical institutions and regulations), *xu tongzhi* 续通志 (supplementary volume of the general reference book of historical events), and *xu wenxian tongkao* 续文献通考 (supplementary volume of the general reference book of historical documents), in addition to *Qingchao tongdian* 清朝通典 (supplementary volume of the general reference book of historical institutions and regulations compiled during the Qing Dynasty), *Qingchao tongzhi* 清朝通志 (supplementary volume of the general reference book of historical events compiled during the Qing Dynasty), and *Qingchao wenxian tongkao* 清朝文献通考 (supplementary volume of the general reference book of historical documents compiled during the Qing Dynasty). Emperor Qianlong's court established a special office for compilation and publication. Later, people added a supplementary volume to *Qingchao wenxian tongkao* 清朝文献通考 (supplementary volume of the general reference book of historical documents compiled during the Qing Dynasty), constituting the series of 10 reference books.

Jean-François Foucquet (1665–1741). Bouvet and Foucquet stayed in Kangxi's palace and translated *Yijing* 易经 (Book of Change) into French. Foucquet returned to France in 1721 with over 4,000 Chinese classics, which he donated to the French royal library, now the Bibliothèque Nationale de France. In October 2011, Taipei's Palace Museum held an exhibition called "Special Exhibition of Emperor Kangxi and the 'Sun King/le Roi-Soleil' Louis XIV 康熙大帝與太阳王路易十四特展," including rare documents and paintings. On display was a letter of Louis XIV addressed to Emperor Kangxi expressing good wishes. The communications between these two prominent rulers of East and West have become a famous event in world history.

**Portrait of Emperor Kangxi**

Beginning at the end of Ming, the so-called "Chinese rites controversy" arose in Europe. This was a debate between the Jesuits on one hand and the Franciscans and Dominicans on the other regarding the method of preaching in Asia, with special reference to China. As China was so incompatible with Europe in culture, Matteo Ricci began to regard Confucius as a sage. He, and subsequent Jesuits, allowed Chinese converts to keep the *Tablet of Deities* 神主牌 for homage to "Heaven 大," "Earth

地," "Monarch 君," "Ancestors 亲," and "Confucius 师." Franciscans and Dominicans were strongly opposed to such a practice. A great debate on this issue raged in the Catholic community throughout Europe. China's prestige was high, and Emperor Kangxi had survived the tenures of many popes of Rome. Though the Jesuits were in the minority, the influence of Emperor Kangxi was considerable in support of them. This influence was indirectly reflected by the fact that the highly authoritative institution "Congregation for the Propagation of the Faith" in Rome initially sided with the Franciscans and Dominicans in 1645, but changed its stance in 1656 to side with the Jesuits. After all, Catholicism was conservative and uncompromising at that time. In 1706, however, Pope Clement XI banned continuation of the Jesuits' practice, which was reaffirmed by Pope Benedict XIV in 1742, who also declared an end to the debate. This European development greatly infuriated Emperor Kangxi. In 1720, he banned Catholic missionary activities in China. Emperor Yongzheng reiterated this ban in 1723 and began to strictly implement it. The significance of this episode is far beyond a mere dispute of religious affairs. It was unprecedented that a Chinese ruler could have such wide influence in Europe within the Catholic community.

Chinese territory expanded to its historical maximum during the "thriving period from Kangxi to Qianlong" with Manchuria (northeast) and Xinjiang (northwest) being added, while Tibet remained firmly within the Chinese common entity. In 1755, Emperor Qianlong fought Junggar and occupied Ili 伊犁. In 1757, the Emperor conquered the northern range of Tianshan 天山 and made Junggar disappear from the earth. Emperor Qianlong named this new addition "Xinjiang 新疆" (new territory) and established an army headquarter at Ili to control Xinjiang. In the wake of the Opium War (1840–1842) and "Treaty of Nanjing 南京条约" (1842), Russia vied with other Western powers to claim a share of China and forced Manchu China to sign the "Treaty of Kulja" (also known as the "Tacheng Protocol 塔城条约"), taking a large area of northern Xinjiang (present-day Kazakhstan, Kyrgyzstan, and Tajikistan). We can see the large expansion of Chinese territory under the reign of Emperor Qianlong.

The "Northeast 东北" of China today is the home of the Manchu race. Ancestors of the Manchu were Nurchen, who severely tortured the Song Dynasty. The Manchu also had kinship with the Mongols. During the "thriving period from Kangxi to Qianlong," Manchu China had cordial relations with Mongol tribes. Thus, the Chinese common entity became free of external invasion from the north. This was an advantage never previously enjoyed by Chinese civilization. In addition, the Korean peninsula was a friendly neighbor of Manchu China (unlike when it threatened the security of Tang China). In comparison with the native dynasties since Han China, Manchu China had the best surrounding international environment, that is, until the Opium War. Unity within the valleys of the two great rivers, Huanghe and Yangtze, was also solid during Manchu China. Manchu Qing represented an enlarged version of the Chinese common entity of destiny.

All treaties signed by China with European powers were unequal, except the "Treaty of Nerchinsk 尼布楚条约" signed in 1689 with Russia, the first modern international treaty signed between China and a power. Four years later, Emperor Kangxi allowed establishment in the capital (Beijing) of a "Russian house 俄馆" and allowed a trade group, not exceeding 200 people, to stay there for 80 days within each year (this facility was not to be shared by any other foreign country). All this indicates that, based on the principle of equality, Manchu China could establish modern diplomatic relations with any country it wished. This fact greatly weakens the theoretical base of Fairbank's Sinocentrism assertion that without using force, Britain and other Western powers could not establish normal diplomatic relations with China because, he alleged, China was obsessed with a traditional "tribute system." Incidentally, participating in the negotiation of the "Treaty of Nerchinsk," on the Manchu

Chapter 8: Manchu China and the Challenge of the Sea

Chinese side, were two European Jesuit fathers, Reverend Thomas Pereira (1645–1708) of Portugal (Chinese name Xu Risheng 徐日升) and Reverend Jean Francois Gerbillon (1654–1707) of France (Chinese name Zhang Cheng 张诚). Both knew the sophistication, treachery, and nuances of modern diplomacy practiced in the Western world. Hence, Russians could not take advantage of the innocent Chinese civilization. This sharply contrasts with the way the "Treaty of Nanjing" was negotiated between Manchu China and Britain in 1842, as well as subsequent unequal treaties in which China was completely manipulated by Western powers. In 1726, a Russian delegation participated in a six-month negotiation in Beijing with Emperor Yongzheng's government and concluded the "Kyakhta Treaty 恰克图条约," which was also an equal bilateral agreement.

Mongol, Manchu, and Tibet formed a close alliance within the Chinese common entity. The Manchu Dynasty worked hard and played a crucial role in consolidating the Tibetan, especially the Dalai administration's, position within this Chinese common entity. The Manchu Qing's appeasement policy toward Mongol was due to Mongol's close affinity with Tibet. All Manchu Qing imperial documents used four languages: Chinese, Manchu, Mongolian, and Tibetan. The largest Lama Temple outside Tibet was the "Yonghegong 雍和宫" (Yonghe Palace) in Beijing. It was the home and birthplace of Emperor Yongzheng, who gave it to the Tibetans as a center for lamas to gather. Emperor Qianlong renovated it, making it into the magnificent Lama Temple. There were also lama temples in the Manchu summer capital of Chengde 承德.

Tibetan culture is firmly built on the concept of rebirth. Today, people in Tibet say: "We rely on the Communist Party for our present life. We rely on the Dalai Lama for our next life." Against a universal background of popular conviction in human evolution, it is rather difficult to manage a society that still regards the Dalai Lama as a deity, while political authorities are in the

hands of laymen. There was once the episode of a "counterfeit Dalai Lama." In 1680, when the fifth Dalai Lama died, the highest officer of the Tibetan local government, Sangye Gyatso, withheld news of the death and continued to issue orders in the name of the fifth Dalai Lama. Sangye Gyatso also secretly installed a boy, Tshangs Dbyangs Rgyamtsho, as the new Dalai Lama. In 1696, Emperor Kangxi was furious when he found out what happened. In 1705, Sangye Gyatso was killed during riots. Emperor Kangxi ordered the arrest of the "counterfeit Dalai Lama," Tshangs Dbyangs Rgyamtsho, who was detained before escaping custody and totally disappeared. According to recent findings, he changed his name and preached in Inner Mongolia until his death.

This was an important lesson for the Manchu Qing court. It subsequently instituted an elaborate procedure for creation of the "living Buddha" Dalai Lama. First, there were rules about discovery of the reincarnated "soul boy 灵 童" and it was determined to draw lots from the Golden Urn to decide the "real reincarnation boy" from among several candidates. Then, the "real reincarnation boy" had to be given pre-novice ordination and approval by the other equally sacred "Banchan Erdeni" (the Panchen Lama). Finally, this had to be approved by the central government of China. During the fourth moon of 1757, Emperor Qianlong sent National Preceptor Canggya to Tibet to find the "reincarnation boy" to be installed as the new Dalai Lama. In 1758, Qambê Gyaco was confirmed as the prospective Holiness. On the 10th of the 7th moon, 1762, there was a ceremony in Lhasa's Potala Palace to install Qambê Gyaco as Dalai Lama. Emperor Qianlong's affirmative edict was read at the ceremony without the specific appointment order. Also, the edict failed to declare that he was the eighth Dalai Lama (because the sixth Dalai was still regarded as the "counterfeit Dalai Lama"). Not until 1781 were the Emperor's golden appointment letter and gold seal received, formally confirming Qambê Gyaco as the eighth Dalai Lama and delegating political power to him to rule Tibet. This confirmation also removed the infamy of "counterfeit Dalai Lama" from the sixth Dalai.

During the 11th moon of 1792, Emperor Qianlong issued the well-known "Imperial Possession of Rehabilitation within the Constitution" (also called "Imperial Possession Statute in the Aftermath Twenty-nine" or "New Order of the Tibet Regulation Twenty-nine" [in Chinese, it is called *qin ding zang nei shan hou zhang cheng er shi jiu tiao* 钦定藏内善后章程二十九条]), which empowered the Manchu resident minister (驻藏大臣) to supervise the Tibetan administration and make political decisions in consultation with the Dalai Lama and Panchen Lama. All officials in the Tibetan government had to obey decisions of the resident minister. It was also the duty of the resident minister to establish and command the Tibetan army, which he would inspect twice per year. Moreover, the important duty of the resident minister was to ensure that succession of the Dalai Lama and Panchen Lama occurred smoothly. This "Imperial Constitution" for Tibet made Tibet an administrative unit within the unified Chinese common entity.

The "thriving period from Kangxi to Qianlong" eliminated the vicious cycle within Tibet between external aggression and internal chaos, hence making an important contribution to the security and stability of Tibet. It vanquished Junggar in Xinjiang and relieved Tibet of northwestern invasions. It sent Manchu troops into Tibet five times to restore law and order. At the end of the Qianlong Era, the Gurkha Kingdom (present-day Nepal) invaded Tibet twice. In 1793, Emperor Qianlong sent troops to repel the Gurkha invasion and made Gurkha, Bhutan, and Dremojong (present-day Sikkim) Chinese vassals.

## II. Continental Common Entity Challenged by the Sea

If the "thriving period from Kangxi to Qianlong" had occurred in isolation, it may have been the golden period of Chinese history. Unfortunately, China was not an isolated island, but instead a close neighbor of the Pacific Ocean with a coastline of 18,000 kilometers. As it was born within the "Himalaya Sphere" and a common geographical entity was carved by Huanghe and Yangtze, which was converted into a common entity of destiny, Chinese civilization grew with a continental mind-set, thinking of the coastline as its outer limit. The ideas of Laozi thought of "water being supremely perfect" and Dong Zhongshu thought of "water sustaining life, while without it there is death" were regarded as eternal truth in Chinese tradition. However, China had overlooked the fact that, on our earth, the home of water is the sea, but the sea water is not "supremely perfect" at all, let alone being "sustenance for life." The sea was the blind spot of Chinese civilization for millennia, and Chinese civilization paid a heavy price for this millennial ignorance of the importance of the sea.

Before the 19th century, China had a peaceful coexistence with the sea, going thousands of years without any aggression via the sea. The challenge to Chinese civilization came from the world of nation-states, from Western powers and hegemons that chose to threaten, harass, invade, repress, and exploit Chinese civilization that was on its odyssey along the civilization highway. It was the innocent Chinese civilization highway being challenged by a wicked highway on the sea that may be termed "Gunboat Road." China was connecting the world with its Silk Road, while the modern Western world was connecting China with its Gunboat Road. Today, as China starts its project of "One Belt One Road" to interconnect the world, it must not forget the historical lessons. The Silk Road, on the continent, may have been a little bumpy and even blocked by high mountains, but it would open gradually. On the high seas, the Gunboat Road would definitely not allow the Silk Road to merrily have smooth sailing.

The earliest Western "nation-state" to invade the East along the Gunboat Road was the Dutch East India Company, which ruled southern Taiwan from 1624 to 1662. The Dutch colonial authority in Taiwan recruited about 10,000 Chinese immigrants from coastal areas of mainland China to Taiwan to reclaim land and develop the economy. The Dutch government appeased

Taiwan's aborigines but heavily taxed immigrant farmers. In 1652, there was an immigrant revolt led by Guo Huaiyi 郭怀一 (?-1652). One quarter of the immigrants (4,000–5,000 people) joined the revolt, which was cruelly put down by the colonialists. Nearly 4,000 immigrants were killed by Dutch bullets or hunger. Holland was a tiny European country relatively civilized, progressive, amicable, and prosperous, yet turned out to be a barbaric colonial nation. This is a typical manifestation of the nation-state rhythm, proving the popular English saying: "Gentlemen at home, scoundrels abroad."

1n 1661, Zheng Chenggong 郑成功 (1624–1662), son of a Ming general (and ex-pirate), called "Koxinga" by the Dutch, drove away the Dutch colonialists and recovered Taiwan. He is remembered by the people of Taiwan as "The sage king who created Taiwan 开台圣王." He settled his family and troops in Taiwan and mobilized large numbers of people from his homeland, Fujian province, as immigrants to Taiwan. He died a year after his victory. His son Zheng Jing 郑经 (1642–1681) succeeded him as King of Taiwan, making it a pro-Ming kingdom independent from the Manchu Empire. Taiwan became a land of traditional China adhering to Confucian teaching and continuing the Ming political system. Chinese culture was disseminated over the entire island. From that time on, Taiwan has really been part of the Chinese common entity.

After great debate in the Manchu court, Emperor Kangxi decided to annex Taiwan into the Manchu Qing fold. He appointed Shi Lang 施琅 (1621–1696), an ex-general of Zheng Chenggong's army who had defected to Manchu, to conquer Taiwan in 1683. The Manchu government put Taiwan under jurisdiction of Fujian province and neglected it. Shi Lang became the ruler of Taiwan and prohibited immigration to Taiwan from Guangdong. Later, the Manchu government promulgated the "sea ban 海禁" order prohibiting Chinese ships from sailing to sea, greatly hurting Taiwan's development. Though they were part of the Chinese common entity, people of Taiwan didn't feel warm affection from the motherland.

Dutch occupation of Taiwan was only the prelude to the sea's challenge to Chinese civilization. The real, severe challenge came from Great Britain. From the reign of Queen Elizabeth I (1533–1603), Britain rose as a strong power. In 1602, she wrote a letter addressed to the *Emperour of Cathaye* (Emperor of China) and entrusted a merchant, George Weymouth, to deliver it to Beijing. Weymouth sailed to China, but turned back without reaching the Chinese coast. The Queen's letter was not delivered, but is preserved today.[2] Queen Elizabeth established the British East India Company to trade with India and the "Far Eastern" countries (mainly China). The Company's huge maritime ships called "East Indiaman" sailed from Britain to India, then to China, and then returned directly to Britain. In 1793, the British government sent George Macartney (1737–1806) as "Envoy Extraordinary and Minister Plenipotentiary" to China, where Emperor Qianlong warmly received him. This first British embassy delegation received by China should have been celebrated as an important international event between Europe and China.

Macartney was a very sharp observer. He praised Emperor Qianlong on one hand, but pointed out some Chinese weaknesses on the other. For instance, while Emperor Qianlong purposely tried to demonstrate Chinese military power before the British guests, the soldiers were using primitive weapons—bows and arrows. The shining helmets worn by soldiers were made of paper, as Macartney discovered. For his part, Macartney wanted to demonstrate the industrial superiority of Britain before his Chinese hosts. Electricity had not been discovered yet. Industrial Europe could make automatic clocks and toys by using simple spring technology (tighten the spring and let it stretch back, creating movement). Because of the attachment of sound devices, these clocks and toys could sing. They were called "singsongs" in

[2]British political activist and geographer John Barrow (1764–1848) published it in his edited book *Captain Cook's Voyages of Discovery* (Edinburgh: Adam & Charles Black, 1860).

the market. A large amount of "singsongs" were carried by the Macartney delegation to China, calculated to impress the Chinese. To his surprise, Emperor Qianlong's palaces in Beijing and Chengde were already well stocked with them as there were European mechanics to make and service the automatic gadgets in the Manchu Chinese palaces.

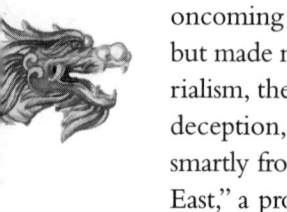

This Macartney embassy delegation was a weather vane of an oncoming hurricane. China's ruling elite saw the warning signs, but made no preparation for it. Wily and inhumane British imperialism, the most powerful in the world, excelled in camouflage, deception, and distortion of facts. It sailed the Gunboat Road smartly from the "Far West" to become the hegemon of the "Far East," a process of greed and cruelty interwoven with hypocrisy and double standards. It has created great confusion for historical analysis within the global academic circle. While successfully obtaining its selfish gains, it demonized the countries, China in particular, that dared to resist it. It muddied international opinion and led the intellectual elite of China and other developing countries down the garden path. By the time you reach the end of this chapter, you will realize this sharp critique from me (based on my decades of research) is no exaggeration.

## III. Opium Imperialism Along the Gunboat Road[3]

Professor Fairbank described the "Opium War" as China's entry into the society of the modern world. He said British gunboats helped open the tightly closed China gate. Fairbank actually

---

[3]Both "Gunboat Road" and "Opium Imperialism" are my coinage. The Gunboat Road phrase is a contrast to the Silk Road. The latter is a highway in peacetime, while the former is a path to war. The latter is a two-way road and the former is a unidirectional charging and assaulting way. The latter is a highway of beneficial commodity transportation, and the former a passageway of colonialism, imperialism, or other forms of international domination. "Opium Imperialism" is a coined term based on my PhD and postdoctoral research decades ago. Let me go ahead and share here something unique from two of my publications: *China and the Brave New World: The Origins of the Opium War* in 1978 and *Triton and Dragon: Studies on Nineteenth Century China and Imperialism* in 1986.

covered the dirtiest page of modern civilization with the blanket of his authoritative observations.

Britain was the pathfinder of the Gunboat Road. The British development strategy was to first obtain supremacy on the high seas, then obtain monopsony in the world trade of Chinese tea, allowing only the "East Indiaman" (the world's largest cargo ships of the British East India Company) to carry Chinese tea from the only port, Guangzhou (Canton), to all major world destinations. World consumption of tea increased by leaps and bounds, but the Manchu Qing government restricted overseas trade of tea to the lone port at Guangzhou/Canton. In addition, only 13 private Chinese companies (known in British records as "Hong merchants") could sell tea to foreigners. This suited the British strategy perfectly (although they complained and protested). The British East India Company would pay any price to drive away all European competitors in buying tea in order to become the sole dealer with the 13 Chinese companies, gaining monopsony (the buyer's monopoly) and making it the British buyer's market for Guangzhou/Canton tea. As the Canton government ruthlessly bled white the 13 companies, the East India Company came to their rescue and made them its Chinese agents. Tea left the Chinese coast via the "East Indiaman" and reached the British Isles first. Then, taxes were paid to the British treasury and the tea was shipped to North America and other British colonies. Britain could exact maximum benefit from this tea trade, but the people in the colonies resented this mercantilist profiteering. On December 16, 1773, the famous "Boston Tea Party" protest broke out. Newly arrived tea chests from Britain were thrown overboard, igniting the revolution of American independence.

The monopsonistic and mercantilist profiteering strategies of Britain, though barbarous, were highly lucrative. However, Britain did not have sufficient money to pay for the ever increasing demand of Chinese tea in the world market. British colonialists then resorted to an even more barbarous and inhumane strategy. The "British Raj" (British-Indian government), established by the East India Company, set up a very important department (a ministry) called the "Board of Customs, Salt, and Opium." Its specific task was to produce opium on Indian soil and sell it to China so the extremely profitable trade of Chinese tea would not be starved of capital. This department/ministry invested money in research for development of this India–China opium trade. Dr D. Butter, an opium expert at the East India Company's Benaras (present-day Varanasi) factory (warehouse), disclosed that their job was to produce opium cake that would create a smell greatly liked by Chinese consumers when the cake was broken for consumption. William Jardine (1784–1843), the world famous/infamous opium trader, testified (to British Parliament in the 1840 debate on waging war against China) that he had been asked by the British-Indian opium ministry to carry the East India Company's opium in various packets to determine the favorite of Chinese opium consumers. The British-Indian government had done an excellent job sending life-killing opium from India to China and making it an attractive commodity for Chinese opium addicts. Britons knew what harm they were doing to humanity, but Britain had to depend on it to establish and consolidate the "sun-never-sets" empire. Britons were, after all, Britons! Apparently, they liked to sustain the "pull of an English gentleman" even when they were taking up the most despicable dealings. The East India Company pretended to have nothing to do with this most deadly drug trafficking. It auctioned company opium at Calcutta (now Kolkata) to British-Indian "private traders" on credit. These British-Indian opium traders shipped the company's opium to China, sold it, and remitted proceeds to the company's "Canton factory" to buy Chinese tea.

Modern Indian writer and thinker Rabindranath Tagore was one of the most severe critics of British opium aggression against China. He described that the British "forced poison down her [China's] throat" with weapons.[4] Though Tagore wrote in a literary style, his description is true to the letter.

---

[4]From Tagore's Bengali writings, *Svadhikara pramattah* (self-arrogance) in 1918, and *Kalantar* (time passing) in 1937. See Tan Chung et al., eds, *Tagore and China* (Beijing: Central Compilation and Translation Press, 2011), 73.

There has always been a way to blame the victim. People might say if the Chinese had no demand for opium, how could anybody force it on them? Of course, Chinese civilization has a fair share of blame for having earned the Chinese people an international reputation as opium addicts, which may be traced back to the hedonistic weakness highlighted earlier in Chapter 6.

Emperor Qianlong's grandson and next-but-one successor Emperor Daoguang 道光皇帝 (reigned 1820–1850) was an opium addict. Earlier, Emperor Yongzheng who led a frugal life had issued an order strictly banning the planting of poppy and opium trade. After his death, the prohibition remained, but was not vigorously implemented, which gave British opium imperialism an opportunity to maneuver. During the Daoguang Era, opium import increased by leaps and bounds, causing increased loss of silver to China. The Manchu government began to take steps to address this rampant British-Indian opium offensive, but the real problem was that the world's most powerful imperialist was creating traffic specifically targeting China for its "primitive accumulation." China was the captured opium importer and victim of Britain's world development strategy, unable to free itself from the claws of the unprecedented opium-trafficking hegemon. This was the true meaning of Tagore's "forcing opium down the Chinese throat" analogy.

Initially, the British–Indian opium ship anchored in the Pearl River estuary off Guangzhou/Canton and Chinese opium vendors went aboard to collect the drug. Later, this was not allowed. The opium ship then moved to "Lintin" (the international name for the Lingding Sea 零丁洋, situated between Macau and Hong Kong), where British–Indian opium traders would send the drug to various points along the Guangdong coast nicknamed *dayaokou* 大窯口 (big kiln mouth) and *xiaoyaokou* 小窯口 (small kiln mouth) to deliver opium to Chinese smugglers. All this was happening under the watch of the Manchu navy, but they did not dare do anything because of the British navy's

**Chapter 8: Manchu China and the Challenge of the Sea**

presence. Delivery boats actually identified themselves using the Union Jack. British naval boats were equipped with guns and rifles, while the Manchu navy had only bows and arrows. How could Manchu China stop this drug trafficking with bows and arrows? In the 1840 British Parliament debate, a member of the opposition Liberal Party, William Edward Gladstone (1809–1898), made the following famous remarks.

> That [British] flag is hoisted to protect an infamous contraband traffic; and if it never were hoisted, except it is now hoisted on the coast of China, we would recoil from its sight with horror.[5]

Gladstone also condemned the Opium War by saying: "A war more unjust in its origin, a war more calculated to cover this country [Britain] with permanent disgrace, I do not know and have not read it."[6] Ironically, later, when Gladstone was British Prime Minister toward the end of the 19th century,[7] he did not yield to public pressure to stop this disgraceful opium trade due to its economic gains for Britain.

In 1974, I published an article entitled "The Britain–China–India Trade Triangle (1771–1840)" in the academic journal *The Indian Economic & Social History Review* that is still remembered and consulted by scholars today. I concluded that as trade ultimately brings balance, the triangular trade balance between China, India, and Britain during the 18th and 19th centuries could be summarized as "Chinese tea for Britons, Indian opium for Chinese, and British Raj for Indians!"

The Opium War (1840–1842), waged by Britain against China, compounded the wrong and injustice. It was a war for endless

---

[5]William Ewart Gladstone, *Hansard's Parliamentary Debates*, Third Series, vol. 53, 800–818; quoted in Tan Chung's *China and the Brave New World*, 215.

[6]Ibid.

[7]He was British Prime Minister for four separate times, 1868–1874, 1880–1885, February–July 1886, and 1892–1894.

continuation of Britain's drug trafficking, with China as the target. Moreover, the Opium War forced China to establish foreign-ruled pockets within the "trade ports" and allowed free entry of foreigners (traders, missionaries, adventurers, and what not), who enjoyed the so-called "extraterritoriality" (free from punishment by Chinese authorities) after they committed crimes on Chinese soil. Foreigners controlled the Chinese customs. Foreign powers continued to wage wars, and force unequal treaties, on China, in addition to charging an "indemnity" against the Chinese government, to be paid from China's customs earnings. Manchu China remained a sovereign entity in name only. The Chinese now had to go through more sufferings than any time in previous history, lamenting that "[T]hey (foreigners) are the chopper and chopping board while we are the fish and meat in between 人为刀俎 我为鱼肉." Under these circumstances, there could not be any Chinese odyssey along the civilization highway.

Similar to the instance cited in Chapter 2, of Professor Fairbank's being misled by his disciples and research assistant, there is another instance, although, like the chicken or egg dilemma, we don't know who misled whom. Fairbank's favorite disciple Hsin-pao Chang (Chinese name 张馨保) published a book *Commissioner Lin and the Opium War* (1964), in which he argued that opium was just an occasion, and not the cause of the war. He remarked: "Had there been an effective alternative to opium, say molasses or rice, the conflict might have been called the Molasses War or Rice War."[8] Have you ever seen an argument as illogical as this? Molasses and rice are essential nutrients for life, while opium is a life killer. How can these two opposite categories be the alternative to one another? We see how desperately Fairbank and his followers tried to whitewash the stain of British "Opium Imperialism" so "Cambridge History" and "Oxford History" can relax and eschew historical details to maintain their purity in history: Whatever blasphemy falls on the image of China is nobody's concern.

---

[8]Hsin-pao Chang, *Commissioner Lin and the Opium War* (1839–1842) (Cambridge: Harvard University Press, 1964), 15.

**Chapter 8: Manchu China and the Challenge of the Sea**

## IV. The Taiping and Boxer Movements

The Taiping Movement (in Chinese, "Celestial Kingdom of Grand Harmony 太平天国," 1851–1864)[9] was an old peasant rebellion with new ideology and Western symbolism. The movement began with the "God Worshipping Society 拜上帝教" organized by Hong Xiuquan 洪秀全 (1814–1864) in Guangdong. Next, in the seventh moon of 1850, Hong Xiuquan asked all members of the God Worshipping Society to assemble at Jintian 金田 Village, Guiping 桂平 County in Guangxi and rise up for an armed rebellion. The uprising unfurled the flag of the "Celestial Kingdom of Grand Harmony" and began its northern expedition. The Taiping army entered Hunan province from Guangxi and received overwhelming support from local peasants. As its fighting strength grew, it continued to march through Hubei, Jiangxi, Anhui, and Jiangsu, conquering Nanjing in 1853. Next, it established a new regime with Nanjing as its capital, ruling a large area of Jiangsu, Zhejiang, Anhui, Jiangxi, Henan, and beyond. It conquered 600 cities before being vanquished in 1864.

**A bronze statue of Hong Xiuquan**

[9]The name of the movement Taiping 太平 could mean "pacifistic" or "grand equality/harmony." Of course, the latter was adopted as the ideal of the new society the movement wished to establish.

Usually, a failed peasant uprising in China was totally suppressed and obliterated. But, the Taiping Movement had the advantage of world coverage, as many foreigners had visited its capital Nanjing. An important document of the movement entitled "Land System of the Celestial Dynasty 天朝田亩制度" was recovered. It was a sort of constitution of the Taiping Kingdom specifically prescribing an ideal society of "sharing land, food, and money 有田同耕，有饭 同食，有衣同穿，有钱同使." It advocated that "[N]o place shall be unequal and no one shall not have enough to eat 无处不均，无人不饱." It was the most progressive scenario ever proclaimed by a Chinese regime.

The Taiping document reiterated liberation of women. It advocated equal status and share for women in land distribution. Women were granted the unprecedented right to join the army and political affairs. The document also advocated the revolutionary practice of "monogamy" (China did not abolish polygamy until the 1950s).

I would say the peasant uprising was both the bright and dark spot in Chinese civilization; bright because it was the only force that could end the bad regime, but dark due to its tremendous destructive power. A few international estimates indicate that casualties among fighters and civilians from the Taiping Movement exceeded that of World War I. Some death toll estimates even go well over 100 million. Even if true, blame cannot be cast entirely on the Taiping Movement. The Taiping uprising had three enemies: The Manchu army, the Hunan Army 湘军, led by Zeng Guofan 曾国藩 (1811–1872), and the Foreign Rifle Brigade 洋枪队. These three forces were as ruthless in killing as were the Taiping fighters. Virtually all the Taiping soldiers died in battle.

As Taiping soldiers did not shave and braid their hair in a queue in the slave-like style imposed by Manchu rule, their long hair fell to their shoulders. The government branded them the "long hair bandits 长毛贼" and their stigmatic image of "terror" was spread (when kids kicked up a row at night, parents would use the image of the "long hair bandits" to frighten them into silence).

Today, these "long hair bandits" have seats on the altar of history. A museum of Taiping history was established in Nanjing in 1958, preserving over 2,000 items left behind by the Taiping Movement.

The name "Boxers" shook the world a 100 years ago. Famous American writer Mark Twain (1835–1910) contributed to their popularity by delivering the "I am a Boxer" speech on November 23, 1900, at the Berkeley Lyceum in New York City. The Chinese name of the movement is *Yi he tuan* 义和团 (literally, a group championing righteousness and harmony) and boxing was the daily exercise of the movement. It broke out at the end of the 19th century and the beginning of the 20th century. Initially, the *Yihetuan* Movement was anti-Manchu. Later, it was utilized by the Manchu regime to target the *yang jiao* 洋教 (literally, ocean religion, that is, Christianity) and *yang ren* 洋人 (literally, ocean people, meaning Europeans and Americans).

**Photograph of a Boxer arrested by Manchu troops**

A special feature of these "righteousness-harmony" Boxers was their belief in the power of "magic boxing 神拳" and its invincibility against foreign bullets. They believed they enjoyed the blessings of the Jade Emperor 玉皇大帝 (the most powerful deity among the non-Buddhist populace), "Patriarch Bodhidharma 达摩老祖," the legendary Guangong 关圣帝君 (of the "Three Kingdoms"), and other deities of folklore. I saw photographs of some tablets of the Boxers preserved in a regiment center in India. One has these 10 Chinese characters *dang lai dong du chuan xiang jiao lao shi zun* 当来东渡传香教老师 尊 (literally, the patriarch of the incense-passing religion who will come to earth and travel east to be with us) inscribed on it. I believe this is the tablet for worshipping Bodhidharma by Boxer fighters. So we see some Indian cultural input in the Boxer Movement.

The Boxer Movement arose from the triangular situation involving government 官, religion 教 (Christianity), and people 民. The last category excluded Chinese Christian converts, regarded as a part of Christian religion. The Movement reflected grievances of the people against the evangelic activities of the Catholic and Christian churches in China in the wake of Western aggression against China.

By the end of the 19th century, a substantial number of the "ocean people," who were bearers of the "White Man's Burden," arrived in China. However, there were a sea of differences between these newly arriving "ocean people" and the earlier Jesuits, such as Matteo Ricci, Diego de Pantoja (1571–1618), Johann Schall von Bell (1591–1666), Ferdinand Verbiest (1623–1688), and many others, who were the cream of Western civilization and virtuous scholars greatly respected by all sections of the Chinese society. These pioneers of the "ocean people" arrived at a time when China was in turmoil, yet no Chinese hated or hurt them. Some happily took government assignments in China during the Ming and Qing dynasties.

"Extraterritoriality" deprived Chinese authorities of the sovereign right to punish lawlessness among foreigners on Chinese soil. Foreign embassies and consulates were busy finding fault with the central and local Chinese administrations in the implementation of treaty provisions. Every treaty signed by the Manchu Chinese government with a Western power had two copies, one in Chinese and the other in the language of the concerned country. If any dispute occurred later, the foreign language version of the treaty would be the authentic document, not the Chinese copy. As Manchu Chinese authorities never had the foreign language expertise to carefully examine the foreign language version of the treaty during negotiation or implementation, whatever the foreign embassies and consulates said about the Chinese "violation" of the treaty provision was unchallenged and the "ocean people" got what they wanted. Also, when any dispute occurred anywhere in China, the foreign mission pressured the Beijing central authority, which in turn pressured the local Chinese government, to resolve the dispute to the satisfaction of the "ocean people." Thus, whenever there was a dispute between Chinese Christian converts and nonconverts, the former would inevitably win. This is how the popular Chinese hatred against "religion" fermented and accumulated.

The Manchu Qing government irresponsibly pampered the Boxers. De facto ruler Empress Dowager Cixi 慈禧太后 (1835–1908), who had just brought an end to the "One Hundred Days Reform 百日维新" in 1898, gave her approval of Boxer activities by writing that "the Boxers are loyal 拳民忠贞" and "their magic can be used 神术可用." The so-called "magic 神术" was that the bare body of the Boxers was bulletproof (which was a myth). As a result, the floodgates were opened in Beijing and Tianjin for the Boxers to unleash terror on the "ocean religion" (Christianity) with the government passively observing.

The Boxers had two targets: *damaozi* 大毛子 (literally, the number-one hairy chaps, meaning the ocean people) and *ermaozi* 二毛子 (literally, the number-two hairy chaps, meaning Chinese who colluded with the ocean people). Actually, only a couple of foreigners were killed by the Boxers. Most of them were protected by the foreign missions. In the "Number-Two Hairy

Chaps" category, the Boxers targeted "One Dragon 一龙" (Emperor Guangxu 光绪皇帝, reigned 1875–1908), "Two Tigers 二虎" (Prince Qing 庆亲王, 1838–1917, and Courtier Li Hongzhang 李鸿章, 1823–1901), and "Thirteen Sheep 十三羊" (high-ranking Manchu Chinese officers). These targets were just symbolic, and the Boxers could not go near any of them. The real victims of the Boxer terror were a large number of common Chinese people. Christian converts bore the brunt, but even students who carried foreign-made pencils and paper were brutalized. There was lawlessness in Beijing and Tianjin especially, with Boxers indulging in arson, looting, and killing while government authorities idly watched.

Eight countries formed a coalition to attack China and occupy Beijing. Boxer fighters were mercilessly killed by foreign bullets (their magic boxing was useless). On September 7, 1901, China signed the most humiliating treaty in history, "Austria–Hungary, Belgium, France, Germany, Great Britain, Italy, Japan, Netherlands, Russia, Spain, United States and China—Final Protocol for the Settlement of the Disturbances of 1900," known as the "Boxer Protocol," or as the "September Seventh National Shame 九七国耻" (to the Chinese people). Clause Six of the Protocol was an indemnity of 450 million taels of silver to be paid to the victors. While the entire Manchu Qing government revenue was only 250 million taels, China had 450 million people, each one of whom had the dubious honor of sharing one tael of the shame and burden for the mischief of the Boxers. It was a heavy loss of Chinese wealth and a great humiliation to Chinese civilization.

Objectively, the Yihetuan Boxer movement demonstrated to the world that Chinese civilization could not be bullied. The insatiably avaricious "nation-state" powers had planned to "cut the Chinese melon" (dividing China into British, French, Russian, German, and Japanese "spheres of influence"), but the Boxer movement burst out to let the world know this could not be done. Fury of the challenge to Chinese civilization by the sea was overwhelmed by the thunder of the Boxers.

**Chapter 8: Manchu China and the Challenge of the Sea**

# CHAPTER 9

# THE AWAKENED LION SHAKING CHINA, NOT THE WORLD

The 20th century was a great century with many firsts: the first motor car, airplane, nuclear power station, bomb, mass production of petroleum and natural gas, high rise and skyscraper, elevator and escalator, organ transplant, in vitro fertilization and Dolly the cloned sheep, computer and Internet service, robot and automation production, and so on, surpassing the previous 20 centuries by 20,000 times in innovation and invention. However, World War I was not fought in 1914 in Europe. It was fought in 1900 on Chinese soil. All the countries of the world that had a respectable modern military force united as "Eight-Nation Alliance" to humiliate China. This was how Chinese civilization inaugurated its 20th century and how the "nation-state" world welcomed Chinese civilization into its midst.

At the end of the 19th century, desire to be rich 富 and strong 强 sank into the heart of Chinese civilization. Realizing that its weaknesses had landed China at the receiving end of the fiercely combatant international environment, it tried to become strong while the decadent Manchu Qing still ruled. In the 1880s, China spent a huge amount to buy two warships from Germany and established its "North Ocean Fleet 北洋舰队," supposedly the strongest in East Asia. This was the same time Japan rose to become a world power. International experts inspected the navies of Japan and China. Japanese warships were smaller, but spic and span, with high battle readiness. The Chinese navy was the opposite, with the sailors' dirty linens hanging on cannons. China's defeat in the China–Japan sea battles of 1894 was a foregone conclusion. China also established a modern army called the "New Army 新军," equipped with rifles made in China. While New Army units were, in most provinces, under command of provincial governors, the overall commander-in-chief was Yuan Shikai 袁世凯 (1859–1916). Ironically, Yuan Shikai and the New Army played a crucial role in stopping China's millennial imperial governance while the "Father of China 国父," Sun Yat-sen 孙中山 (1866–1925), devoted his entire life to creating a new China without success.

# I. Awakening of the Chinese "Sleeping Lion"

"Let the lion sleep, for when she wakes, she will shake the world" is a famous adage attributed to the 19th century French hero Napoléon Bonaparte (1769–1821), which, however, cannot be confirmed. For nearly 200 years, this observation, legendary or historical, has served as a strong analeptic for rejuvenating China.

The world famous "1911 Revolution 辛亥革命" was actually launched by a bunch of enthusiastic soldiers from the New Army in Wuchan 武昌, Hubei province to respond to the revolutionary call of Sun Yat-sen, who was then outside the country. They easily occupied the headquarters of the commanding general of the Hubei–Hunan–Guangdong area, but had no leader of social standing to declare the birth of a new regime. They wanted the commander of the 21st Brigade Li Yuanhong 黎元洪 (1864–1928) to be their leader. Brigadier Li became frightened when his own soldiers were looking for him. He hid in a friend's house, but was dragged from under a bed to assume the role of commanding general of the Hubei–Hunan–Guangdong area and declare creation of the Republic of China 中华民国. This revolutionary call was quickly responded to by 17 commanding generals of China. Their representatives met in Nanjing on New Year's Day of 1912 and elected Sun Yat-sen as the president of the provisional government. Sun immediately negotiated with Yuan Shikai who, in turn, forced the Manchu government to step down and then took the seat of president of the Republic vacated by Sun Yat-sen. Thus, as soon as the new Republic was established, it fell under the control of a warlord.

As Sun Yat-sen was only the provisional president, the first formal president of the Republic of China was warlord Yuan Shikai, sworn in on October 10, 1913, for a five-year term. On December 12, 1915, Yuan Shikai changed the name of the country from "Republic of China 中华民国" to "Empire of China 中华帝国," but did not enthrone himself. This change infuriated the entire country. Cai E 蔡锷 (1882–1916), a

progressive political and military activist, immediately launched a military campaign from Yunnan to overthrow Yuan Shikai. Yuan, seeing his emperor ambition untenable, changed the country's name back to "Republic of China" in March 1916. Three months later, he died.

The biggest event during Yuan Shikai's regime was his being forced to conclude an agreement with Japan conceding to their "Twenty-One Demands." Yuan did try to resist Japanese pressure by leaking the secret negotiations to the United Kingdom and the United States, hoping they might intervene (which they didn't because they were fully engaged with the rising Germany). When Japan realized that Yuan was playing games, it issued an ultimatum that Yuan's government reply within 48 hours, by 6 pm, May 9, 1915. All Japanese civilians in China abruptly withdrew and Japanese warships menacingly arrived at Bohai 渤海 Bay. Japan, the pupil of Western imperialism, surpassed its gurus in ferocity and aggressiveness.

There is a Chinese motto: "Better to be broken jade pieces than an unimpaired mud tile 宁为玉碎，毋为瓦全." Yuan Shikai chose to be just the opposite. He yielded to the Japanese demand and signed on May 9 before the deadline. A student in Hunan province named Peng Chao 彭超 (1896–1915) was overtaken by anguish and cried: "My country is dead!" He cut his finger and wrote with his blood: "I swell not to see my country and family being thus ruined 立志不愿看到国破家亡" and drowned himself in the River Xiang 湘江. Meanwhile, teachers and students in Hunan organized themselves into the "Society of National Shame 国耻会." In Beijing, 200,000 students held a protest. The popular fury also moved Yuan Shikai, who declared May 9 as the "Day of National Shame" for people to remember forever. In fact, it was Yuan Shikai, not Peng Chao, who should have committed suicide with shame. That would have cleansed the stigma of a "traitor" in public opinion.

After Yuan's death, the young Republic of China still remained under warlord control. However, when the Manchu Empire

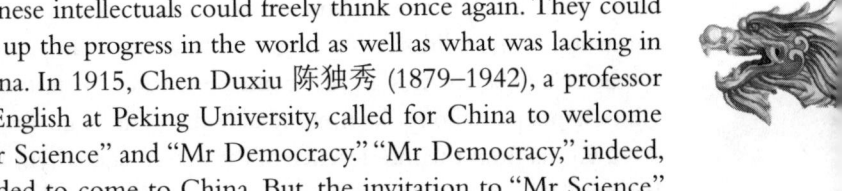

ended, so did its repression on Chinese culture and wisdom. Chinese intellectuals could freely think once again. They could size up the progress in the world as well as what was lacking in China. In 1915, Chen Duxiu 陈独秀 (1879–1942), a professor of English at Peking University, called for China to welcome "Mr Science" and "Mr Democracy." "Mr Democracy," indeed, needed to come to China. But, the invitation to "Mr Science" was rather questionable. Being ahead of other states in productive skills for most of history, China had already been the home of "Mr Science." Scientific spirit in pursuing truth and reality has always been a part of Chinese civilization. The three words *satyam, shivam, sundaram* (the truth, the good, and the beauty) chanted by the Hindus every day in their prayers were disseminated in China over a millennium ago. Chen Duxiu, who went to Japan three times to study English, French, and European literature was, perhaps, not aware of the millennial quintessential Chinese civilization. The "Mr Science" he wanted to invite to China must be a man with blue eyes and a high nose. He seemed to have forgotten the native "Mr Science" or was ignorant of his long existence. I hasten to add that I do not wish to demean Chen Duxiu's contribution to China's modern awakening. But, his weak roots in Chinese civilization was a great handicap for China's real awakening.

Although China did not politically recover from this nightmarish situation, Chinese civilization was slowly awakening. Under the leadership of Chen Duxiu, Hu Shi 胡适 (1891–1962), Lu Xun 鲁迅 (1881–1936), and other progressive Chinese intellectuals, there came a "New Literature Movement 新文学运动" advocating a colloquial in lieu of classical style of writing. This movement, combined with popularization of new types of educational institutions, newspapers and magazines, and so on, spread knowledge and culture to the lower strata and remote areas of China, uplifting hundreds of millions of illiterates and semi-illiterates to the level of the intellectuals. Though people no longer wrote in classical styles, they still loved to read ancient works of art, especially classical style poems. Chinese civilization grew richer, more vibrant, and more robust.

Chapter 9: The Awakened Lion Shaking China, Not the World

Chinese script mistakenly became a target during the movement. The nonalphabetic Chinese script functions as a cultural construction in addition to its linguistic function as an auditory symbol. Such script was a great centripetal force. It united the Chinese people who spoke innumerable different languages and saved China from the interference of the nation-state rhythm. In January 1923, the journal *Chinese Language Monthly* 国语月刊 carried a special piece on *Reform of the Han Script* 汉字改革 in its seventh issue. Contributors included Hu Shi, Cai Yuanpei 蔡元培 (1868–1940), Qian Xuantong 钱玄同 (1887–1939), Li Jinxi 黎锦熙 (1890–1978), Zhao Yuanren 赵元任 (1892–1982), and Fu Sinian 傅斯年 (1896–1950), all eminent intellectuals and linguists. Most of them believed that nonalphabetic Chinese script should be locked in a museum as a heritage of "feudal culture 封建文化" and China should use the Latin alphabet. Thirty years later, the Chinese government simplified Chinese script and made it easier for beginners of the language. However, this also created difficulties in reading ancient books and obstacles in communication between the people of China's mainland and the people of Taiwan, Hong Kong, Macau, and overseas. In today's information society and digitization of cultural environment, where the special form of Chinese script is no longer a burden or obstacle, no one talks about script reform any more.

## II. Sun Yat-sen and the Guomindang

Sun Yat-sen was, doubtlessly, the inspiration and brightest star of the Republic of China. However, he didn't do much for construction of new China as he was only the provisional president for a few months. Since he was not in power during warlord rule, even if he was the most active statesman among the people, he was not able to achieve much.

By 1917, the scramble for supremacy in the capital, Beijing, among warlords, led to dissolution of Parliament. Sun Yat-sen went to Guangzhou to convene an "extraordinary Parliamentary session" and was elected commander-in-chief of the army, navy,

and air force to prepare for a "northern expedition 北伐." His move was sabotaged by the warlords of Guangdong and Guangxi, and his commander-in-chief position was annulled. Sun went back to Shanghai to lie low. In January 1923, he met with the special envoy of the Soviet Union, Adolf Abramovich Joffe (1883–1927), and the two issued the "Joint Manifesto of Sun and Joffe." Then, Sun Yat-sen began political and military activities with pomp and show at Guangzhou, which became the "Red Capital 赤都" of China, and the Republic of China regained new life. Two events distinguished this new chapter of Chinese history. The first was formation of the "Chinese Nationalist Party/Guomindang 中国国民党," while the second was establishment of the "Whampoa Military Academy 黄埔军校" to train military officers in new ideas. Connected to these two events was Sun Yat-sen's policy of "Uniting Russia and Uniting the Communists 联俄联共." Guomindang allowed members of the Communist Party of China (CPC) to join it as card-carrying members. This inaugurated the first "Guomindang–Communist cooperation 国共合作."

**Photo of Sun Yat-sen at the Whampoa Academy**

In October 1923, Mikhail Markovich Borodin (1884–1951) arrived in Guagnzhou from Moscow as adviser and trainer for

the Guomindang. With Soviet help, Sun Yat-sen finally had his office of commander-in-chief. In January 1924, the "First National Assembly of Guomindang" convened in Guangzhou. Among the 165 delegates to the Assembly were 24 Communists, led by Chen Duxiu, Li Dazhao 李大钊 (1889–1927), Mao Zedong, Lin Boqu 林伯渠 (1886–1960), and Tan Pingshan 谭平山 (1886–1956). As the Assembly had been designed by the Soviet adviser Borodin, it replicated the National Congress of the USSR. The Assembly passed many important resolutions, the most famous of which was the "Declaration of the First National Assembly of Guomindang." It called for "Abolition of all unequal treaties, including foreign concessions, consular jurisdiction (the 'extraterritoriality'), foreign control of Chinese maritime customs, and foreigners' enjoying all political power on Chinese soil impinging on Chinese sovereignty." Soon after, in October 1924, the warlord Feng Yuxiang 冯玉祥 (1882–1948, who had received aid from the Soviets to build a powerful "Northwest Army 西北军") launched a coup in Beijing and overthrew the reigning warlord's regime. When he came to power, he changed the name of his army to the "National People's Army 国民军" and invited Sun Yat-sen to Beijing for consultation. Sun jumped at this invitation, left Guangzhou, and sailed to Beijing via Japan. Unfortunately, he fell ill upon reaching Beijing and died in March 1925.

Sun Yat-sen lit the fire of the Chinese dream that inspired the entire country. He also contributed to uniting his own Guomindang movement with the Chinese Communist movement. But he did not clearly understand the Chinese odyssey along the civilization highway and tried to transform China into a nation-state. The slogan "Rejuvenation of the Zhonghua Nation 振兴中华民族" is his legacy that led to the growth of nationalism in China which was detrimental to fulfilling the Chinese dream to become a perfect "civilization-state."

Sun Yat-sen's presence in Beijing could have brought revolutionary fever to North China. This prospect was quashed by his

untimely death which, at the same time, took away the unifying umbrella from his revolutionary base in Guangzhou. Chiang Kai-shek 蒋介石 (1887–1975) emerged as his successor and led the "northern expedition." When he entered Shanghai with his troops in 1927, he began to cleanse the Communists from the Guomindang. The Communists responded to Chinag Kai-shek's offensive by establishing a base of the "Red Army for Workers and Peasants 工农红军" at Jinggangshan 井冈山 in Jiangxi province, challenging the sovereignty of the Guomindang. Mao Zedong was a hero in creating this first "revolutionary base area 革命根据地." Then, in 1934, Chiang Kai-shek drove the Red Army out of Jiangxi and the latter elected Mao Zedong as their supreme leader, commencing the historic "Long March 万里长征," marching 25,000 *li* (about 8,000-plus miles) to establish a new revolutionary base among the caves of Yan'an 延安 in Shaanxi province (close to the historic city of Xi'an (ancient Chang'an). Interestingly, Chiang Kai-shek, who had visited the Soviet Union for three months in 1923, still maintained cordial relations with the USSR, while the Communist force led by Mao Zedong pledged to strive for fulfillment of Sun Yat-sen's ideals. The Yan'an regime, opposed to Chiang Kai-shek's Nanjing regime, advocated pursuit of "New Democracy 新民主主义." Mao said this was the new version of the "Three People's Principles 三民主义" of Sun Yat-sen. Another interesting phenomenon was that Song Qingling/Ching-ling Soong 宋庆龄 (1893–1981), married to Sun Yat-sen, was always left-leaning, while her younger sister Song Meiling/Mailing Soong 宋美龄 (1897–2003) married Chiang Kai-shek in 1927, the year Chiang expelled the Communists from the Guomindang. Thus, even after Sun Yat-sen passed away, the two political rivals in China—the Guomindang and the CPC—still had some bonds of affinity.

## III. Sleeping Lion Pricked by Japanese Militarism

Japan should not have joined the European–US coalition force to attack China in 1900 as it had neither Christian missionaries

nor evangelic activities in China (it did not have a case to settle the score with the Boxers as the other nations in the "Eight-Nation Alliance" did). While other nations had grievances against the Boxers, Japan joined for the obvious purpose of avarice and aggression. In the wake of the "Boxer Protocol," Japan began to station substantial troops near Beijing and Tianjin. In 1905, Japan forced the Manchu government to sign a Sino-Japanese "Treaty on Matters of the Three Provinces of Northeast China 东三省事宜条约." In that same year, the Russo-Japanese War broke out, ending in Japanese victory. In 1907, Japan and Russia concluded both open and secret agreements virtually allowing Manchuria to become Japan's sphere of influence. In June 1928, the Japanese planted explosives at the Huanggutun 皇姑屯 Station of the Southern Manchurian Railway, killing powerful Chinese warlord Zhang Zuolin 张作霖 (1877–1928). Zhang Zuolin's son Zhang Xueliang 张学良 (1901–2001) succeeded him as commander-in-chief of the "Northeastern Army 东北军." He joined the camp of Chiang Kai-shek's "National Revolutionary Army 国民革命军" and adopted the latter's insignia of "the blue sky with a white sun 青天白日." Japan tried, in vain, to stop him. In 1931, Japan created the "September 18 Incident 九一八事变," internationally known as the "Mukden Incident." The term "incident" was a pretext for Japan to annex the three Chinese provinces of the Northeast (Heilongjiang 黑龙江, Liaoning 辽宁, and Jilin 吉林) and create an independent "Manchurian state 满洲国." In this "Manchurian state," Japan adopted the policy of erasing memories of China by migrating Chinese children to Japan to be raised newly as Japanese, cutting off their Chinese cultural roots. On July 7, 1937, Japan created another "incident"—the "Marco Polo Bridge Incident 卢沟桥事变," claiming that during an exercise, a Japanese soldier went missing. The Japanese wanted to enter the city of Wanping 宛平, near Beijing, to search for the missing soldier. They attacked the city when Chinese garrison troops refused their request. This was the beginning of the Sino-Japanese War.

**Chinese troops on the Marco Polo Bridge**

Warlord Zhang Zuolin had a strong army, navy, and air force of 300,000 men, with substantial money and ammunition. Zhang Xueliang inherited it. When Japan created the "Mukden Incident," Zhang Xueliang wanted to fight, but he was restrained by the overall leader of the "National Revolutionary Army," Chiang Kai-shek, whose strategy was "First consolidate China internally, then resist external aggression 攘外必先安内." In other words, Chiang wanted to annihilate the CPC armed forces before taking up resistance against Japanese aggression. Under Chiang's order, Zhang Xueliang withdrew his 300,000 soldiers from the three northeast provinces without firing a shot.

Had this been Ming China in the 16th century, or the Manchu Qing in the 19th century, Chiang Kai-shek may have had his way. But, during the 20th century, when the Chinese sleeping lion was awakening, this amounted to setting the clock back and rousing the sleeping lion. All of China was angry about this nonresistance and loss of territory. When I was in junior primary school in Changsha 长沙 (Hunan province), I learned a popular song entitled "On the Songhua River 松花江上." This song was created by Zhang Hanhui (张寒晖, 1902–1946) in 1936. He was born and raised in the lost territory of the northeast and was teaching in the Second Provincial Middle School in Xi'an. When

Chapter 9: The Awakened Lion Shaking China, Not the World

he created the song and sang it with his students, they broke down and cried. All this, of course, I learned only now. But, I must have learned the song itself just a couple of years after its creation, before I was age 10. During the Anti-Japanese War, I sang the song quite often, alone or with my schoolmates. For seven decades since, I did not sing it, yet I still remember every word. I translate a portion of it as follows:

> The eighteenth of September,
>
> that was the sad time,
>
> I left every family member,
>
> And endless treasure behind.
>
> Wandering, wandering,
>
> Whiling my days away
>
> from place to place.
>
> O, what year, what month,
>
> can I return to my lovely home?
>
> What year, what month,
>
> can we regain our endless treasure?
>
> O, My dad and mom,
>
> when can we again be together
>
> in our sweet home with joy and calm?"

（九一八，从那个悲惨的时候。脱离了我的家乡，抛弃那无尽的宝藏，流浪！流浪！整日价在关内流浪！哪年，哪月，才能够回到我那可爱的故乡？哪年，哪月，才能够收回那无尽的宝藏？爹娘啊，爹娘啊，什么时候，才能欢聚一堂？!）

Even without the music, you may feel the sadness and excitement of those days when this song reverberated all over China.

After the sad "September 18th Incident," Chiang Kai-shek sent Zhang Xueliang and his huge force to Xi'an to fight the Communist base at Yan'an. Chiang flew to Xi'an on December 7, 1936, to urge Zhang Xueliang and Yang Hucheng 杨虎城 (1893–1949), commander-in-chief of the "Northwestern Army," to reinvigorate the civil war. On December 9, students in Xi'an gathered to commemorate the "December 9 Movement."[1] From their assembling place, demonstrators marched to the guesthouse where Chiang Kai-shek was staying. They sang the aforementioned song with emotion and sadness. Zhang Xueliang reached the site to drive the protesters away. But, when he heard the students singing, he and the soldiers with him (who had all left behind loved ones in northeast China) felt their hearts melt. A softened Zhang Xueliang did not use force against the students. Instead, he said, "Please have confidence in me that I want to fight the Japanese…I shall reply to your demands with action within a week." Three days later, Zhang Xueliang and Yang Hucheng shocked the world by creating the "Xi'an Incident 西安事变". We see the power of a song to create history. Later,

**A scene of the Xi'an Incident**

---

[1] The movement began a year earlier, on December 9, 1935, when students in Beijing demonstrated to urge the government to stop the civil war and jointly fight Japanese aggression.

Chapter 9: The Awakened Lion Shaking China, Not the World

Mao Zedong commented that this song was worthy of the fighting power of two army divisions. The song was the roar of the awakened China. While Chiang Kai-shek slept with his personal career dreams, China was awake and roaring like a lion.

Never had Chiang Kai-shek, as highest leader of a regime, been thrown into such panic and embarrassment as during the "Xi'an Incident." On the night of December 12, 1936, Zhang Xueliang's 17th Army raided the guesthouse where Chiang was staying. The resistance of his guards was quickly put down and Chiang was captured in a pavilion at the foot of the hill behind the guesthouse, which is a very popular tourist attraction today. As he escaped through a window wearing only his sleeping gown, he shivered in the cold winter night. He lost his dentures while trying to escape. So he spoke incoherently when captured. The soldiers escorted him to Zhang's official residence, and Zhang politely kept him under house arrest. When the incident was reported the following morning, the entire world was shocked. International concern focused on the life and safety of Chiang Kai-shek, while China was faced with a serious Japanese threat. The crisis also impacted the future development of the civil war between the Guomindang and Communist forces.

**The pavilion where Chiang Kai-shek was captured in 1936 (Upper photo shows the 1936 scene and lower photo the present scene)**

Soong Mei-ling, who was also known as Madame Chiang Kai-shek, played a crucial role in the Xi'an Incident. It was her intervention that made the episode end to the satisfaction of all concerned. What she actually did was defuse tempers, especially those of Chiang Kai-shek and Zhang Xueliang. She transformed the initially hostile atmosphere into an amicable environment. As soon as she heard about the Incident, she secretly sent Chiang Kai-shek's Australian private adviser William Henry Donald (1875–1946) to Xi'an with a letter consoling Chiang. When Chiang saw Donald and read his wife's letter, he immediately calmed down and Donald telegraphed to Soong that Chiang was safe. Soong Mei-ling used the telegraph to placate agitated political circles in Nanjing and suppress the war cries of extremists within the Guomindang government. Then, on December 22, Madame Chiang flew to Xi'an in the company of her elder brother, Song Ziwen, who was also known as T. V. Soong (1894–1971). She took control of the situation and negotiated with the two generals, Zhang Xueliang and Yang Hucheng (on behalf of the host army), and Zhou Enlai (on behalf of the CPC). Chiang Kai-shek said nothing publicly while his wife assured the other two parties that he had agreed to fight Japanese aggression. Zhang Xueliang began and ended the Incident. He escorted Chiang Kai-shek back to Nanjing, where he was immediately arrested and thereafter completely disappeared from public life. He died a centenarian in the United States.

The Xi'an Incident preceded the Marco Polo Bridge Incident by only six months. It helped China mobilize all political factions to fight Japanese aggression. When the Marco Polo Bridge Incident occurred, Chiang Kai-shek raised the standard of "fighting Japanese aggression." He became supreme leader of China's eight-year War of Resistance against Japan. Japanese militarists went insane, riding the tide of victory in China and extending the war front to Southeast Asia and South Asia. Then, in 1941, they attacked Pearl Harbor and forced the United States to join World War II. Chiang Kai-shek became Generalissimo of the Far Eastern Theater of the Allied Forces. In 1943, he attended the Cairo Summit of the four major leaders with President

Roosevelt, Prime Minister Churchill, and Marshal Stalin. This was the finest hour for Chiang Kai-shek personally and the first time China enjoyed the status of a world power.

The eight-year Anti-Japanese War was the most sorrowful and heroic epic in China's 5,000-year history. According to estimates, Chinese military and civilian casualties topped 35 million people (the total population of Australia, New Zealand, and all the Pacific Islands) with incalculable loss of wealth. No one can say how many years of Chinese progress were sacrificed by such loss. During World War II, France surrendered after only six weeks of fighting. Other small countries, like Belgium and Holland, resisted only a couple of days. The Japanese army was so strong, yet it could not crush the resistance of the weak Chinese people, even in eight years. This surprised the entire world. Never had there been such a total mobilization of China against external aggression. Never had China shown such courage and persever-ance in fighting its enemy. People organized the "Broadsword Brigade 大刀队" and children raised their "red tassel spears" (红缨枪). The savage atrocity and cruelty of Japanese troops in China were the worst anywhere and anytime on earth. They were not content with their deadly weapons. They had their "Unit 731," conducting research on biological and chemical warfare in China. The unit experimented on Chinese, Koreans, Mongols, Southeast Asians, Pacific islanders, Russians, and other enemy captives, killing over 10,000 of them. The most inhumane Japanese atrocity was the "Nanjing Massacre," which was human savagery of insane proportion. On November 13, 1937, when Japanese troops ended Chinese resistance in Nanjing and cap-tured this capital city of the Republic of China, they went around the city killing whoever they met, burning whatever houses they saw, and raping women, including the old and children. After being raped, victims were killed by bayonet. In total, 300,000 innocent people were killed, 20,000 women were raped, and a third of Nanjing was razed to the ground. Such Japanese savages deserve to die 10,000 deaths. Even Yamaraja, Lord of Death, would not condone them.

**A graphic scene of the "Nanjing Massacre"
(Japanese soldiers killed a Chinese child)**

Though China was an awakened lion, it was not yet powerful enough to qualify for that description. Besides, Japan had been preparing for the invasion for a long time. It controlled the iron and coal mines of China's northeast to develop the armament industry. It trained male subjects in Korea, Taiwan, and Manchuria, and organized them into the Japanese invasion army. Then, Wang Jingwei (汪精卫 1883–1944) established the puppet pro-Japan government in Nanjing called the "People's Government of the Republic of China 中华民国国民政府," which also had an army. All these pro-Japanese Chinese army units were called "fake troops 伪军" by the Chinese media, while genuine Japanese soldiers were called "devils 鬼子." During the Anti-Japanese War, Chinese troops fought two million Japanese "devils" and over two million "fake troops." This phenomenon of such a large number of Chinese joining enemy ranks to destroy their own motherland was rare in world military history. This was really the Achilles' heel of Chinese civilization.

All told, China was no peer to Japan during the war. Had Japan not made the mistake of attacking the United States and instead concentrated on conquering China, it would have

Chapter 9: The Awakened Lion Shaking China, Not the World

possibly repeated the history of Mongol Yuan and Manchu Qing. Even after making that mistake, Japan did not surrender due to Chinese resistance. It was instead due to the collapse of Germany and that the Soviet Union launched a massive attack on the Japanese base in Manchuria, overtaking it. Meanwhile, the United States started bombing the Japanese islands. US aircraft carriers sailed into Japanese territorial waters and heavy bombers took off to bomb Japanese cities. After dropping the bombs, US bombers flew to China's mainland and crash-landed in the fields. These US pilots were rescued by Chinese people and sent to US camps in China. Finally, on August 6 and 9, 1945, two US atomic bombs were dropped on Hiroshima and Nagasaki. Ultimately, Japan had to surrender.

I recall that the Nationalist Government did a very poor job organizing the Anti-Japanese War. The government never told the truth. Half of the country fell under Japanese occupation, but one never saw in the news media the loss of a single city. If Nanjing was lost, the news would say: "Our troops turned a direction in advance from Nanjing." This phrase "turned a direction in advance 转进" means "withdraw" and is the most ridiculous way of saving face by the then Chinese government, amounting to self-deception. When Japanese troops made moves for strategic and tactical reasons, there would be big news of a Nationalist Army victory. The commander of the army would treat his unit as a personal asset and would fight sincerely only for his own reputation. But, he would be least willing to render help to a sister unit at the cost of his own force to boost the morale of others. The typical example was the fierce battle in defending Hengyang 衡阳 City in Hunan from June to August 1944. Fang Xianjue 方先觉 (1903–1983), commander of the Tenth Army, the garrison force of Hengyang, fought bravely in defending the city. His army was besieged by the Japanese and supplies were cut off. Chiang Kai-shek sent many armies to lift the siege. These armies reached the railway station, but would not enter the city to fight shoulder to shoulder with Fang's unit (they wanted to preserve their own strength). Finally, Fang

Xianjue had no ammunition and few soldiers left, so he accepted the Japanese terms and surrendered. This was the fate of a real hero of the War of Resistance against Japan. China was a huge territory, too large for tiny Japan to swallow. Japanese troops fell into a quagmire of prolonged exhaustion. The Japanese war front was too extended to avoid Chinese attacks. Army units, led by the Eighth Route Army and New Fourth Army (under the command of Mao Zedong), actively fought behind the Japanese frontline. They engaged the invaders with guerilla warfare and upset the stability of the Japanese rear. In the front, Guomindang troops persevered and endured, and became stronger and stronger.

China established its air force with backup from the United States, the USSR, and other countries. Japan lost its air superiority in China. In the final two years, hard battles were fought in Changde (常德) and Changsha (长沙) in Hunan province and also in western Hunan to prevent the Japanese invaders from reaching the war capital of Chongqing (重庆).

China was on the side of justice, while Japan was on the side of evil. Mencius said, "A just cause gets plentiful aid while an unjust cause gets few or none (得道者多助，失道者寡助)." International opinion supported China and denounced Japan. The great Indian poet Tagore had a famous debate in 1938 with his old Japanese friend Yone Noguchi (1875–1947). Tagore admired Noguchi and invited him to his university at Santiniketan (in Bengal, India) with a red-carpet welcome. Japanese militarists wanted to use Noguchi to win Indian support and had Noguchi write to Tagore first on July 23, 1938, advocating Japan's dream for a "co-prosperous" East Asia. Tagore wrote his reply on September 1. Then, Noguchi sent a second letter, written on October 2, to which Tagore replied in the same month (date unknown). Tagore's letters were simultaneously carried by the Indian press and read worldwide. In his first reply, Tagore wrote: "In launching a ravaging war on Chinese humanity, with all the deadly methods learned from the West, Japan is infringing every moral principle on which civilization is based." Focusing on

**Chapter 9: The Awakened Lion Shaking China, Not the World**

Noguchi's keenness to whitewash Japanese aggression, Tagore humorously wrote: "I suppose the bombing of Chinese women and children, and the desecration of ancient temples and universities, is a means of saving China for Asia..." Tagore continued:

> I speak with utter sorrow for your people. Your letter has hurt me to the depths of my being. I know that one day the disillusionment of your people will be complete, and through laborious centuries, they will have to clear the debris of their civilization wrought to ruin by their own warlords run amok.

In his second reply, Tagore lamented: "I suffer intensely because the reports of Chinese suffering batter against my heart and I can no longer point out with pride the example of a great Japan." These words reveal sincere sentiment and great vision. Today, after so many decades, the debris wrought by the Japanese "warlords run amok" has yet to be cleared and the Japanese people don't seem to know how to do it (unlike the Germans, who have admirably done so).

## IV. Mao Zedong Roared Like a Real Lion

On October 1, 1949, when Chairman Mao Zedong proclaimed the founding of the PRC from the Tiananmen Rostrum 天安门, he said: "Chinese people have stood up!" It sounded like an echo of Napoleon's adage—the roar of the awakened lion. Recall the opening of Chapter 1 with Mao's poem's "My country is an enchanting bride, heroes woo her with craving eyes." I should have translated the last line of that poem, in which he rhymed: "Can we find the real romantic man? Yes, here and now, you can! 数风流人物，还看今朝！" Few great Chinese poets, if any, have proclaimed themselves as a "romantic man 风流人物." Thus, we see Mao's dual character of a ruthless hard side and romantic soft side. Mao was the founding father of the PRC in 1949 and died in office (as China's supreme leader) in 1976. This 27-year period (1949–1976) known as the "Mao Zedong Era" had a hard and soft side as well.

A very big event of the "Mao Zedong Era" that was forced upon him was the Korean crisis created by the adventurism of North Korean leader Kim Il-sung (1912–1994) and the pampering of Joseph Stalin. Kim's adventurism of trying to unite the Korean Peninsula by force resulted in American military intervention under the flag of the United Nations. North Korea was on the verge of being written off. On the other hand, Stalin was unwilling to risk a third World War with nuclear America. He kicked the ball into the Chinese court. While the majority of Chinese leaders were opposed to any involvement, Mao chose to stand firmly behind China's fraternal neighbor and friend in need. Mao's China, which had barely completed its task of recovering the territory from the remnants of Guomindang forces, started the movement to "Resist US Aggression and Aid Korea 抗美援朝" in November 1950. Chinese forces, dubbed "Chinese People's Volunteers," crossed the Yalu River 鸭绿江 and engaged the US army and its allies in a fierce war. The US army was far superior in terms of weaponry and commanded greater air supremacy. China requested the Soviet Union to provide air support, but in vain. With numerical superiority on the ground and a smart strategy, China fought the United States to a tie. From that time on, the US government and public began to respect China.

**Chinese troops marching toward Korean battlefield in 1950**

Chapter 9: The Awakened Lion Shaking China, Not the World

From the Korean battlefield, the United States learned that Mao had inherited the art of war from the ancient strategist, Sunzi. The Pentagon had Sunzi's classic, *Sunzi bing fa* 孙子兵法 (literally, "War Method of Master Sun"), translated into *The Art of War* for the rank and file to study. Even today, it remains an important textbook in American military training institutions. Based on Sunzi's teaching of "know thine enemy 知己知彼," American universities enthusiastically started a new discipline called "Area Studies" in which East Asian study dominated. The Korean War, one of the few wars America did not win, was not of Mao's making. Mao's China suffered the collateral damage of the war which, dubiously, looked like a blessing in disguise.

Tan Yun-shan (1898–1983, my father), a fellow student of Mao at the First Normal School in Changsha in the early 1920s, proposed to Mao (for whom Tan had great admiration since childhood), when he wrote from India in 1950, that China should develop a great relationship with India. Mao accepted the suggestion and confirmed it when he met my father in 1956. China's special gesture was quickly reciprocated by Jawaharlal Nehru (1889–1964), modern India's founder and first prime minister. In 1954, one million Beijing residents lined the streets from the airport to the guesthouse to welcome Nehru and his daughter Indira to Beijing.[2] Prem Bhatia (1911–1995), renowned Indian journalist and diplomat, wrote the following words about the grandiose welcome he personally witnessed (in the breaking news on the front page of *The Statesman*, New Delhi and Calcutta, October 20, 1954).

> Never has your correspondent seen Nehru greeted in such a cheerful, but orderly, manner.... A million people, with hardly 50 unarmed policemen to control them.... As we passed in the procession, laughing and jumping boys and

---

[2] If one million Beijing residents (the actual number may be less) went to the streets to welcome Nehru, there wouldn't have been many people left indoors. Such grandiosity was not only unprecedented in world history, but may never happen again in China or elsewhere.

girls clapped their hands and shouted "Long live India–China friendship." Yet an hour before, covering the same route to the airport, we saw no trace of these crowds. Where they emerged from in the interval and how they stood there without causing a riot would be regarded a miracle in India.

**One million people welcome Nehru in Beijing in 1954 (Chinese Premier Zhou Enlai rode with Nehru from the airport to the guesthouse)**

Mao met Nehru four times for cordial conversation and dinner in Beijing during that trip. He recited a famous ancient Chinese poem when he bid Nehru farewell in the following words.

In life, parting with the dear one is the saddest

while gaining a bosom friend is the gladdest.

(悲莫悲兮生别离，乐莫乐兮新相知。)

Mao's China had a love–hate relationship with the Soviet Union. Mao used to disobey Stalin's directives, while Stalin described Mao as a "peasant leader" and "marginal communist." "You can't wage a revolution in the ravine!" was Stalin's comment on Mao's establishing "revolutionary base areas" under Chiang Kai-shek's regime. In December 1949, Mao went to Moscow for a formal visit (and also to attend the 70th birthday of Stalin).

However, the Soviets did not treat it as a "state visit" of an equal state and important ally. Stalin remained at his seaside resort in Crimea when Mao arrived in Moscow. When Stalin received Mao a couple of days later, Mao complained about past Soviet criticisms to which Stalin responded: "The victor does not deserve criticism"—thereby paying high tribute to Mao's revolutionary victory. Stalin also graciously asked Mao what he would like to carry back from the Soviet Union as a gift. To this, Mao expressed his wish for Soviet aid for China's industrial development. After that meeting, a large number of Soviet experts arrived in China and Soviet aid to China's industrialization plans was in full swing during the regime of Nikita Khrushchev (1894–1971). Then came the Sino-Soviet split in 1960.

Before the split, over 1,000 Soviet experts arrived in China with blueprints, mostly working in the armament industry. Khrushchev promised to provide a sample bomb, which was never delivered. On the contrary, all the Soviet scientists withdrew abruptly, along with the blueprints, in 1960, leaving over 200 projects to languish. All 233 Soviet experts involved in the atom bomb project, including eight in the Academy of Nuclear Designs in Beijing and five engineers in the Lanzhou Factory for Enriching Uranium, departed. The Soviets waited for the Chinese nuclear project to collapse. They predicted that China would not be able to make the bomb for another 20 years. Khrushchev said that the Chinese would have no trousers to wear should they continue with the project. To this, China's Foreign Minister Marshal Chen Yi 陈毅 (1901–1972) replied that even if the Chinese people had no trousers to wear, the bomb must be made. China made it in 1964. Mao humorously said that Khrushchev deserved a one ton medal because he taught China how to be self-reliant.

While in the Yan'an caves, Mao accepted the request of any American who wished to see him and would spend days talking to them. He also expressed a keen desire to visit the United States. In 1969, Mao wanted to emerge from the embarrassment of facing both superpowers as enemies and asked Marshals Chen Yi, Ye Jianying 叶剑英 (1897–1986), Xu Xiangqian 徐向前 (1901–1990), and Nie Rongzhen 聂荣臻 (1899–1992) to form a study group analyzing the world situation. The four marshals submitted the following two reports: (a) "A Tentative Estimate of the War Situation 对战争形势的初步估计" and (b) "An Analysis of the Current Situation 对目前局势的看法." They concluded that: Sino-Soviet contradictions were greater than Sino-American contradictions and it was unlikely that the United States and USSR would singularly or jointly wage a large-scale war against China. They also proposed to engage the United States for normalizing relations. This development coincided with the move of President Nixon, and the initiative of National Security Advisor Henry Kissinger, to break the ice between the United States and China. The Sino-US détente enabled Mao to quickly exit the "anti-American" stage.

As a believer in dialectic materialism, Mao believed in the possibility of converting willpower into energy. In the fantastic year of 1958, Mao launched a campaign in which "all people of China produced steel 全民炼钢铁." Beijing's Zhongnanhai 中南海, the residential area of China's top leaders, set the example by erecting a "little blast furnace 小高炉" to produce steel (leaders, their secretaries, service personnel, and family members played the role of steel workers). Government offices, educational institutions, and communities throughout China followed suit. Steel is usually produced in a scientific way according to rules of physics and chemistry. In China that year, one-sixth of its population (100 million in number), the overwhelming majority of whom had very little knowledge of science and technology, joined the venture with the goal of raising China's steel production from 4 million to 10 million tons within just a few months. They haphazardly set up thousands of improvised blast furnaces. In some cases, where iron ore was not available, people threw household iron utensils and implements into the furnace (making useful instruments scrap). Finally, by December 1958, China's total production of iron and steel was 8 million tons, which included over 3 million tons of substandard scrap. This result ended the Chinese enthusiasm for steel production.

Of course, not all the economic constructions of the Mao Era were conducted in this manner. Operating shops and workshops has been China's cup of tea for thousands of years. All the steel, machine tools, and heavy chemical factories of the Mao Era were built well according to blueprint. There was also the famous Daqing 大庆 Oil Field. However, everything in the Mao Era was subject to political considerations; thus, it was called "Politics in Command 政治挂帅." But economic construction had substantial development in the macroclimate of "politics in command." By the end of the Mao Era, all machine tools in China's factories, locomotives and ships in transportation, and so on were made in China with few imports.

The less-than-three-decade Mao Era was turbulent. Within China, it was, indeed, "Turning Heaven and Earth upside down 天翻地覆," as Mao used to say. China went from one movement to the next. But, all political movements paled in comparison to the fervor, impact, and damage to the "movements" called the "Great Cultural Revolution 文化大革命." Lin Biao 林彪 (1907–1971), who held the number two position next to Mao during the Cultural Revolution, said that a single sentence from the chairman was as good as 10,000 from others. People no longer read books, not even the *Selected Works of Mao Tse-tung* 毛泽东选集. They had, in hand, the small red book that was the "Quotations of Chairman Mao 毛主席语录" and gathered in public places for the "loyalty dance 忠字舞."

Mao purposely created a brief period of anarchy, allowing the "Red Guards 红卫兵" (young students and factory workers) to denounce and sideline heads of their respective institutions and take the law into their own hands. They targeted people in authority and eminent public figures for "struggle," humiliating them in public. Red Guards broke into private houses at will in search of evidence of "counterrevolution." People began to panic

and burnt books, manuscripts, diaries, and letters. Overnight, tons of valuable historical information turned into ash. Red Guard organizations started fighting among themselves, even in battles with real weapons, which they had looted from military depots. Red Guards in Chongqing 重庆 staged a mini-civil war with cannons and tanks. Mao saw that things had spiraled out of control and ordered a stop to such activities. Red Guards were disbanded and all factories, educational institutions (the den of the Red Guards), and other organizations were brought under control of the armed forces. In this way, China came out of the self-inflicted mess of anarchy.

After the Mao Era, China gradually returned to the normal life of peacetime under leadership of Deng Xiaoping 邓小平 (1904–1997), whose internationally famous adage was "It doesn't matter whether the cat is black or white, so long as it catches mice 不管黑猫白猫，捉到老鼠就是好猫." Deng's down-to-earth mind-set returned China to its odyssey along the civilization highway. Recalling Napoléon's adage, China was, indeed, the awakened lion and roared for a while (loudest during the Mao Zedong Era). After Mao, the lion shrank into a good cat—one good at catching the mouse of economic development. The world was not shaken (perhaps only experiencing a small tremor), but China was joining the comity of the "nation-state" world as a distinct common entity of destiny.

# CHAPTER 10

# CHINA JOINS THE COMITY OF THE "NATION-STATE" WORLD

CHINA: A 5,000-YEAR ODYSSEY

The world beckons post-Mao China while it continues its odyssey along the civilization highway. The 100-year desire to be rich 富 and strong 强 remains ever so strong lest China again goes under in the international nation-state environment and faces challenges from the sea. The PRC, born in war, automatically had sufficient strength, as demonstrated in the Korean War. The lessons of the Soviet Union have been enlightening. As a socialist state, the USSR single-mindedly went for power at the cost of riches. The United States ultimately forced a poor superpower, the Soviet Union, into bankruptcy by waging a fierce armament race with it. Even before the demise of China's erstwhile socialist "Big Brother," Deng Xiaoping made the sensible observation that "poverty is not socialism 贫穷不是社会主义." Recall that during the Sui–Tang–Song period, the Chinese aspiration was to get rich, which has become one of China's obsessions in present times. This is the heritage of the Chinese odyssey along the civilization highway.

To an observer like myself, who left China in the 1950s, almost entirely cut ties for a quarter century, and began visiting my homeland again from the 1980s onward, I feel China is "casting off its old, and taking a new body and soul 脱胎换骨"—to quote a Chinese description. From the 1980s on, we see a China developing on a fast track, doubling its GDP every 10 years, and becoming more and more unrecognizable to anyone whose image of China is decades old. While commenting on China's economic progress, people arrive at different conclusions. There seems to be a host of contradictory aspects coming together. In 2012, a Chinese scholar pointed out that in total GDP terms, China ranked second in the world after the United States, but in per capita GDP terms, it ranked 100th after Albania. However, anyone who travels to China's medium cities can see they're all much more developed and advanced than Tirana, the capital of Albania. Viewed objectively, China's place in the world is neither number 2 nor 100. It is at X, a special spot for China that always differs from other states of the world and is difficult for people of the world to size up, including Chinese intellectuals.

# I. Three Decades of "Reform and Opening-up"

In general, Chinese view the latest phase, from the 1980s until today, as an extended period of "reform and opening-up 改革开放." This description is internationally recognized and India has emulated it from the 1990s onward. However, development models of the two countries are distinct given their respective idiosyncrasies. Professor Pranab Bardhan, my colleague at Delhi University in the 1970s, who joined the University of California at Berkeley in the 1980s, is a renowned economist whose book *Awakening Giants, Feet of Clay: Assessing the Economic Rise of China and India* (2010) is well known in Chinese academia. He told us of an interesting experience. When he was in his home state of West Bengal (India), he gained the impression that Chinese were better socialists than Indians. Then, in the United States, he gained the impression that Chinese were better capitalists than Indians. I can quite understand this dichotomy. In international circles, the rapid progress of China's "reform and opening-up" has been regarded as the extraordinary achievement of "socialist China having capitalist development." I see online that many Chinese netizens believe China is a capitalist society.

During the 1980s, a paradigm shift occurred in the United States and other developed countries to outsource capital and industries. China welcomed this with an enthusiastic strategy of what is known as "building the nest to attract the phoenix 筑巢引凤." Foreign capital was the phoenix and the nest to attract it was the modernized infrastructure. The popular Chinese saying during the 1980s was "First build the road, then get rich 要致富，先修路."

Deng Xiaoping's "opening-up" strategy initially targeted Hong Kong, Macau, and Taiwan. Four special economic zones (SEZs) were created to beckon them (Shenzhen 深圳 facing Hong Kong, Zhuhai 珠海 facing Macau, and Xiamen 厦门 and Shantou 汕头 facing Taiwan). Subsequently, Hainan became a SEZ and a separate province. In creating these special zones, China no longer

felt threatened by the challenge of the sea. The government promulgated a host of special policies in the SEZ to encourage establishment of new enterprises and welcome foreign capital. Some Chinese veterans of the revolutionary period broke down after visiting Shenzhen in the 1980s, crying that the revolutionary martyrs had not shed their blood to create such capitalist models. This ignited public desire for a debate on the merits of capitalism versus socialism, which Deng Xiaoping did not allow.

In today's reality, we see Chinese civilization discarding old notions. For instance, the 2002 revised Party Constitution of the CPC defines the CPC as the "vanguard party" of not only the working class but also the Chinese nation. It is the core leadership for the socialist cause with Chinese characteristics. It represents the demands of an advanced production force in China, the direction of China's advanced culture, and the fundamental interests of the Chinese people. The CPC being the vanguard party of the Chinese nation means it has discarded the class element and opened its membership to citizens from all walks of life. The CPC has 90 million members, amounting to 7 percent of the total Chinese population. However, 40 percent of China's private entrepreneurs (top capitalists) are CPC members, and this number is rising. When half of Chinese entrepreneurs are CPC members, we can no longer regard the Chinese private sector as capitalist.

Some CPC members were mass leaders in the past, leading their followers to become "moderately prosperous." They are now private entrepreneurs and their enterprises are collectively owned and socialist in nature. They are socialist activists contributing to China's "reform and opening-up." They have made the people of larger areas prosperous while also enriching themselves. A notable example was Wu Renbao 吴仁宝 (1928–2013). He was a government cadre who joined the CPC in 1954 and was party secretary of the Huaxi 华西 Brigade of the Huashi 华士 People's Commune in Jiangyin 江阴 County, Jiangsu province. During the early years, when the overwhelming majority of China's people's communes were disbanded, the

Huaxi Brigade, under leadership of Wu Renbao, decided to carry on with the common goal of getting rich collectively. In 1987, the Huaxi Village Group Corporation 华西集团公司 was formed with Wu Renbao as its founder and CEO. Apparently, he became an entrepreneur, but actually he was a party leader at the village and county levels until his death. Huaxicun 华西村 (Huaxi Village), a poor village three decades ago, is now the "Number One Village of Tianxia 天下第一村", leaving the difference between socialism and capitalism blurred. The per capita GDP of Huaxi Village in 2010 was 85,000 Yuan (double that of national leader Shanghai that year). Wu Renbao's feat of making the Huaxi Village, and neighboring areas, moderately prosperous began to be emulated by the entire country.

**Huaxicun: "The Number One Village of Tianxia"**

Recall that China's initial base was the irrigated areas of the third and fifth longest rivers on Earth. Consequently, from time immemorial until now, China has had the world's largest population (at times as high as one-third of humanity, but never below one-sixth of the world's population). Mao Zedong basically believed population was an asset, not a burden, hence, the more people the merrier. When Ma Yinchu 马寅初 (1882–1982), president of Peking University and a famous demographer, proposed

to slow China's population growth, Mao rejected the idea outright. But population increased too rapidly as there was no war and the death rate fell substantially. With population increasing at a rate of nearly 2.8 percent, Chinese authorities, including Mao, were forced to take measures to control it. Stringent measures were announced during the 1980s and, in 1982, "family planning" was written into the revised Constitution. In 2000, Chinese population growth went down to 1.3 percent. In 2001, the Chinese government enacted the "Law of Family Planning."

The "One-child Policy" of Chinese family planning was stringently enforced in the cities and suburbs, with little flexibility. It was known as the "one-and-a-half children" (一胎半) policy that was practiced quietly, allowing couples (if both were single children of their parents) to have a second child if the first was a girl. In Yunnan and Qinghai, rural families with difficult living conditions were allowed to have a second child. In Hainan 海南, Ningxia 宁夏, and Xinjiang 新疆, the "two children" policy was adopted. In fact, Uighurs and Tibetans could have as many children as they want.

According to tradition, every Chinese family must have a son to pass from generation to generation because daughters get married into another family. In this way, the one-child Chinese policy collided with traditional values.[1] There were other negative impacts as well. In a family with parents and two sets of grandparents, the child did not have a sibling to play and grow up with. Thus, the child was always pampered and behaved like a so-called "small emperor." Such a child easily grew to become greedy and unable to endure hardships, opposite to the merits of Chinese culture.

---

[1]The Chinese tradition of overvaluing the male child died hard. The government prohibited the hospital (or doctor) from revealing the gender of the fetus to the parents to avoid feticide, but could not eliminate it. One way to circumvent this was to send a blood sample of the pregnant mother to Hong Kong or abroad for examination. As a result, killing the female child by abortion was not uncommon. A World Bank report in 2012 noted that the male–female ratio in China was 119:100, the most serious among all countries. In some Chinese areas, the ratio became as abnormal as 177:100.

为革命实行晚婚和计划生育

**Government propaganda for the one-child family
(The child in the drawing is a girl to balance popular
preference for a son)**

Chinese society, especially the intellectual elite, enthusiastically supported the government's determination to halt rapid population growth. In cities, implementation of the One-child Policy was smooth and many single daughter families lived happily, treating the daughter as a treasure. The saying "expecting the daughter to become a phoenix 望女成凤" was as popular and vigorous as "expecting the son to become a dragon 望子成龙." During the past few decades, a "super-women 女强人" phenomenon has emerged in China, with the wife/mother assuming an outside role in the family, while the husband/father shares household chores and babysitting. An increasing number of female judges, department heads, school principals, singing and movie stars, intellectuals with doctoral degrees, diplomats, powerful personalities, entrepreneurs, and billionaires have emerged. In 2014, a Shanghai research institute published a world survey it conducted regarding female billionaires who started from scratch: China had the most, including the top three. In international sporting competitions, female Chinese athletes won far more medals than their male counterparts. Mao Zedong's statement that "women hold up half the sky" is increasingly true in China. I am not attributing all this to the impact of the One-child Policy, but Chinese civilization is developing in the right direction to achieve gender equality.

Chapter 10: China Joins the Comity of the "Nation-state" World

Yi Fuxian 易富贤, a Chinese-American demographer at the University of Wisconsin, first published a book in Hong Kong in 2007 entitled *Empty Nest in a Great Power* (大国空巢). In 2013, the China Development Press, affiliated with the State Council's Development Center, published a revised edition of the book that strongly urged revision of the One-child Policy. Yi Fuxian's appeal was warmly received by the Chinese public and listened to by Chinese leadership.

In October 2015, the Fifth Plenary Session of the 18th CPC Central Committee decided to discontinue the one-child family planning policy. In December 2015, the Standing Committee of China's People's Congress approved the revised family planning act drafted by the State Council. The new law took effect January 1, 2016. Today, a Chinese family is allowed to have two children and most of the tension of the one-child family planning policy is gone.

**New Chinese propaganda for a 2-child family**

Imagine hundreds of millions of Chinese girls growing up in a country with unlimited opportunities to advance to a dreamlike future, yet the social setting is traditional. Chinese civilization has disciplined them to face problems in life and love with courage and a harmonious approach (involving self-sacrifice). They are reared within and raised to maintain and fortify the family system.

Chinese women, by and large, belong to the model of "good wife and loving mother 贤妻良母." This model remains vibrant through any social changes because Chinese civilization will not allow it to be weakened. I think China and India stand out as countries having such a fine tradition. Many Chinese women are devoted to their careers on the one hand while playing the role of family helper for their husband on the other. Chinese women pay great attention to the education of their children. Chinese children are raised under supreme maternal guidance and have well-rounded development of character and skill with minimal bad habits. This displays the steadfast steps of China's odyssey along the civilization highway.

Industrialization and urbanization are the twin sisters of modern economic development. China has created megacities and urban agglomerations (city groups). The most prominent example is the urban agglomeration around the three famous cities of Shanghai, Nanjing, and Hangzhou, China's most prosperous, developed, and avant-garde area. This area has the most developed means of communication and transportation. To commute between Shanghai and Nanjing (300 kilometers) by bullet train takes just 1.5 hours and between Shanghai and Hangzhou (180 kilometers) takes just one hour. The area also has the most intimate connection with the world. Shanghai is the largest industrial and commercial center in China and wants to become the economic high ground of the world—to become the world model in "Shanghai quality," laboratory research, industrial renovation, and other fields, as well as the "global civilization city 全球文明城市" by 2050. Shanghai aspires to be the leader and model in the second half of the 21st century, with the same world status as London in the 19th century and New York in the 20th. All this is excellent, but we must look back to the vast space within and beyond the Huanghe and Yangtze valleys that had "agriculture as the basis" for millennia during China's odyssey along the civilization highway. In the new China, new epoch, new economy, and new culture, this vast space has been relatively neglected. There is an observation that many

Chinese cities have become Europe and many Chinese villages have become Africa.

On the whole, the PRC has done a marvelous job in 60-plus years to eliminate poverty in Chinese villages and has been universally praised. In 1981, 730 million of the rural population in China lived below the poverty line, with a per capita daily income of less than $1.00. In 2008, that number decreased to 100 million. To some commentators, 630 million people being lifted out of poverty within 27 years is rather miraculous. Credit goes to the PRC government for paying close attention to the problems of the countryside with increasing input into rural development. In 2003, the government budget for improving peasant conditions was 214.4 billion yuan ($25.88 billion). By 2007, this budget progressively increased to 391.7 billion yuan ($53.66 billion). In those years, the government established experimental "civilization villages 文明村" and "tourism villages 旅游村" in poor areas. Scientific methods of pig rearing were introduced, biogas facilities installed, and attractive local products for export developed, etc. Modern roads have been built to link these experimental villages with towns and cities. New residences have been designed for peasants (with modern showers and toilets, some even with a garage, and, of course, a pigsty). Government guidelines for the new villages read: "Developed production 生产发展," "comfortable life 生活宽裕," "civilized custom 乡风文明," "clean outlook 村容整洁," and "democratic administration 管理民主."

In October 2015, the Fifth Plenary Session of the 18th CPC Central Committee decided to eliminate the stigma of "poor and difficult county 贫困县" in rural areas wherever it may and to lift the remaining 70-plus million Chinese out of poverty. In concrete terms, these 70-plus million Chinese will not have to worry about food and warmth, will enjoy free education and medical security, and will have an increasingly daily income. No family will be left out. There will be a combined "care-protect-service" system for stay-behind women, children, and the elderly in the countryside. High school education will be popularized in these areas. The Chinese government plans to ensure that all this is done within five years.

China's focus on building megacities along the east coast has created the horizontal mobility of 150 million "peasant workers 农民工" from Central and Western China into the cities of Eastern China. Of them, 60 percent are the younger generation who joined since the end of the 20th century. Like the "old generation" of "peasant workers," they come to the cities and earn money to remit to their rural homes. Unlike their elders, they cherish the hope to be urban residents. This is not difficult in other countries, but not easy in China. For 1,000 years, China has maintained a system of people having a *hu kou* 户口 (household identity). The PRC has exceeded all previous regimes in this "household identity" administration. In 1958, the "PRC Household Registration Ordinance" became law. People who have their household registration in their original home place have to get the registration transferred to other places through the government. The mobile population can go anywhere easily, but transfer of household registration is not so easy. When people live in a new place without *hu kou*, they cannot enjoy the welfare, education, and medical care like local residents can. In 2015, urban population in China reached 56.1 percent of China's total population. But only 37.5 percent of the Chinese population had urban *hu kou*. That means 18.6 percent of those who lived in cities had no *hu kou*; hence, they were being discriminated against as "second-class citizens." They had difficulty buying property, setting up businesses, and even renting a place to stay. Earlier, the older generation of "peasant workers" tolerated this discrimination, but the newer generation does not. At the moment of writing, we see Chinese authorities being seized by the problem and trying to resolve it. Ultimately, the *hu kou* system will have to be abolished.

## II. Two-way Globalization

China is drawn in by the world and vice versa. This is what I mean by "two-way globalization" between China and the world.

Chapter 10: China Joins the Comity of the "Nation-state" World

China is now globalized. It is still China, but also an integral part of the world—a member of the comity of the globe. China is increasingly feeling the impact of the world, while the world increasingly feels the existence of China. The tie between China and the world is increasingly greater and stronger, with neither wanting to break it.

The message of globalization to China was a basket with two eggs, one marked "peace" and the other marked "development." China was particularly keen on obtaining the proverbial goose that laid golden eggs, that is, foreign capital. China obtained the golden eggs by paying substantially high prices for investment in infrastructure and labor. China modestly began its globalization in the 1980s by making sports shoes for the famous American company Nike. While a pair of Nike shoes sold for dozens of US dollars, China earned only $1 for making it. This reminded people of China's paying for every ton of Soviet heavy machine tools with a ton of soybeans. A Soviet machine could weigh 1,000 tons, while it took millions of Chinese peasants, through enormous labor, to produce 1,000 tons of soybeans. It probably took Chinese workers many hours to make a pair of Nike shoes to get just $1. But China had to pay two to three hundred million US dollars to buy a Boeing passenger plane. China did not hitchhike to get onto the globalization wagon. Every iota of benefit from globalization was earned through the sweat, tears, and sometimes even lives of Chinese laborers.

**Some 150 million "peasant workers"
migrating to China's cities**

For over three decades, "Made in China" has created a sensation in the markets of the United States and other countries. Prices of goods for many famous American brands have greatly decreased, benefitting American consumers. Some years ago, the ABC television network in the United States launched a movement, in vain, to not buy "Made in China" products. In fact, what had been targeted by the American media were not actually Chinese products, but instead American products processed in Chinese factories with cheap Chinese labor. Some of these products are no longer produced in the United States. If America is no longer interested in allowing China to process products, then it must allow other countries to process. Today, China is no longer content with "Made in China." Since 2015, Chinese Premier Li Keqiang 李克强 and other leaders have reiterated transforming "Made in China" into "Created in China." China is starting its "13th Five Year Plan" from 2016, which will symbolically be extremely important for China's development. It will materialize China's first "one hundred year dream" (in 2021, the Chinese Communist Party will celebrate its 100th birthday). During this "13th Five Year Plan" (2016– 2020), a scheme called "Made in China 2025" is being implemented. This is a long-term development plan with three phases. The first phase is making China a great manufacturing country by 2020. The second phase is for China to reach the middle level of the world's great industrial powers by 2035. The third phase is to make China a frontline manufacturing

**Chinese workers making clothes**

Chapter 10: China Joins the Comity of the "Nation-state" World

country by 2049 and fulfill its second "one hundred year dream," when the PRC celebrates its 100th anniversary.

I have been saying "China is China," which is not saying much. India is India, Russia is Russia, and America is America. No force on earth can change such a rule. America, Russia, or India should not expect China to become "un-China" through globalization. This is not to say China is not globalized. China has been globalized and is continuing its globalization process. Foreign friends who live in Shanghai, Beijing, Shenzhen, Guangzhou, Nanjing, Qingdao, etc., feel as if they are in New York, London, Frankfurt, or Tokyo. English is spoken in all big cities. All Chinese airports and airlines make announcements in Chinese and English. In large and medium Chinese cities, people can watch TV newscasts and movies in English, as well as BBC and CNN programming. McDonalds, Kentucky Fried Chicken, and Starbucks are found in many Chinese cities and always draw more crowds than their counterparts in the United States. Birthday parties are everywhere in Chinese cities and the countryside, with guests singing "happy birthday to you" in English. Christmas has become a major festival in China while Valentine's Day is celebrated with gusto, to the surprise of Europeans, some of whom have not heard of it. Valentine's Day in 2017 in China was classy. Young, rich Chinese paid thousands of yuan to buy roses to present to their lovers. China is the world's largest market for desktop computers, laptops, and notebooks, overtaking the US market. The Chinese market of American automaker General Motors is larger than that of America. The China market contributed, in no small measure, to the recovery of General Motors after 2008, and United Airlines and American Airlines after 2001.

China is one of the great countries of the world for coffee drinking. Yet this in no way detracts from China's 1,500-year tea drinking tradition. Similarly, China's globalization does not substantially impact China's political tradition of many millennia. For instance, President Reagan's famous observation "Government is the problem, not the solution" can never convince the Chinese

people, who have been acclimatized for 4,000 years (since the Great Yu) in the Chinese political environment of looking to the government and political leaders to solve societal problems. The Chinese governance will remain the odd man out in the globalized world which, in many ways, is a help (rather than a hindrance) in tackling the complex problems of today's perilous international situation.

Traditionally, ideal Chinese sociopolitical conditions are "elect the sagacious and give power to the talented 选贤与能." During "reform and opening-up," a convention has been established that the CPC Party Congress elects the Standing Committee of the Politburo, the highest echelon of Chinese leadership, for five years (can be reelected for another term) with the General Secretary of the Party and Chairman of the country (through an election process of the People's Congress). This post of Party General Secretary and State Chairman looks formidably powerful, but does not even have one-tenth of the freedom enjoyed by the US president to say things and hold events. There is a changing of guards every 10 years. The Jiang Zemin 江泽民 team passed the baton to the Hu Jintao 胡锦涛 team, who, in turn, passed the baton to the current Xi Jinping 习近平 team. This has been the best leadership succession practice in Chinese history, freeing China from the not-infrequent power struggles and palace coups of yesteryear and ensuring prudent and mature policy decisions. It has been an important contributing factor to China's rapid economic growth in the past three decades. China would not have been so politically stable and united had it mimicked Western "democracy" to create an arbitrary opposition for the sake of "democracy." The phenomenon of divided states of America (DSA), accentuated by the 2016 presidential election, is demoralizing many zealots of Western democracy. The "greatest democratic country" in the world, the United States, is creating problems for the peace and stability of the entire world.

The "reform and opening-up" inaugurated by Deng Xiaoping signified a significant transformation of China from the "rule of

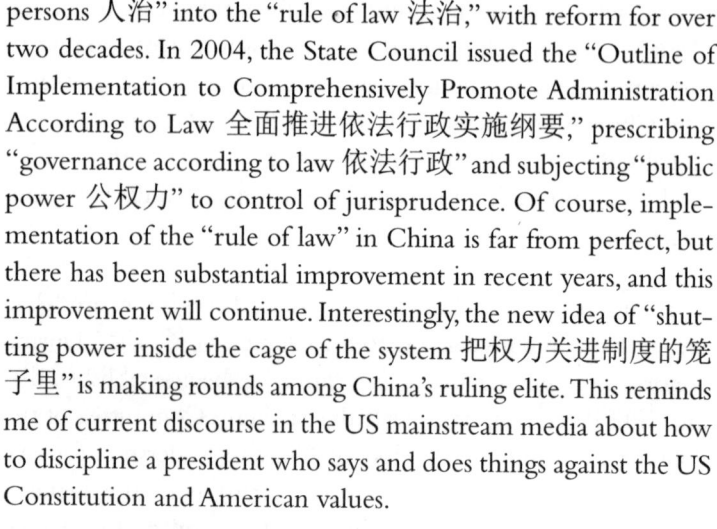

persons 人治" into the "rule of law 法治," with reform for over two decades. In 2004, the State Council issued the "Outline of Implementation to Comprehensively Promote Administration According to Law 全面推进依法行政实施纲要," prescribing "governance according to law 依法行政" and subjecting "public power 公权力" to control of jurisprudence. Of course, implementation of the "rule of law" in China is far from perfect, but there has been substantial improvement in recent years, and this improvement will continue. Interestingly, the new idea of "shutting power inside the cage of the system 把权力关进制度的笼子里" is making rounds among China's ruling elite. This reminds me of current discourse in the US mainstream media about how to discipline a president who says and does things against the US Constitution and American values.

We live in the Information Age. In the past couple of decades, China has had a steady increase in personal computers and smartphones, as well as having the world's largest netizen population today. The population distribution between urban and rural areas is nearly balanced. Three-fourths of the 700 million urban citizens of China own computers or smartphones and go online. One-fourth of the rural Chinese population goes online. This means China has 650 million netizens/cybercitizens (500 million in the cities and 150 million in the countryside). The huge Chinese population of netizens who now participate in cyber discourse on governance is a very new phenomenon. The Chinese tradition of "[H]e who wins the hearts and minds of the people can rule Tianxia 得民心者得天下" is making this cyber discourse increasingly powerful. The Chinese government is increasingly responsive to the demands and aspirations of the common people. This is a welcoming sign of China's democratization.

China is China, and can only be China. The so-called "special Chinese characteristics" (中国特色) is often used as China's self-defense in international debate, sometimes with a sense of pride. Foreign friends should be able to appreciate such pride, which is a response to the repressive Western critique on China's not following Western nation-state development. The Western world should be thankful China is still China, not being transformed into a Western power competing for supremacy and hegemony. Meanwhile, China must be given time to integrate into the comity of nations, which promotes friendship and mutual respect between countries, accepting each other's laws, political systems, and customs. If the international community respects China's idiosyncrasies to a greater degree, it will hasten its progress of integration into the world comity.

## III. China and the World Common Entity of Destiny

We are familiar with China's being made a gigantic common entity by two great rivers and the Chinese feeling they have been living in a Tianxia or a kind of universe beyond their own country. Such feeling is reflected in a poem of Wang Bo 王勃 (about 650–676): "Within the four seas we have bosom friends. People are our neighbors even when they live on the other side of the earth 海内存知己，天涯若比邻." We know the Chinese concept of "within the four seas" is a synonym for Tianxia. Chinese have also conceived, for 1,000 years, of the idea of "the edges of Heaven and corners of the sea 天涯海角." But, they have never reached such remoteness until today. Chinese people have started going to every place where "Made in China" commodities have reached. China is connecting, engaging, and understanding the world with expansion of foreign trade—being the number one country in foreign trade today. China's integration into global development is mainly due to its increasing economic importance apart from its diplomatic initiatives in uniting with other countries. The "Made in China" phenomenon is, of course, crucial. However, there are also monetary and financial factors involved. China and Japan are the world's two greatest creditors. The Chinese government has a great deal of foreign exchange reserve. Chinese enterprises also have a great deal of money. Though China remains a country attracting the largest amount of foreign investment, it has been also increasing its investment in other countries, including "merger and acquisition" (M&A) investment. In 2016, China's outbound M&A investment nearly reached the level of the United States. China is buying high-tech German firms and operating them with German scientists and technicians as well, not just for the purpose of economic expansion but also for the purpose of making strides in high-tech industries.

The well-known Chinese initiative "Promoting the Silk Road Economic Belt and the 21st Century Maritime Silk Road", known as "One Belt One Road 一带一路," has not been clearly defined, causing confusion, if not apprehension, in many countries. No doubt, it relates to trade and economic contacts. Use of the term "Silk Road" seems to reveal the Chinese intention of reviving the thriving international commerce during the Sui–Tang–Song period. The professed goal is "win-win" for all participants. If there is an ulterior motive, it is China's eagerness to develop fast train services worldwide, which would be beneficial not only for China's development but also for other countries and people.

China is helping other countries stabilize their economies. Being the largest country in foreign trade, China has gained importance vis-à-vis countries substantially involved in trading with China. Also, the Chinese currency, RMB, is now an international reserve currency of the IMF with "Special Drawing Rights" (SDRs) and will become a hard currency of the world. Huawei 华为 (Huawei Technologies Co. Ltd.), a private Chinese company, has headquarters in Shenzhen and research and development (R&D) connections with the United States, the United Kingdom, Canada, France, Germany, Sweden, Belgium, India, Pakistan, Russia, Turkey, Columbia, Israel, and Ireland. It is the Chinese version of the world famous Swedish company Ericsson (Telefonaktiebolaget L. M. Ericsson).

International estimates show that the number of Chinese household having an annual income exceeding $35,000 (the threshold of the middle class) is 40 million (over 100 million

people) and is likely to increase to 160 million (400–500 million people) by 2025. Even if half of this is true, it is unmistakable that China is a very rich country today in a world of depressed economic growth. China is in a position to provide public good for the world.

Over three decades ago, China began interconnecting Japan, Taiwan, and overseas Chinese entrepreneurs, mainly from Southeast Asian countries along with Hong Kong and Macau. Thereafter, China started taking over "sunset industries" out-sourced from the United States and other developed countries. China's interconnectivity with the United States reached a new height. China is America's second largest trade partner (after Canada), second largest source of imports, and fourth largest overseas market. America is China's second largest trade partner (after the EU), sixth largest source of imports, and largest overseas market. Behind the statistics, China is crucial to America. For instance, many spare parts used by the US automotive industry are supplied by China. Apple's iPhone is entirely assembled in China. China also has increasing trade and economic ties with the United Kingdom and EU.

China's odyssey along the civilization highway is on the same page as its globalization. China is enjoying peace and development, engaging in talks and transactions with a large number of countries, and creating a China-related world order of "within the four seas" friendship. There may be fear in some quarters about the so-called "Thucydides Trap," referring to an age-old theory initiated by Thucydides (460–400 BCE), the Greek historian and author of the *History of the Peloponnesian War*. The fear underscores an inevitable clash between the rising great power and the status quo great power, insinuating what may happen between China and the United States. The scenario is far-fetched. China is much less than a "rising great power" and the United States is a shaky "status quo great power." In terms of military power, China will not be any match to the United States within the next 25 years. In terms of economic power, views differ. I illustrate this in the following table (based on information supplied by the United States).

## China–US Comparison in Economic Power

|  | China | US |
| --- | --- | --- |
| Population | 1,373,541,278 | 323,995,528 |
| GDP (PPP) | $21.27 trillion | $18.56 trillion |
| Per Capita GDP (PPP) | $15,400 | $57,300 |

*Source*: Information provided by the World Fact Book of the US Central Intelligence Agency, consulted on February 6, 2017.

The CIA used "Purchasing Power Parity" (PPP) to calculate GDP in this table to show that China has the largest GDP, surpassing the United States. But, no one seriously believes the Chinese economy is larger than the United States. China will not be able to match the United States for a long time yet. We see that in per capita GDP, it will take China at least two decades to catch up with the United States. Even if China replaces the United States (that is, the 15th highest in the world) in per capita GDP, it does not mean the United States will cease to be a superpower. Thus, the "Thucydides Trap" scenario is irrelevant in Sino-US relations.

An alternative scenario to the "Thucydides Trap" is "John Tyler Hope." Decades ago, I would read the US presidents' public pronouncements and I have copied some words from an undelivered letter (dated July 12, 1843) from John Tyler, the 10th US president, to the Emperor of China.

The rising Sun looks upon the great mountains and great rivers of China. When he sets, he looks upon mountains and rivers equally large, in the United States…. Now, my words

are that the Governments of the two such Great Countries should be at peace. It is proper, and according to the will of Heaven, that they should respect each other, and act wisely....[2]

The letter expresses hope for "peace" between the United States and China, and suggests that the US and Chinese governments "respect each other, and act wisely." I think this "John Tyler Hope" scenario is relevant and ready to guide Sino-US relations for the time being and for many years to come.

China's memory of the sad 19th century scenario "They are the chopper and the chopping board, we are the fish and meat on it" remains fresh. China doesn't want history to repeat; hence, it must maintain a modern and efficient fighting force to meet any eventuality. This is the basic justification for China's acquiring and making aircraft carriers and extending the defense line to the South China Sea. However, developing military strength may be likened to a tiger tasting blood. It is dangerous and difficult to exercise self-restraint. An international environment featuring the "shock-and-awe" attack on Saddam Hussein's Iraq in 2003, regular US–Japan–Australia naval exercises in the western Pacific Ocean, maneuvers of the US Seventh Fleet near the Taiwan Strait, deployment of the Terminal High Altitude Area Defense (THAAD) System on South Korean soil, and so on, surely disturbs the sleep of Chinese national defenders. The world, especially the United States, should help make Asia-Pacific *pacific*, instead of one-sidedly blaming China. On the other hand, Chinese authorities have work to do to prevent the public from becoming zealous shouters of nation-state slogans. In becoming a member of the comity of nation-states world, China must not go astray and veer down the nation-state path. The progressive

---

[2] *See* Tan Chung, *Triton and Dragon*, 368, citing Robert H. Ferren, ed., *Foundations of American Diplomacy, 1775–1872* (Columbia, South Carolina. University of South Carolina Press, 1968), 219–220.

**Chapter 10: China Joins the Comity of the "Nation-state" World**

and enlightened world community can help preserve the oasis of the "civilization-state," that is, China instead of seeing it sink into the quicksand of the nation-state desert.

After joining the nation-states world comity, China has pursued a foreign policy of maintaining a friendly, peaceful coexistence with all countries. It has selectively collaborated with some countries without forming an alliance. One type of collaboration (such as Sino-Pakistan relations) is to develop a close partnership, whereas another type is to form a loose union, such as the "Shanghai Cooperation Organisation" and five-state "BRICS" (Brazil, Russia, India, China, and South Africa) organization. There are regular summit meetings and consultations at the ministerial level and interstate cooperation programs. These organizations may gradually develop into a kind of "common entity." The G20 Summit in Hangzhou, held in September 2016, was an important stepping stone for China's ambitious "common entity" drive. G20 countries constitute two-thirds of the world's population, 60 percent of its territory, and 85 percent of its GDP. If the present trend of unity and interconnectivity continues, there is hope that a huge "common entity" may emerge, with China playing an increasingly positive role. China's advocacy for an "Innovative, Invigorated, Interconnected, and Inclusive World Economy" at the 2016 G20 Summit indicates its desire to sell the made-in-China "common entity of destiny" to the world. There is no sign that the other 19 states will come on board soon, but none have resisted this Chinese initiative. To begin anything is difficult. If China persistently pursues this ideologically, emotionally, and concretely, there will be economic and cultural progress.

In Chapter 5, I described China, India, Japan, and Korea as being in the same "common civilization entity" during the Tang Dynasty. The situation today shows there is still close geo-cultural affinity within this belt (being East Asia and the Indian Peninsula of South Asia). We can even extend this belt to Southeast Asia, and China has already formed a semi-common entity of destiny

with Pakistan. China and North Korea had long been a semi-common entity of destiny, but Kim family rule has created a puzzle for Chinese policymakers, posing difficulty for mutual trust between the two erstwhile fraternal countries. Additionally, China has rapidly improved relations with South Korea in recent years. The two countries have maintained deep-rooted historical and cultural ties and share co-prosperous economic development, though some competition exists. China and Vietnam had formed a semi-common entity of destiny at one point, but their 1980s war has damaged their solidarity. Vietnam has always been a hardy nation-state for itself and maintained a safe distance regarding China to avoid being swallowed by the Chinese giant. Both China and Vietnam are ruled by one party with identical theory and thinking, with Vietnam emulating China time and again since the days of Ho Chi Minh (1890–1969). Myanmar is China's very close neighbor. The two countries have interacted for millennia with few conflicts. During World War II, there was a famous strategic highway connecting them. Today, China and Myanmar collaborate well in economic constructions. China has a special emotional bond with Singapore. The founder and prime minister of Singapore Lee Kuan Yew (1923–2015) miraculously transformed a tiny city-state into one of the developed countries of the Western world. Yet he was conscious of his Chinese cultural roots. Singapore has helped China forge and broaden friendship and cooperation with the ASEAN countries. China should not have much difficulty forming a semi-common entity of destiny with all the countries discussed before.

Sino-Indian relationship is my main academic field and life-long career. I have written voluminously in this area, and those concerned with China and India may have seen some of my writings. In this book, I have repeatedly highlighted the influence of Indian civilization on the development of Chinese civilization. I quite agree with Ji Xianlin's observation that without the millennial intercourse between the two great civilizations of China and India, Chinese society would not have been what it is today. I have also done my best to popularize the concept of "Chindia."

Sino-Indian relations developed to a climax of *Hindi Chini Bhai Bhai* (Chinese and Indians are brothers) during the 1950s. However, 1962 brought the border dispute that was aggravated into a war. The civilizations of China and India are the twins of the Himalaya Sphere. How unfortunate that the progenies of the two civilizations turned mother Himalaya into a battleground! The two "civilization-states" that advocated "Panchsheel" (the five principles of peaceful coexistence) today behave like "nation-states," maintaining a tit-for-tat armed coexistence. A greater tragedy of history I have not seen! It is wrong if either India or China accuses the other of being the perpetrator of this tragedy. Both countries have committed blunders and are responsible for righting this historic wrong. My father, Tan Yun-shan (known as the "modern Xuanzang"), went to India in 1928 and dedicated his life to promoting Sino-Indian friendship until his death in India in 1983. I went to India and inherited his legacy before his retirement. The 90th anniversary of this episode will soon be here. I think I understand both China and India. I know the Indian people think of China as a country of primary importance to India, and many Indians admire China while most want to have friendly relations with it. This is one side of the picture. The other side is the misunderstandings of China among Indian people due to Western propaganda, exile of the Dalai Lama in India, the 1962 war, Chinese public opinion, and messages sent by China. When these misunderstandings disappear, China and India will become a natural common entity of destiny.

I saw a report of a September 2016 conference under the auspices of the think tank "Pangu Academic Committee 盘古智库" of the International Institute for Strategic Studies of the CPC Central Party School. The conference theme was trade opportunities for China arising from India's "Make in India" projects. An expert from the "Academy of Asia-Pacific and World Strategy 亚太与全球战略研究院" of the Chinese Academy of Social Sciences 中国社会科学院 commented that China could not predict the direction of development of India's strategy. But it could ensure a normal course for future Sino-Indian

strategic relations through collaboration in India's economic projects. She (the expert) said this resonated with what Xi Jinping proposed for promotion of people's understanding. She went on to say that China had neglected this aspect and should make amends. Her conclusion was when China had the support of the Indian people, there would not be many problems in Sino-Indian relations no matter what political forces ruled India. She sees things through the strategic prism, and her observation shows there is uncertainty in the continuity of Sino-Indian relations. I always feel China must behave as a civilization-state to pursue a geo-civilization relationship because the geostrategic relationship belongs to the arena of the geopolitical paradigm of the nation-states, which is a zero sum game that cannot go far.

In this same conference, an India expert from the Academy of Contemporary International Relations Studies 现代国际关系研究院 said that since India is very unreceptive toward the slogan "One Belt One Road," China should avoid it to cooperate with India. The earliest "Silk Road" went from Sichuan through Yunnan and Myanmar to India and developed further afield from India. The primary builders of this Silk Road were Indian merchants, while Chinese merchants made negligible contribution. Additionally, the aforementioned "Dharmaratna Marg" developed from India and created a trans-regional artery of trade and cultural interaction: This artery was the Silk Road people have been talking about. Thus, in our book, the Dharmaratna Marg was the Silk Road. If China thinks of the "One Belt One Road" from this historical perspective and recognizes the important contributions of India, then our Indian friends would not become antagonistic toward it. During the Tang Dynasty, many eminent Chinese monks and Chinese diplomatic missions traveled to India across the Himalayas. Today, railway lines of China and India are very close to one another and can easily link in Nepal or at the Nathula Pass, thus providing a shortcut to development of Sino-Indian relations. Linking the railways between the two countries and resolution of the border dispute are mutually complementary. With the link of Sino-Indian railways across Himalaya, "One Belt One Road" will be in

sight and we shall see the prospect of a Sino-Indian common entity of destiny on the horizon.

China's security is ensured when there will be no war between China and Japan. In history, Sino-Japanese relations shifted from extreme cordiality during Tang to Japanese aggression against China during the 19th and 20th centuries. In modern times, Japan has admired the West, but the West is far away from Japan. China was close to Japan, but Japan looked down on China. The Asian portion of Eurasia lay near Japan, but Japan dreamed of "de-Ami On" (getting out of Asia). We don't know if this Japanese dream still prevails. Now, in many ways, Japan has developed beyond Europe; thus, Europe may not be attractive to the Japanese any longer. It was ironic that the Japanese dream of becoming a part of Europe ultimately pushed Japan to the position of enemy of the Western powers during World War II. This is the mischief of the nation-state mind-set. The fatal defect of the nation-state is to climb to the top of the pyramid alone and build one's own bliss upon the misery of others. Indian poet Tagore, and many Indian intellectual elite, once admired Japan's vigorous self-strengthening, social harmony, soft culture, and so on. Japanese aggression against China exposed the ugly monster within Japan, frightening away Tagore and other Indian admirers. The image of the rising sun dropped into the Pacific Ocean. This episode should serve as a lesson to China and all future emergent countries. I think, ultimately, the Japanese people will realize this and become ardent lovers of peace and intimate partners with China in forever pursuing the ideal of co-prosperity.

Having a different civilization background has prevented, and will prevent, people of the Western world from intimately embracing Chinese civilization. But, this is not so with people of East, South, and Southeast Asia. If China tries hard to unite these neighboring areas, it will forge a common entity. When there is an Asian common entity of destiny, the world atmosphere will change and the Eurasian common entity of destiny will emerge as a corollary. When that day arrives, the prospect of a world common entity of destiny will no longer be an illusion.

# CONCLUSION

Many thanks to my readers for joining me for this bird's-eye view of the 5,000-year history of Chinese civilization. China's history is so long, its political stage and players so large and many, its events so numerous, and its problems so complex that I cannot detail and itemize everything in this overview. Western culture likes anatomy, which can only be performed on a dead body. If a living person is dissected, life is lost and putting all the dissected parts together again won't resurrect the person. That is why Western anatomy methodology in historical studies often fails to obtain a correct picture of human history. In Eastern culture, people prefer the holistic prism. Indians think there is only one life that manifests in all living beings (humans, animals, vegetation, and even minerals). The Indian philosophy of "ahimsa" is built on the theory that when you hurt other lives you hurt yourself. This logic is identical to the adage of *Laozi* that "Dao (truth) creates one, one creates two, two creates three, and three creates all beings on earth." In this book, we adopt macro and holistic methodology to grasp China's development rhythm, not being led astray and going into the blind alley.

Evaluation of historic events and personalities is no easy task. Today, people have too irreconcilably divergent opinions about contemporary events and personalities to arrive at an objective assessment. It becomes more difficult to do so for history. My basic perception is based on the Chinese saying: "As there is no 100% gold ingot, there is no immaculate and perfect person 金无足赤，人无完人." The prominent imperial rulers highlighted in this book, like Qin Emperor Shihuang, Han Emperor Wu, Tang Emperor Taizong, and Tang Empress/Emperor Wu, are always controversial. But there would not have been a Chinese civilization enduring 5,000 years without them. Demeaning their greatness means debunking Chinese civilization. Tang Empress Wu was a marvel, if not a miracle, to, as an ordinary woman among commoners, realize the legendary ideal of having a "Chakravartin/universal ruler" on earth: She is the only person of this category in world history. While Chinese history books refused to recognize her "son of heaven" status, teachers of Chinese history worldwide make it a pastime to describe her as an immoral, lascivious ruler when she was the Empress Dowager and Empress. Actually, she did not do anything immoral except show a little affection to male courtiers and scholars she liked, while all her male counterparts in Chinese history had a huge harem. In modern times, a woman of her feminine charms and affection with a romantic nature would be the brightest star with innumerable fans.

Readers must have marked the various milestones we passed from the Sanxingdui and Great Yu until today. Such a lengthy and enduring continuity of history is hard to find elsewhere, except in India. Throughout this discourse, we described the odyssey embarked on by Chinese civilization along the civilization highway to distinguish it from development of "nation-states." Chinese civilization has repeatedly interacted with the "nation-state" dynamics. Twice it encountered tremendous confrontation from, and then integrated into, nation-state dynamics. The first time was during the Mongol Yuan and Manchu Qing dynasties. Apparently, nation-state rhythm hijacked China's civilization-state development while, in reality, the two dynamics converged and marched ahead, albeit in a rather unhappy, even agonizing, mood. The second time was aggression and repression from Western powers and then aggression and repression from Japanese militarists. In 1949, China stood again and repulsed the material and spiritual repression of the nation-states. From the 1980s onward, China ascended the central stage of the world and merged with the world of nation-states, joining the comity of nations. Such a development has been quite unusual, totally at odds with the nation-state "rise–apex–decline" trilogy.

Chapter 3 is titled "A Unified Empire sans Imperialism," which may sound strange if we don't compare the unified Chinese Empire with the Roman Empire, British Empire, and so on. The latter, being in the realm of nation-state, represented an aggressive, powerful nation using force to colonize other nations. But the Qin–Han Empire and its new version during the Sui–Tang–Song dynasties were just political organizations within the domain of China. As I have reiterated, nation-state type empires inevitably stage the "rise–apex–decline" trilogy. If people today don't visit Rome and its ruins, the Roman Empire is out of sight, out of mind. The British Empire is being forgotten by new generations in former British colonies such as India, Singapore, Myanmar, and Bangladesh. But, in China, memories of the Chinese Empire are revived time and again by very popular TV dramas. Mao Zedong made a wise observation that after the 1911 Revolution, no one can become emperor of China again. In fact, even during the Chinese Empire period, the Emperor's situation was very similar to that of new US President Donald Trump, who wants to do whatever he likes, but is restrained by the US Constitution and System of Checks and Balances. There was truly a hidden system of checks and balances within the erstwhile Chinese Empire.

We may, for the sake of clarity, liken China to an oasis and the world of nation-states to a desert that repeatedly tried in vain to devour China. When Mongolia conquered Song China, the Mongol nation-state temporarily disappeared, not Chinese civilization. China's Manchu conquerors completely lost their identities: The Manchu "nation/race," along with the Manchu Dynasty, is gone. Not that Manchu people were annihilated, but they harmoniously transformed themselves into the Chinese race. Viewed from another angle, the 1.3 billion Chinese today have no singular ancestral origin. They are the posterity of Qiang, Xianbei, Turk, Tatar, Nurchen, Mongol, Manchu, and what not. Chinese civilization does not recognize these identities, and "Han" is not an ethnic identity at all. So China certainly is not a "nation," nor a "nation-state." In India, ethnic identities are also blurred. But linguistic differences are outstanding, even assuming the importance of "race/nation." In India, there is "diversity in unity," while in China it is a kind of "unity in unanimity and diversity."

An awakened lion of China did not shake the world, but only transformed itself. There is some belief within US mainstream media that during the Mao Zedong Era, China joined the *yin* of hating America with the *yang* of loving China. If that were true for a while, Mao's historic talks with President Nixon in 1972 at his Beijing residence stopped it. Today, the *yang* of loving China remains strong, but the *yin* of hating America has largely disappeared among the people, except for a tiny minority who still take pride saying no to America for dubious patriotic vanity.

It was the theory of "Sinocentrism" that kindled my desire to write this book, and the aim of this book is to demolish this theory. We hardly mentioned Fairbank's "Sinocentrism" because through the prism of the geo-civilization paradigm, "Sinocentrism" is totally irrelevant to the 5,000-year odyssey of Chinese civilization along the civilization highway. "Sinocentrism" is not even a tiny speck on the giant image of China. It falls out of sight and mind when we focus on China's long endured development as a common entity. Recall in Chapter 8 when I highlighted attempts by Fairbank and company to whitewash Britain's centuries' involvement in "opium imperialism." In fact, "Sinocentrism" is designed to make China the whipping boy for the wrongdoing of British "opium imperialism." I am sure that Fairbank's "one stone killing two birds" master stroke doesn't work on the minds of my readers. China has been punished as a whipping boy innumerable times in Western media. However, China does not want to settle the score—whatever is past is past. The Mongol and Manchu "nation-states" invaded, insulted, repressed, and ruined China. Yet China ultimately forgot, forgave, and embraced them as brethren. Western powers did the same to China (using different methods and styles), yet China created a happy ending by revering the erstwhile perpetrators as "guru" and making itself into a new entity. If Professor John King Fairbank were alive today to write on China, he surely would withdraw his theory of Sinocentrism, which he propounded during the height of the Cold War. At that time, everyone in US and China study circles was obsessed with the intense "challenges and responses" between one nation-state and the other, and between one bloc and the other. Everyone, including Fairbank, missed the crucial point that it was the two great rivers, Huanghe and Yangtze, which first carved the contours of China and created the Chinese common geographical entity, which evolved into a common civilization entity and common entity of destiny during Qin–Han and Sui–Tang–Song. Without such basic understanding, Fairbank and others noticed the Chinese concept of "Tianxia" and arrived at "Sinocentrism" by viewing China through the nation-state prism. Fairbank and other international China scholars imagined a "Chinese center" and a solar system functioning in China with hundreds of millions of people revolving around the solar center in China. They missed the phenomenon of the affectionate embrace of the "fish of Yin and Yang," as we saw from the picture of *Taiji*.

While we can put the "Sinocentrism" theory to rest, we notice the emergence of "reverse Sinocentrism" in world politics. Today, China is often placed at the center of the world for the wrong reasons. I noticed from 1992 onward, during the yearlong US presidential campaigns, that China was being used as a whipping boy. I remember Bill Clinton would suddenly condemn the "butchers from Beijing to Baghdad" to brag about himself being a "human rights" fighter without any provocation from China. George W. Bush's election speeches were not free from anti-China remarks, with the purpose of discrediting the China policy of the Clinton administration. Donald Trump, who won the 2016 election by attacking dozens of enemies (China inevitably occupying a prominent place), alleged that China had "stolen" jobs from America. China has become accustomed to such attacks during every US presidential campaign because it knows Washington's US–China harmony and etiquette always takes a vacation during the election year. We can see that, nowadays, it is the United States, not China, who suffers from "Sinocentrism."

A country embarking on its odyssey along the civilization highway beyond the rhythm of "nation-state" will not become a hegemon. The Chinese "awakened lion" has not proved Napoleon's fear, even if he really made the "China shaking the world" remark. Chinese tradition has always believed that "peace and harmony are the most precious 和为贵" and the millennial Chinese dream is "grand harmony in Tianxia 天下大同." China has forged a cordial international relationship in the spirit of "me in you and you in me 你中有我、我中有你"—the main tenet of Chinese Chan Buddhism.

We can recall the image of China's "future Buddha" in Chapter 7, with his excessive fat and round belly. Do you think he would inspire China to invade other countries and conquer the world? Anyone who sees that image (seen everywhere in China) would not fear the alleged "China threat." Somehow, China is not represented by this image (although it should be), but instead illogically by the image of a fire-breathing dragon. We discovered, in Chapter 7, that China's "future Buddha" is the reincarnation of Indian bodhisattva Maitreya. Indian readers know that Maitreya, in Indian legend, would never have that obese image, which is 100 percent Chinese imagination. On the other hand, Chinese would never agree with international media that the fire-breathing dragon is the true image of China. We scrutinized Chinese historical development and did not find any trace of the fire-breathing dragon at any point in time. The obese Maitreya/future Buddha image and fire-breathing dragon image demonstrate the wide gap between the civilization-state mind-set and nation-state mind-set.

American public opinion during the climax of the Cold War provided fertile soil for "Sinocentrism" theory to grow. However, times have changed. Today, China has integrated into the nation-state world to become a member of the comity of nations. Because of Tianxia tradition, China is getting along amicably with other members of the comity. Chinese are keen and good at learning and adopting languages and cultures of others. Today, most American flags, and quite a large portion of the idols consumed during festivals in India, are made in China. Today, there is a fever in China for sending children abroad to study. The call of "going out 走出去" beckons Chinese entrepreneurs and others, enterprises as well as institutions. The well-to-do take foreign tours and avail themselves of increasing visa-free privileges abroad (meaning countries that waive visa regulations for Chinese tourists to target their money for shopping). Conversely, Chinese tradition of welcoming foreigners into their midst is reinvigorated everywhere. Foreign visitors, students, and job seekers in China are increasing. The number of foreigners marrying Chinese in China is steadily rising.

In my Introduction, I quoted Professor Warren I. Cohen's comment that Chinese were "the most ethnocentric people in the world." On China's odyssey along the civilization highway, ethnic consciousness has been totally absent, except for periods when Mongol Yuan and Manchu Qing imposed ethnic repression on Chinese people. My readers ignored Cohen's siding with "civilization seekers" from the northern steppe to censure China for wrongdoing. On the contrary, my analogy of "a big fishbowl with fish swimming merrily and gluttonous cats waiting upon it" is a sharp reflection of how Cohen's "most ethnocentric" Chinese were devastated by conquerors from the northern steppe. Being a China expert, Cohen perhaps never had empathy for the over 100,000 corpses floating offshore in Guangdong to mark the end of the Song Dynasty, as my readers have lamented with me.

We must also recall how the ardent patriotic general Yue Fei died tragically, and, with his death, Southern Song had no will and strength to resist foreign aggression. As a civilization-state, China has always been insufficient in patriotism. Manchu conquerors were actually invited by Ming Chinese General Wu Sangui to rule China. During the anti-Japanese War (1937–1945), over half the Japanese invaders were from puppet army.

Now that China has joined the comity of nation-states, our analogy of the big fishbowl with gluttonous cats waiting upon it seems no longer relevant. China is open with large numbers of foreign friends coming to tour, visit, and attend meetings to have dialogues and enjoy Chinese cuisine. The wider China's interactions are with the world, the more English will be spoken and the more foreign friends China will have. Foreign elements in Chinese culture are also growing. Meanwhile, China deals with a complex world. There are pro-China people and anti-China people. There are foreigners who think they are superior to Chinese and also foreigners who respect, admire, and befriend China. We still don't see among them the gluttonous cats, such as the Xiongnu, Nurchen, Mongol, and Manchu of the past. Whether the cats emerge in the future is still a big question. The world situation is rather uncertain and fluid. In the Introduction, I alluded to the "Westphalian Regime" that smiled with a dagger at the ready. This "regime" is still there. China must not lower its guard.

In the 1960s, there was a malicious description of China in Western media as the "empire of the blue ants" because Chinese in those years wore only blue tunics, creating a feeling of monotony. Today, China is colorful and outdoes European and American countries in gorgeous attire. Chinese stores are equally colorful, well stocked with a great variety of native products and imported goods. China is vying with the United States, France, Japan, and many other countries to increase color in material life and lifestyle. The sumptuous fare of color, aroma, and taste produced by the restaurants in China is hard to surpass in other parts of the world.

Increasingly, the Chinese are buying houses, driving private cars, sightseeing abroad, and feasting in restaurants. Their consumerist standard has overtaken Japan and European countries and is catching up with the United States. More and more Chinese enterprises are competing with one another. Universities of the state (private universities are yet to begin) run enterprises and star-class guesthouses. Publishers and other cultural institutions of the state have become private enterprises of sorts, becoming increasingly profit oriented and smelling commercialism. Chinese society has returned to the merrymaking pacifism of the Sui–Tang–Song period. As the Chinese pie grows, there is a stronger combination of commercialism, consumerism, and hedonism with self-interests taking a front seat and virtue a back. These developments are worrisome. Chinese "wine culture" links with corruption and waste. Public money has been used in banquets under all kinds of pretexts. In the past couple of decades, the total liquid Chinese drank from bottles of famous (and expensive) brands of alcohol such as "Maotai 茅台," "Wuliangye 五粮液," and so on equaled (according to expert estimates) the entire West Lake of Hangzhou. Presently, the government, led by Xi Jinping, has strictly banned feasting on public accounts, resulting in a bit of astringency.

We recall from my favorite poem, which I translated in Chapter 5 (by Luo Yin), that "Tomorrow, if there is worry, let me worry tomorrow." This is not optimism, but complacency. Confucius warned that "those who have no anxious thoughts for the future are bound to encounter trouble at their door 人无 远 虑必有近忧." Had the Sui–Tang–Song Chinese adhered to this Confucian teaching, Chinese history would have been much different—the tragedy at the end of the Song Dynasty would not have happened. Today, while Chinese leadership adheres to this Confucian warning, China's populace is rather complacent (somewhat like their Indian counterparts). While the world is not afraid of the rise of India, it also has no reason to fear the rise of China.

Seeing through the holistic prism, the United States is still the Judas goat of the world's thinking, information, wisdom, and culture. However, it is unable to lead a new movement to overcome the crisis of the nation-states world. We need a renaissance going beyond the development rhythm of nation-state. I think this renaissance can lead the world out of the vicious cycle of violence begetting violence, compounded by US bombs and terrorist IEDs. Who should lead this renaissance? I think the leader should be "*Bodhicitta*/the enlightened mind." This leadership is not a post attained through competition, nor a prize to win. It is there waiting for the "Enlightened One" to emerge and take. Whoever takes it, Chinese civilization will be there to vindicate

**Conclusion**

and lend a mighty hand. The 1.3 billion Chinese (one-fifth of humanity) will form a huge column in the marching procession. The renaissance will emerge and succeed.

In the Introduction, I mentioned that China is trying to gradually create a "Shanghai Cooperation Organization Common Entity of Destiny," "China–India Common Entity of Destiny," "China–South Asia Common Entity of Destiny," "China–ASEAN Common Entity of Destiny," "East Asia Common Entity of Destiny," "BRICS Common Entity of Destiny," and "Eurasia Common Entity of Destiny." From cover to cover, this book presents a civilization (civilization-state) ready to embrace the entire world and take all nations (nation-states) together to forge a global "common entity of destiny." China does not want to be the Judas goat (the US Judas goat should go ahead, but not lead the world down the garden path). China just wants the world to become an ideal globe.

Do you feel you have gone through a commentary written by a Chinese person who looks at China through a holistic prism? A commentary displaying a mind infused with ideas and passion vis-à-vis one's own civilization. However, there is no "frog-in-the-well" attitude. As author of this book, I may describe myself as a sea frog having seen the sea and world. I probably know China inside and out, and know too well its merits and demerits. Every civilization has its merits and demerits, and I look at them judiciously without discrimination. I see China as China, albeit my China. I want China to be your China, dear readers! China is no *Devapura*/paradise from where the devi/fairies shower flower petals. It is not a piece of jade without defect. The author of this book loves China, as do the readers who spent so much time perusing the book. You must have had a rapport with the author throughout these pages. In world opinion, we see affection and appreciation for China. We hear critical voices too. That is good! China must listen to the critiques. Chinese people should understand their own country—what it is, and is not. Only Chinese who understand their country well can tell a good story about China.

# APPENDIX

## RECOMMENDED BOOKS ABOUT CHINESE CIVILIZATION BY OTHER AUTHORS

### Chinese Books

袁行霈、严文明、张传玺、楼宇烈编：《中华文明史》，2006 年北京大学出版社

范文澜：《中国通史简编》（修订本），1978 年，北京：人民出版社范文澜、蔡美彪：《中国通史》，1994 年，北京：人民出版社钱穆：《中国史大纲》，1940 年，上海商务印书馆翦伯赞：

1. 《中国史纲要》，1961 年初版，2006 年新版，北京大学出版社
2. 《中国史论集》，2008 年新版，中华书局

白寿彝：《中国通史》，1999 年，上海人民出版社吕思勉：《中国通史》，1992 年，上海：华东师范大学出版社　《中国断代史系列》丛书，2003-2004 年，上海人民出版社

1. 王仲荦：《隋唐五代史》
2. 陈振：《宋史》

任继愈主编：《中国佛教史》，1997 年，北京：中国社会科学出版社姜义华：《中华文明的根柢—民族复兴的核心价值》，2012 年，上海人民出版社

## English Books

**Allan, Sarah, ed.** *The Formation of Chinese Civilization: An Archaeological Perspective* 中国文明的形成. New Haven, CT: Yale University Press, 2005.

**Brook, Timothy.** *The Troubled Empire: China in the Yuan and Ming Dynasties* 元明时代：受困的帝国. Cambridge, MA: Belknap Press of Harvard University, 2013.

**Cambridge History of China Series** 剑桥中国史系列: General Editors: John K. Fairbank and Denis Twitchett, published by Cambridge University Press.

### Volume 1:

**Twitchett, Denis and Michael Loewe, eds.** *The Ch'in and Han Empires, 221 BC–AD 220* 秦汉帝国, 1986.

### Volume 3, Part 1:

**Twitchett, Denis C., ed.** *Sui and T'ang China, 589–906 AD* 唐代中国, 1979.

### Volume 5, Part 1:

**Twitchett, Denis and Paul Jakov Smith, eds.** *The Sung Dynasty and Its Precursors, 907–1279* 宋朝及前代, 2009.

### Volume 5, Part 2:

**Chaffee, John W. and Denis Twitchett, eds.** *Sung China, 960–1279 AD* 宋代中国, 2015.

### Volume 6:

**Franke, Herbert and Denic C. Twitchett, eds.** *Alien Regimes and Border States, 907–1368*, 1994.

### Volume 7, Part 1:

**Mote, Frederick W. and Denis Twitchett, eds.** *The Ming Dynasty, 1368–1644* 明朝, 1988.

**Lewis, Mark Edward.** *China Between Empires: The Northern and Southern Dynasties* 中国南北朝. Cambridge, MA: Belknap Press of Harvard University, 2008.

———. *China's Cosmopolitan Empire: The Tang Dynasty* 唐朝都会帝国. Cambridge, MA: Belknap Press of Harvard University, 2009.

**Li Feng** 李峰. *Early China: A Social and Cultural History* 早期中国社会文化史. Cambridge: Cambridge University Press, 2013.

**Mote, Frederick W.** *Imperial China 900–1800* 中国帝国时代. Cambridge, MA: Harvard University Press, 2003.

**Murowchick, Robert E., ed.** *China: Ancient Culture, Modern Land* 中国：现代国土古代文化. Norman, OK: University of Oklahoma Press, 1994.

**Pomeranz, Kenneth.** *The Great Divergence: China, Europe, and the Making of the Modern World* 中国和欧洲形成当今世界异端. Princeton, NJ: Princeton University Press, 2000.

**Westad, Odd Arne.** *Restless Empire: China and the World Since 1750* 一七五零年开始的中国与世界不得安静. New York, NY: Basic Books, 2012.

**Williams, Samuel Wells.** *The Middle Kingdom: A Survey of the Geography, Government, Education, Social Life, Arts, and History of the Chinese Empire and Its Inhabitants* 中央之国. London: W. H. Allen, 1883.

# ABOUT THE AUTHOR

The author of this book, **Tan Chung**, is a typical "Chindian" in both metaphoric and real sense. Born in Malaysia in 1929, his nine decades long life can be divided according to the Indian ashrama life stages into the brahmacharya (celibate student) phase from 1930 to 1954 living in China, the grihastha (householder) phase from 1955 to 1999 living in India, and the sannyasa (wandering recluse) phase from 1999 to date living in the United States. His body chemicals were built by Chinese air, water, and food, and his brain cells were climatized by the environment of Chinese culture. He was a witness of the birth of a new China as well as the "ancien regime" overthrown by it. His celebrated father, Tan Yun-shan, was welcomed by Gurudeva Rabindranath Tagore at Santiniketan in India as an emissary of Chinese civilization. Tan Chung's arrival at Santiniketan in 1955 began the gradual process of stepping into the shoes of his father. He started his career as a Chinese instructor at the National Defence Academy at Khadakvasla in 1958 and some of his pupils of the 15th, 16th and 17th courses retired in the general's rank in the Indian defence forces. He continued his chalk-consuming career until he retired from Jawaharlal Nehru University in 1994 with a seven-year stint as the Head of Chinese Studies in Delhi University in between. Many of his students have affectionately regarded him as a father figure. In 2010, he received the Indian civil award Padma Bhushan from Indian President Pratibha Patil and also the award of outstanding contribution to China–India friendship from Chinese Premier Wen Jiabao in New Delhi. In 2013, he was conferred the honorary degree of Deshikottama by Visva-Bharati University. He was also the recipient of the award for "outstanding contribution to China studies" at the 6th World Forum of China Studies in Shanghai in 2015. That Forum generated the inspiration and energy for the production of this *Odyssey*.

**Volume 8, Part 2:**

**Twitchett, Denis C. and Frederick W. Mote, eds.**
*The Ming Dynasty, 1368–1644* 明朝, 1998.

**Volume 9, Part 1:**

**Peterson, Willard J., ed.** *The Ch'ing Empire to 1800*
满清帝国, 2002.

**Volume 9, Part 2:**

**Peterson, Willard J., ed.** *The Ch'ing Dynasty to 1800*
满清帝国, 2016.

**Volume 10, Part 1:**

**Fairbank, John K., ed.** *Late Ch'ing 1800–1911* 晚清, 1978.

**Volume 11, Part 2:**

**Fairbank, John K. and Kwang-Ching Liu, eds.** *Late
Ch'ing, 1800–1911* 晚清, 1980.

**Volume 12, Part 1:**

**Fairbank, John K., ed.** *Republican China, 1912–1949*
中华民国, 1983.

**Volume 13, Part 2:**

**Fairbank, John K. and Albert Feuerwerker, eds.**
*Republican China 1912–1949* 中华民国, 1986.

**Volume 14, Part 1:**

**MacFarquhar, Roderick and John K. Fairbank, eds.**
*The People's Republic, The Emergence of Revolutionary China,
1949–1965* 中华人民共和国：革命中国涌现, 1987.

**Volume 15, Part 2:**

**MacFarquhar, Roderick and John K. Fairbank, eds.**
*The People's Republic, Revolutions Within the Chinese
Revolution, 1966–1982* 中华人民共和国：中国革命中
的革命, 1991.

**City University of Hong Kong.** *China: Five Thousand Years of History & Civilization* 中国五千年历史文明. Hong Kong: City University Press, 2007.

**Cosmo, Nicola Di.** *Ancient China and Its Enemies: The Rise of Nomadic Power in East Asian History* 古代中国宿敌：东亚游牧势力. New Zealand, 2002.

**Ebrey, Patricia Buckley.** *The Cambridge Illustrated History of China.* Cambridge: Cambridge University Press, 1996.

**Fairbank, John King** 费正清. *Trade and Diplomacy on the China Coast: The Opening of Treaty Ports (1842–1850)* 中国沿海贸易与外交. Cambridge, MA: Harvard University Press, 1953.

————. *The Chinese World Order: Traditional China's Foreign Relations* 中国世界秩序. Cambridge, MA: Harvard University Press, 1968.

**Fairbank, John King and Merle Goldman.** *China: A New History* 中国新史. Cambridge, MA: Belknap Press of Harvard University, 1992.

**Gernet, Jacques.** *A History of Chinese Civilization* 中国文明史. Cambridge: Cambridge University Press, 1996.

**Goodrich, L. Carrington.** *A Short History of the Chinese People* 中国人民简 史. New York, NY: Harper & Brothers, 1943.

**Keay, John.** *China: A History* 中国史. London: Harper Press, 2009.

**Lewis, Mark Edward.** *The Early Chinese Empires: Qin and Han (History of Imperial China* 秦汉帝国史. Cambridge, MA: Belknap Press of Harvard University, 2007.